Food Dehydration

Volume I
Principles

other AVI books on food processing

Food Dehydration

Edited by WALLACE B. VAN ARSDEL, B.S.

Assistant Director

and MICHAEL J. COPLEY, Ph.D.

Director

*Western Utilization Research and
Development Division, Agricultural Research Service,
U. S. Department of Agriculture,
Albany, California*

Volume 1 — Principles
by W. B. Van Arsdel

WESTPORT, CONNECTICUT

THE AVI PUBLISHING COMPANY, INC.

1963

104542

Printed in the United States of America
BY MACK PRINTING COMPANY, EASTON, PENNSYLVANIA

Preface

This volume is designed to be the first of a pair of books dealing with food dehydration. The present volume is devoted to an exposition of the underlying scientific principles, while the second one will describe dehydration technology, both as applied in the many kinds of drying equipment and processes and as reflected in specific methods for dehydrating particular food commodities.

Although the technical and scientific literature relating to the phenomena and operation of *drying* is very extensive, few books have dealt with the subject comprehensively, and none of the recent ones is in English. The two-volume "Trocknungstechnik" (1956, 1959), by O. Krischer and K. Kröll, is by far the most complete treatment of drying theory and drying equipment that has been published anywhere. Food dehydration is given some attention (especially the dehydration of potato pieces), but primary emphasis is placed on the drying of industrial materials and products. The only other fairly recent book, by A. W. Lykow (in Russian, 1950, translated into German, 1955), is concerned mainly with industrial drying and gives only secondary attention to the problems of food dehydration. The present volumes, on the other hand, are directed specifically at these food problems.

Two books on the subject of food dehydration have been published during the past twenty years, both in English: "Drying and Dehydration of Foods," by the late Harry W. von Loesecke (Reinhold Publishing Corporation 1943, Second Edition 1955), and "The Dehydration of Food," by T. N. Morris (Chapman and Hall, London, 1947). Both are highly condensed summaries of current technology. Neither book makes any attempt to go deeply into the underlying principles of drying.

An important contribution to the literature on principles of food dehydration was the bound volume of papers presented at a symposium held in Aberdeen, Scotland, March 25–27, 1958, under the auspices of the Society of Chemical Industry. The general title of the symposium was "Fundamental Aspects of the Dehydration of Foodstuffs." The present volume makes extensive use of the ideas presented there.

Most of the published work on principles of dehydration, whether of foods or of industrial products, has appeared in the pages of the scientific and engineering journals. Important contributions have also been published in paper-back bulletins issued by the British Department of Scientific and Industrial Research and by the U. S. Department of Agriculture. The British Ministry of Agriculture, Fisheries, and Food has very recently published a slender hard-cover book which specifically describes the "Accelerated Freeze-drying" method of dehydration.

The author's purpose in this volume is to present in one place a rather complete description of the physical phenomena of drying, a discussion of the significance of the phenomena in the light of current physical and chemical theory, a presentation of the quantitative relationships between such factors in air drying as temperature, humidity, and velocity, a discussion of the several kinds of difficulty with product quality related to the drying conditions, and a survey of the application of these principles in each of the dozen or more different drying methods employed for food dehydration. The author's presentation of principles has naturally been colored by his own experience, most of which has been gained through contact with the wide-ranging research on vegetable dehydration and the somewhat less extensive work on egg dehydration and fruit dehydration carried on at the Western Regional Research Laboratory of the U. S. Department of Agriculture from 1941 onward. The tray drying of piece-form materials receives special emphasis.

After an introductory chapter on the history and present status of the food dehydration industry, the physical and thermal properties of humid air are summarized, humidity measurement and the use of the psychrometric chart are discussed. The phenomena of heat transfer and mass transfer, as seen in a body undergoing drying, are described next, with particular attention to the mechanism of water transport within the moist body. The next section considers the characteristics of the organic materials we use for food, both as they affect the drying behavior of the material and as they may be responsible for some kinds of damage to product quality inflicted by the drying operation itself. Drying phenomena observed in experiments under controlled laboratory conditions are then analyzed, and the quantitative relations between drying rate and various environmental factors are presented. Thermodynamic relationships within typical air convection driers are next derived, applied first to formulation of procedures for estimating the drying time to be expected in a particular drier under specified conditions, and then more generally to description of the theoretical behavior of common types of tunnel drier. In the concluding section the general principles stated in preceding sections are applied in discussion of the theoretical behavior of other types of driers used for dehydrating various foods.

The student who approaches the technical literature of drying for the first time may get the impression that the big work has all been done, the important discoveries made, and the theoretical basis of dehydration practice thoroughly understood, so that only details remain to be filled in.   Nothing could be further from the truth.   The field is full of puzzles, inconsistencies, disputed observations, and conflicting interpretations.   An enormous amount of well designed experimental work needs to be done, leading into many lines of theoretical inquiry and technological advance.   Only the simpler practical drying methods are now accessible to theoretical analysis. In equipment design and process operation, empirical procedures have so far been much more useful than the predictions of basic physical theory.   In the long run this situation will undoubtedly be reversed; understanding of the real mechanism of drying processes will point the way to major practical developments.

The author gratefully acknowledges his debt to the numerous present and past colleagues at the Western Regional Research Laboratory who have contributed so greatly to development of many of the ideas expressed here.   Special thanks are due to his long-time associates, W. D. Ramage and M. J. Copley, both of whom read the first draft of the manuscript and made important suggestions for its improvement.

W. B. VAN ARSDEL

Albany, California
June 4, 1962

Contents

CHAPTER 1

Introduction

SCOPE

The two volumes of this work will present a statement of the principles and practice of food dehydration, as understood by specialists familiar with different aspects of the subject.

The scope will correspond approximately with the breadth of meaning commonly attached to the phrase "dehydrated food." For example, we do not include the cereal grains (wheat, corn, rice, etc.) or grain products (flour, dry cake and pastry mixes, etc.), dry beans or peas (except as these are used in certain dry soup mixes), tree nuts, dry active yeast, and some other dry food products, even though some of these on occasion do require a drying or conditioning treatment prior to storage. The fruits and vegetables discussed are only those that have significant commercial importance in the United States.

We do not insist on a rigidly limited definition of "dehydration" or "dehydrated," and often use the words as synonyms of "drying" or "dried." A "dehydration plant," however, is always more than just a "drier"; it includes also a variety of other equipment and facilities, for example to handle the raw material into the plant, prepare it by cleaning, scalding, cutting, or other preliminary operations, and handle, inspect, package, and store the dry product. In this sense a study of the dehydration of a food commodity may be a great deal broader than just a study of drying. "Dehydration" is sometimes meant to signify "artificial drying," as contrasted with "sun drying," but we have not made that distinction in dealing with fruits in this book; the "dried fruits" of commerce are relatively high in moisture content, but they may have been produced either by sun drying or by hot-air drying in a mechanically ventilated dehydrator.

DEHYDRATION AS A HISTORICAL METHOD OF FOOD PRESERVATION

The drying of foods in order to preserve them during seasons of abundance for consumption during seasons of shortage is an ancient art; its origins are unrecorded, but many of its practices have been handed down even into the present day, and in some cases form the basis of modern food manufacturing processes. Sun-dried dates, figs, apricots, and raisins must have been almost as highly prized by the aboriginal inhabitants of the Mediterranean Basin and Near East as the wild honey which was the other principal sweet. Mankind's unremitting search for things edible undoubtedly led to countless minor discoveries and inventions that by trial-and-error gradually broadened the list of traditional food processing methods. Salaman (1940) believes that "chuño," prepared from native potatoes in the Andean highlands, may have been invented as long as 2,000 or 3,000 years ago, and is possibly the first food product ever to be specially processed by man for storage into the hungry winter and spring months. Pemmican, air-dried lean venison or buffalo meat, mixed with fat, was invented by pre-Columbian American Indians. Die-mair (1941) says that the household preservation of fruits, vegetables, and mushrooms by drying has been common in many primitive cultures.

The first record of the artificial drying of foods, according to Prescott and Proctor (1937) appears in the 18th century. J. Graefer, according to a British patent of 1780, treated vegetables with hot water, then held them under drying conditions. Eisen dried vegetables on racks in a stove-heated room. Vegetables dried by Edwards according to British Patent No. 8597 of 1840 are said by Allen *et al.* (1943) to have been shipped to British troops in the Crimea (1854–1856), but the quality left much to be desired. One of the prime needs was a diet that would prevent scurvy among the troops; the dried vegetables then available proved to have little or no antiscorbutic activity when finally consumed. Eventually it was found that scalding the vegetables before drying improved their stability.

E. N. Horsford (1864), who was Professor of Chemistry at Harvard University, was a strong advocate of the use of dried vegetables in military rations, and was responsible for the procurement of a considerable amount of dehydrated food which was used by the Union troops during the Civil War. "Erbswurst," pea sausage, which contains condensed pea soup, was used in German rations during the Franco-German war of 1871. Prescott (1919) says that during the Klondike gold rush, dried potatoes were imported from Germany. Onions dehydrated by W. A. Beck, at the Pajaro Valley Dehydrating Co. in Watsonville, Calif., were also shipped to the Klondike; hermetically sealed cans opened 50 years later had kept the contents pungent and edible (Anon. 1959). Dried vegetables produced in Canada were shipped to South Africa for the British forces in the Boer War (1899–1902), and some of the unused supplies were consumed by the British expeditionary force in France early in World War I

(Prescott 1919). Relatively small amounts were produced in the United States during that war. According to Chace *et al.* (1941) about 4,500 tons of dehydrated vegetables were shipped to the U. S. forces overseas. The 1920 U. S. Census showed some 5,500 tons of dehydrated vegetables processed in the United States in 1919; materials included green beans, cabbage, carrots, celery, potatoes, spinach, sweet corn, turnips, other vegetables, and soup mixture. The industry was much further advanced in Europe; in 1914 there were 488 dehydration plants in Germany and by 1916 this had increased to 841 plants. Prescott makes the remark, "War seems to be a great stimulator of methods of food preservation." Chace *et al.* (1941) list 96 U. S. patents on various aspects of dehydration dating between 1915 and 1940. Falk *et al.* (1919) described extensive research done during the first war on the vacuum drying of various foods, including meat and fish.

Fruit dehydration experienced a somewhat different history in the United States, mainly because it was based largely on traditional sun-drying methods. Some of these are still widely used, with only minor improvements in technique and appropriate modernizing in materials handling, packaging, and quality maintenance. A major change occurred, however, in the dried prune industry. In the States of Oregon and Washington, where weather during the harvest season is not dependably dry, various types of artificially heated driers had come into use. According to Cruess (1938) the "Oregon tunnel" was invented by Allen about 1890, and was widely known and used. Prune producers in California, equipped only for sun drying, became convinced of the economic necessity of artificial dehydration after experiencing serious losses from untimely fall rains in 1918 and 1919. Engineers and research workers associated with the University of California (Ridley 1921; Cruess and Christie 1921 A, B; Christie and Ridley 1923; Christie 1926, revised by Nichols 1929) worked with industrial equipment builders and developed a very simple "tunnel" design which eventually became almost standard in the prune-growing area and exerted a strong influence on the design of many of the vegetable dehydrators built during World War II.

Even before the Second World War other drying methods were being vigorously investigated and developed. Drum drying had been applied to whey and buttermilk, soup mixtures, and tomato flakes and powder. Spray drying had come into extensive use on milk products, especially non-fat milk, and was being increasingly used to make certain egg products, particularly dried egg yolk, because of the economy and convenience of dried egg in commercial baking. A few fruit products were being vacuum dried to low moisture content for a relatively small civilian market. Several attempts had been made to produce and market other dehydrated foods, such as pumpkin and squash powders and onions, but without lasting success until about 1923, when a new group undertook onion and garlic dehydration in California (Pardieck 1960). By 1941, dehydrated onion production was solidly established in the civilian market; the products had found steadily expanding use, especially for remanufacture in a variety of other processed foods; several plants were in regular production.

Enormous logistic problems were encountered by the opposing forces in World War II; armies of millions of men had to be supplied, maintained, and fed in every quarter of the globe, from the Arctic to the tropical jungle. Among all the possible food preservation methods, dehydration especially commended itself to military planners because of its space-saving and weight-saving possibilities. Rapid expansion of dehydrated food production facilities was undertaken by all the warring nations. Co-ordination of planning and execution of needed research on dehydrated foods was achieved early between the United States and the British Commonwealth nations. In the United States a Joint Dehydration Committee made decisions on behalf of the War Production Board, the Agricultural Marketing Administration, and the Office of the Quartermaster General, regarding production goals, location, design, and construction of plants, and allocations of scarce materials and equipment. Intensive research was undertaken by the U. S. Department of Agriculture, concentrating on vegetables and eggs at the Western Regional Research Laboratory in Albany, Calif., and on meat at the Department's laboratories in Beltsville, Md. A vast expansion of plant capacity for dehydrating some six vegetables and spray drying whole egg was quickly carried out. According to von Loesecke (1955) there were 139 vegetable dehydration plants in the United States in 1943, and they produced 115 million pounds of dry product, worth nearly 50 million dollars. Pardieck (1960) says that by the end of the war some 375 companies, located in 34 states, were set up to dehydrate vegetables. Peak rate of production was reached with an output of 132 million pounds of dehydrated potatoes and 76 million pounds of other vegetables in 1944 (Anon. 1961). The German dehydrated potato industry reached a maximum production of 66 million pounds in 1944 (Völksen and Wegner 1951).

As might have been foreseen, not all of the hastily built new plants, many of them using makeshift equipment, were successful in getting into satisfactory production; likewise, not all of the dehydrated product delivered overseas was acceptable after months of storage under field conditions. In egg dehydration, particularly, the stability of the whole egg powder was found to be so unsatisfactory that by the summer of 1943 all production had been stopped and intensive search for a remedy had been undertaken by public and private agencies in the United States, Canada, and Great Britain. Greatly improved procedures were discovered and put into large-scale use before the end of the war.

While the new dehydration plants were being designed and built, much effort was put into training a large number of people in the complex technology of food dehydration. Training schools provided a large group of managers and superintendents with the basic knowledge and empirical practices developed by the small previously existing industry. Official Dehydration Manuals, concerned mainly with the technology of vegetable dehydration, were published and widely disseminated in the United States (1941 and 1944), Great Britain (1943 and 1946), Australia (1944), and New Zealand (1944). These Manuals, although now long out of print, and in some respects outdated by various technical advances, still represent the most complete published statement of the detailed technology of vegetable dehydration. The British experience was summarized in a book by Morris (1947). The U. S. Manual was supplemented by several bulletins published by members of the staff of the Western Regional Research Laboratory and by a Management Handbook (U. S. Department of Agriculture 1959).

Many people in the new dehydration plants realized that the industry would experience severe cutbacks at the end of the war. An Inter-Bureau Committee of the U. S. Department of Agriculture and the War Food Administration estimated even before the end of the war (Samuels 1945) that from 25 to 30 million pounds of dehydrated vegetables (including potatoes) might be sold in the peacetime market. That output had already been reached ten years later, after a period of little activity, and was surpassed in every year after 1955 by an increasing amount; totals reported by the Canner/Packer Yearbook (Anon. 1961) for 1960 were 80,000 tons of dehydrated potatoes and 34,000 tons of dehydrated "other vegetables." Current practices for vegetable and fruit dehydration for military procurement, applicable to possible emergency conditions, were outlined in the widely disseminated Management Handbook (1959), prepared by the staff of the Albany laboratory at the request of the Quartermaster Corps.

Egg dehydration remained active for several years after the end of the war, mainly because of relief shipments, but dropped nearly to nothing during the years 1952–1958. Non-fat dry milk production, in contrast, expanded rather steadily during the whole post-war period. In general, the dried onion and other specialty manufacturers who had developed a pre-war business continued to expand their market in many lines of processed food manufacture. A few well financed and well located potato plants made a determined and successful bid for a new civilian market; expansion of this market has by no means reached its crest. Several potato products developed near the end of the war and afterward have come ahead fast, especially potato granules and flakes; also dry mixtures for the quick kitchen preparation of scalloped, au gratin, and hash-brown dishes. Vacuum puff-dried orange and grapefruit powders are in commercial production. Dry mixes for various kinds of cake, pie, and other desserts have become an important outlet for dehydrated egg products. Instant coffee and instant tea are widely used "convenience items." Freeze drying, long supposed to be too costly for the practical drying of foods, is now used commercially to dehydrate red meats, chicken, shrimp, mushrooms, and other high-valued foods; this method of dehydration is undergoing intensive evaluation for military field ration items, and is stimulating much industrial activity and wide public interest. Industry sources estimate that 1.5 million pounds of spray-dried and freeze-dried chicken meat was produced in 1960. Most housewives have become familiar with non-fat dry milk, onion and garlic powders, and a wide range of dry soup mixes, some of which contain pieces of freeze-dried meat, chicken, or mushrooms. Highly sophisticated formulation, packaging, advertising, and merchandising have combined to bring dehydrated foods out into the main stream of modern large-scale food processing.

THE FOOD DEHYDRATION INDUSTRY

Production of dehydrated foods in the United States, sometimes slightingly dismissed as a mere "war baby," has finally become a vigorously growing branch of the peacetime food processing industry. The annual wholesale value of the products shown in Table 1 is already two-thirds of a billion dollars, and at its current rate of growth will very soon reach the billion-dollar level. The field is a greatly diversified one, comprising many products which are not yet reported in census figures or trade estimates, so the specific production and value figures are fragmentary. Table 1, which refers generally to the period about 1959–1960, is based in part on official statistics,

TABLE 1

RECENT YEARLY PRODUCTION OF THE MAIN CLASSES OF DRIED AND DEHYDRATED
FOODS IN THE UNITED STATES (1959–1960)

Commodity	Production (Thousands of Tons[1])	Value (000 Omitted)[2]
Egg solids[3]	30	$ 72,000
Milk solids[4]	960	400,000
Potatoes[5]	80	45,000
Other vegetables[6]	34	40,000
Raisins	220	55,000
Prunes	110	40,000
Other fruits[7]	70	21,000
Totals	1,504	$673,000

[1] At customary market levels of moisture content.
[2] Wholesale, institutional pack, at point of origin.
[3] Composite value of whole egg, whites, yolk.
[4] Composite value of non-fat and whole milk.
[5] Composite value of mashed and piece forms.
[6] Most of the value and tonnage is contributed by onions, garlic, and peppers.
[7] Including both conventionally dried and low-moisture products.

in part on industry estimates, and leaves out of consideration entirely
a number of the smaller items.

The great importance of milk solids in the total production stands
out prominently. Table 2, listing production of six dehydrated
foods by years from 1941–1960, shows that non-fat dry milk has gone

TABLE 2

UNITED STATES PACKS OF DRIED AND DEHYDRATED FOODS[1]
1000 Tons

Year	Egg Solids	Whole Milk	Non-fat Milk	Potatoes	Other Vegetables	Dried Fruits
1941	23	23	183	1	6	491
1942	118	31	283	10	17	526
1943	131	69	255	36	27	688
1944	160	89	291	66	38	582
1945	53	109	321	38	27	539
1946	63	94	327	10	17	503
1947	43	82	339	18	7	579
1948	22	85	341	83	7	455
1949	38	63	467	25	9	474
1950	47	62	441	20	10	359
1951	9	66	351	10	12	469
1952	9	51	432	5	13	463
1953	10	52	607	5	16	423
1954	11	47	701	5	18	380
1955	12	55	702	10	17	409
1956	11	58	774	23	20	434
1957	14	55	839	27	19	368
1958	13	44	855	43	21	315
1959	27	45	862	60	30[2]	403
1960	23	49	909	80	34	...

[1] Data selected from Canner/Packer Yearbook, Sept. 25, 1961, and Agricultural Statistics.
[2] 1959 pack of dehydrated "other vegetables" estimated as 10,000 tons onion, 5,000 tons garlic, 5,000
tons peppers, 10,000 tons all others.

ahead without substantial setbacks during the entire period. Egg
solids were produced on a very large scale during the war, and on a
somewhat reduced scale for several years thereafter. Production
during the years 1951–1958 was on a much lower level, mainly because Government purchases were greatly curtailed. Potatoes and
other vegetables experienced the wartime expansion already described.
Dehydrated potatoes, in particular, underwent a great surge of
overseas shipment during the period of the Berlin crisis of 1948 and
the Korean War (Anon. 1959 A). Dehydration of potatoes and other
vegetables shows evidence of healthy new growth during the past
five or six years, reaching peacetime production levels hitherto con-
fined to war periods. Statistics of dried fruit production reflect
a long-time decline in the output of these foods; recently-developed
low-moisture fruit products have not yet attained a high enough
volume to affect the trend.

Tables 3 and 4 show the quantities of various vegetables and fruits

TABLE 3

QUANTITY OF PRINCIPAL VEGETABLES DEHYDRATED, 1960, AND TOTAL U. S.
PRODUCTION OF THESE VEGETABLES

Thousands of Tons, Fresh Weight Basis		
Product	Dehydrated	Total Production
Garlic	18	23
Onion	112	1,312
Potato	410[1]	12,871

[1] Estimated.
Source: Canner/Packer Yearbook, Sept. 25, 1961.

TABLE 4

QUANTITY OF PRINCIPAL FRUITS DRIED, 1960, AND TOTAL U. S. PRODUCTION
OF THESE FRUITS

Thousands of Tons, Fresh Weight Basis		
Product	Dried	Total Production
Apples	69	2,553
Apricots	53	244
Dates	23	23
Figs	52	60
Grapes	776	3,018
Peaches	36	1,157[1]
Pears	9	637
Prunes	348	461

[1] Freestone.
Source: Canner/Packer Yearbook, Sept. 25, 1961.

used for drying in 1960, and also the total quantities of the same commodities produced commercially in the United States.

BIBLIOGRAPHY

ALLEN, R. J. L., BARKER, J., and MAPSON, L. W. 1943. The drying of vegetables. I. Cabbage. Soc. Chem. Ind. Trans. *62 T*, No. 10, 145–160.

ANON. 1959. Gentry Serenader *10*, No. 7, 1.

ANON. 1961. Canner/Packer Yearbook Number *130*, No. 10, September 25.

AUSTRALIA DEPT. OF COMMERCE AND AGRICULTURE. 1944. Dehydration of Vegetables—Factory Manual. Commonwealth Food Control, Melbourne.

BRITISH DEPT. OF SCIENTIFIC AND INDUSTRIAL RESEARCH, and MINISTRY OF FOOD. 1943. Dehydration. U. K. Progress Reports, London.

BRITISH MINISTRY OF FOOD. 1946. Vegetable Dehydration. H. M. Stationery Office, London.

CHACE, E. M., NOEL, W. A., and PEASE, V. A. 1941. Preservation of fruits and vegetables by commercial dehydration. U. S. Dept. Agr. Circ. *619*.

CHRISTIE, A. W. 1926. The dehydration of prunes. Calif. Agr. Expt. Sta. Bull. *404*. Revision by P. F. Nichols, December 1929.

CHRISTIE, A. W., and RIDLEY, G. B. 1923. Construction of farm dehydrators in California. J. Am. Soc. Heating, Ventilating Eng. *29*, 687–716.

CRUESS, W. V. 1938. Commercial Fruit and Vegetable Products. Second Ed. McGraw-Hill Book Co., New York.

CRUESS, W. V., and CHRISTIE, A. W. 1921 A. Dehydration of fruits—a progress report. Calif. Agr. Expt. Sta. Bull. *330*.

CRUESS, W. V., and CHRISTIE, A. W. 1921 B. Some factors of dehydrator efficiency. Calif. Agr. Expt. Sta. Bull. *337*.

DIEMAIR, W. 1941. The Preservation of Foodstuffs. (In German.) F. Enke Verlag, Stuttgart.

FALK, K. G., FRANKEL, E. M., and McKEE, R. H. 1919. Low temperature vacuum food dehydration. Ind. Eng. Chem. *11*, 1036–1040.

HORSFORD, E. N. 1864. The Army Ration. Second Ed. D. Van Nostrand Co., New York.

MILES, W. D. 1961. The Civil War—chemistry and chemists. Chem. Eng. News *29*, No. 14, 108–115; No. 15, 116–123.

MORRIS, T. N. 1947. The Dehydration of Food, with Special Reference to Wartime Developments in the United Kingdom. Chapman and Hall, London.

NEW ZEALAND DEPT. OF SCIENTIFIC AND INDUSTRIAL RESEARCH. 1944. Vegetable Dehydration. Auckland.

PARDIECK, J. B. 1960. My four decades in dehydration. Activities Report, QM Food and Container Inst. *12*, Second Quarter, 142–147.

PRESCOTT, S. C. 1919. Relation of dehydration to agriculture. U. S. Dept. Agr. Circ. *126*.

PRESCOTT, S. C., and PROCTOR, B. E. 1937. Food Technology. McGraw-Hill Book Co., New York.

RIDLEY, G. B. 1921. Tunnel driers. Ind. Eng. Chem. *13*, 453–460.

SALAMAN, R. N. 1940. The biology of the potato, with special reference to its use as a wartime food. Chem. and Ind. *59*, 735–737.

SAMUELS, J. K., Ed. 1945. Post-war adjustments in processing and marketing dehydrated fruits and vegetables. Inter-Bur. Comm. of Post-War Planning, U. S. Dept. Agr. and War Food Admin.

UNITED STATES DEPARTMENT OF AGRICULTURE. 1944. Vegetable and Fruit Dehydration—A Manual for Plant Operators. Misc. Publ. *540*.

UNITED STATES DEPARTMENT OF AGRICULTURE. 1959. Management Handbook to Aid Emergency Expansion of Dehydration Facilities for Vegetables and Fruits. Western Utilization Research and Development Division, Agricultural Research Service, Albany, Calif.

VÖLKSEN, W., and WEGNER, H. 1951. Potato Drying. (In German.) Neumann Verlag, Radebeul and Berlin.

VON LOESECKE, H. W. 1955. Drying and Dehydration of Foods. Second Ed. Reinhold Publishing Co., New York.

CHAPTER 2

Properties of Water, Water Vapor, and Air

Introduction

The characteristic operation in food dehydration is *drying*, the evaporation of nearly all of the water normally present so that the food product is converted to a dry solid. The nature of the raw material, the kind of product desired, and the characteristics of available processing equipment will modify various stages of a dehydration process drastically—but always there will be a removal of water. The operation of drying is essential to many non-food manufacturing processes as well, and frequently another liquid than water is to be vaporized. However, we shall deal here only with processes wherein water is removed by *evaporation*, rather than by pressing, centrifuging, or freezing; where the operation is continued down to dryness, to distinguish it from the *concentration* of a liquid solution or suspension; and where the purpose is recovery of the dry solid, not just the generation of water vapor as in operation of a steam boiler.

Pressure-Volume-Temperature-Enthalpy Relations; the Gas Laws

A number of the pertinent properties of water and air are collected in Table 5. In most cases the values are given to a greater degree of precision than is required in drier calculations.

The volume occupied by unit mass of a gas or vapor is known as the specific volume; it is the reciprocal of the density. For example, the specific volume of dry air at a temperature of 200°F. and normal sea-level pressure (1 atmosphere, 14.696 lbs. per sq. in., 29.92 in. of mercury barometric height) is 16.62 cu. ft. per lb. Water vapor is lighter than air; a pound of it occupies about 60 per cent greater volume than a pound of dry air at the same temperature and pressure. Moist air is therefore a little lighter than dry air.

Dry air behaves substantially as a perfect gas in this range of temperatures and pressures. Water vapor and moist air depart significantly from the simple relations described by the laws of perfect gases (Goff and Gratch 1945 and 1946; Scott 1958), but the departures are taken into account in most psychrometric tables and charts and are frequently neglected entirely for approximate calculations.

The following "gas laws" are most frequently applied:

11

TABLE 5

PROPERTIES OF WATER AND AIR

1 Atmosphere Pressure

	Liquid Water				Water Vapor	Dry Air				
Temperature (°F.)	32	100	200	212	212	32	100	200	212	300
Specific volume[1]	0.0160	0.0161	0.0166	0.0167	26.80	12.39	14.10	16.62	16.90	19.14
Specific heat[2]	1.0074	0.9986	1.0057	1.0076	[6]	0.240	0.240	0.242	0.242	0.244
Thermal conductivity[3]	0.319	0.363	0.393	0.393	0.015	0.014	0.016	0.018	0.018	0.020
Viscosity[4]	4.35	1.90	0.76	0.68	0.032	0.042	0.046	0.052	0.053	0.057
Surface tension[5]	5.19	4.79	4.13	4.04	...	...	...	...	...	...

[1] Specific volume, V, (cu. ft.)/(lb.).
[2] Specific heat at constant pressure, c_p (B.t.u.)/(lb.)/(°F.).
[3] Thermal conductivity, k (B.t.u.)/(hr.)(ft.)(°F.).
[4] Viscosity, μ (lb.)/(hr.)(ft.).
[5] Surface tension, σ [(lb. force)/(ft.)] $\times 10^3$.
[6] Mean specific heat of superheated water vapor at common drying temperature is 0.440 (B.t.u.)/(lb.)(°F.).

Boyle's Law.—At a constant temperature the volume of a perfect gas is inversely proportional to the pressure of the gas.

Charles' Law.—At a constant pressure the volume of a perfect gas is proportional to the absolute temperature ($°F. + 459.7$, symbol $°R$, degrees Rankine).

Dalton's Law.—In a mixture of gases each component exerts the same pressure that it would exert if it were present alone at the same temperature in the volume occupied by the mixture (additive pressures). The pressure exerted by any component of a mixture of gases is known as the partial pressure of that component.

Amagat's Law.—The volume occupied by a gas mixture is equal to the sum of the volumes occupied separately by each constituent at the same temperature and pressure as the mixture (additive volumes).

Avogadro's Hypothesis.—Equal volumes of perfect gases contain the same number of molecules.

A combination of these principles leads to the following general expression for the pressure-volume-temperature relations of gases (including, approximately, moist air):

$$MPV = RT \tag{1}$$

The symbols have the following meanings, along with a consistent set of English engineering units:

M = molecular weight (pure component or mean molecular weight of a mixture)
P = pressure (atmospheres)
V = specific volume (cu ft.)/(lb.)
R = gas constant (atmos.)(cu. ft.)/mole-weight (lb.)($°R$.)
T = absolute temperature = $°F. + 459.7$ ($°R$)

In these units the numerical value of the gas constant, R, is 0.7302. At the standard conditions of one atmosphere pressure and a temperature of $32°F.$, or $491.7°R.$, $MV = 358.97$; that is, one pound-mole of the perfect gas occupies 358.97 cu. ft. under the standard conditions. Instead of solving Equation (1) to determine the volume of a given mass of gas under specified conditions of temperature and pressure, it is frequently more convenient to multiply the volume of the gas under standard conditions by the appropriate ratio:

$$V = V_0 \cdot \frac{P_0}{P} \cdot \frac{T}{T_0} \tag{2}$$

remembering that under standard conditions $P_0 = 1$, $T_0 = 491.7°R$.

Again, in a mixture of gases the proportion of any constituent by volume is equal to the ratio of its partial pressure to the total pressure of the mixture and also is equal to the mole-fraction of that constituent

—*i.e.*, the proportion of the number of molecules of the constituent to the total number of molecules in the mixture. Then if there are x moles of water vapor and y moles of air in a mixture, and since the molecular weights are 18.02 and 28.97, respectively, the proportion of water vapor by weight = $[18.02\ x/(18.02x + 28.97y)]$, and the proportion of air by weight = $[28.97y/(18.02x + 28.97y)]$. The proportion of water vapor by volume, or mole fraction of water vapor, is simply $x/(x + y)$. We shall denote this by the symbol w.

Furthermore, in moist air,

$$P = p_a + p_w \tag{3}$$

where p_a is the partial pressure of dry air in the mixture and p_w is the partial pressure of water vapor.

The mass of water vapor per pound of dry air in a mixture is,

$$H = \frac{p_w}{p_a} \cdot \frac{18.02}{28.97} = 0.622 \frac{p_w}{p_a} = 0.622 \frac{p_w}{P - p_w} \tag{4}$$

This quantity is known as the absolute humidity. Under all ordinary outdoor conditions it is a small fraction, rarely greater than 0.02 lb. of water vapor per pound of dry air, but in some commercial driers it may rise as high as 0.20 or more. In air conditioning work the absolute humidity is generally expressed as *grains* of water vapor per pound of dry air (1 lb. = 7,000 grains). At low values of humidity we often simplify Equation (4) by taking

$$p_a = P - p_w = 1 \text{ (approx.)}$$

so that we have

$$H = 0.622\ p_w \text{ (approx.)} \tag{5}$$

The relation between absolute humidity and mole fraction of water vapor is seen to be,

$$H = 0.622 \frac{w}{1 - w} \tag{6}$$

The enthalpy of moist air (usually called the "total heat of the air" in the early texts on drying and air conditioning) is defined as the sum of the sensible heat and the latent heat of vaporization of the water in the mixture. At not too high levels of humidity it can be computed with fair accuracy by the following formula:

$$E = c_{pa}(t_a - 32) + H\ [c_{pv}(t_a - 32) + \lambda_{32}] \tag{7}$$

where

E = enthalpy of the moist air (B.t.u.)/(lb. dry air)
c_{pa} = specific heat of dry air, very nearly 0.24 (B.t.u.)/(lb.)(°F.)—see Table 1

t_a = temperature of the mixture (°F.)
λ_{32} = heat of evaporation of water at 32°F., 1,076 (B.t.u.)/(lb.)
c_{pv} = mean specific heat of water vapor, approximately 0.44 (B.t.u.)/(lb.)
        (°F.)

Here the enthalpy is measured from 32°F., instead of from 0°F. as it is usually shown in charts and tables used for air conditioning calculations (Goff and Gratch 1945, 1946; ASHRAE Guide and Data Book 1961).

The heat of evaporation at temperature t°F. can be approximated for many purposes in the range of 50° to 200°F. by the linear expression,

$$\lambda_t = 1,096 - 0.593\ t \text{ (approx.)} \tag{8}$$

The humid heat of moist air is defined as the amount of heat required to increase the temperature 1°F. in a quantity of the mixture containing one pound of dry air.

$$c_s = c_{pa} + Hc_{pv} \tag{9}$$

where c_s is the humid heat of the mixture (B.t.u.)/(lb. dry air) (°F.).

The humid volume of moist air is defined as the volume of one pound of dry air plus the water vapor accompanying it.

$$V_h = V_a + HV_v = 0.7302\ \frac{T}{P}\left(\frac{1}{28.97} + \frac{H}{18.02}\right)$$
$$= 0.0405\ \frac{T}{P}\ (0.622 + H) \tag{10}$$

Comprehensive tables of the properties of moist air have been published by Marvin (1941); Goodman (1938, 1939, 1940, 1944); Goff and Gratch (1945); Grubenmann (1958); and American Society of Heating, Refrigerating, and Air Conditioning Engineers (1961).

Vaporization and Evaporation

The familiar phenomenon of evaporation of water from a wet object may be regarded from the standpoint either of the kinetic behavior of molecules or the macroscopic relations characteristic of the transport properties—that is, heat and mass transfer. We shall have occasion to use both approaches. In general, study of heat and mass transfer is largely empirical and affords little insight into mechanisms, but usually has the more immediate application. The mechanism of water movement within the moist object itself will be considered in Chapter 3.

In the German literature on drying, the words "Verdunstung" and "Verdampfung" are rather sharply differentiated (Krischer and Kröll 1956, 1959). The former corresponds to our "evaporation," the latter to "vaporization," but we tend to use the words interchangeably. Insofar as they represent shades of meaning, "evaporation" implies that another gas, such as air, besides water vapor is present in the space over the wet surface, while "vaporization" means that only water vapor is present, although perhaps at very low pressure, as in vacuum drying.

According to the kinetic theory, a phase transition like the evaporation or vaporization of water corresponds to the passage of molecules of the evaporating substance from the liquid mass to the vapor phase. This is not a one-way traffic, but is accompanied by the return of some molecules from the vapor to the liquid. On the average, molecules which pass from the liquid to the vapor will be those which possess higher than average velocity and energy, while those that are recaptured by the liquid will be those of relatively low velocity and energy. Whether there will or will not be a net evaporation from the liquid will depend on the temperature at the phase boundary and the temperature gradient through that boundary, the presence of air or other gas along with the water vapor, the presence of dissolved substances in the liquid, and the shape and curvature of the liquid surface.

The rate of evaporation from the surface of water or a completely wet flat porous object like a wick has been very extensively investigated (Carrier 1921; Hinchley and Himus 1924; Sherwood and Comings 1932; Powell and Griffiths 1935; Shepherd et al. 1938; Powell 1940; Smith 1943). It is well known that even a trace of a non-evaporating immiscible liquid which will spread on the water surface, like a film of oil, will reduce the rate drastically, and this expedient is being used to reduce the rate of evaporation from water storage reservoirs. However, even when the surface is as clean as it can be made experimentally, observed rates of evaporation into air are lower by many orders of magnitude than would be calculated by the methods of the kinetic theory, and even under high vacuum the rate is less than one per cent of the theoretical. The factor that imposes this limitation is the slow diffusion of water vapor through the stagnant film of adsorbed air at the surface (see the discussion of freeze drying, pp. 157–161). The reason we are interested is that the *initial* rate of evaporation from the wet surface of a body of typical food material, whether it be liquid or solid, is the same as the rate of evaporation from a water surface if the temperature, pressure, and

air velocity are the same.   Eventually, as drying progresses, the body
ceases to act as though it were completely wet, and the rate of drying
decreases.

Vapor Pressure and Humidity

Saturation, Relative Humidity.—When, according to the
kinetic picture, the rates of molecular escape from and recapture by
the water surface are equal, we have a condition of dynamic equilibrium.   The vapor space is said to be saturated with water vapor at
whatever temperature prevails there.   If conditions remain unchanged, no further net evaporation takes place.   Careful experiment
has shown that the amount of vapor in any given volume of the
saturated space is very nearly the same whether air is also present in
that space or not; it is as though it is the *space* which becomes saturated with water vapor.

At saturation, the water vapor exerts a perfectly definite partial
pressure, the vapor pressure of water,[1] which rises rapidly as temperature increases.   At 212°F. the vapor pressure of water is one
standard atmosphere; that is, 212° is the boiling point of water.
Table 6 gives the vapor pressure of water at 10° intervals from 0° to

TABLE 6

VAPOR PRESSURE OF WATER

Tempera-ture (°F.)	Vapor Pressure		Temper-ature (°F.)	Vapor Pressure	
	Atmos-pheres	Inches of Mercury		Atmos-pheres	Inches of Mercury
0 (ice)	0.001257	0.0376	160	0.323	9.656
10 (ice)	0.00210	0.0629	170	0.408	12.20
20 (ice)	0.00345	0.103	180	0.511	15.29
30 (ice)	0.00552	0.165	190	0.637	19.02
32	0.00602	0.180	200	0.786	23.47
40	0.00830	0.248	210	0.968	28.75
50	0.01210	0.362	212	1.000	29.92
60	0.01745	0.522	220	1.170	35.0
70	0.02470	0.739	230	1.414	42.3
80	0.03455	1.032	240	1.697	50.8
90	0.0476	1.422	250	2.030	60.7
100	0.0647	1.933	260	2.41	72.1
110	0.0869	2.597	270	2.84	85.1
120	0.1152	3.447	280	3.35	100.1
130	0.1515	4.527	290	3.92	117.2
140	0.1966	5.884	300	4.56	136.4
150	0.2533	7.572	...	...	...

[1] The pressure of a vapor in equilibrium with its liquid depends not only on its
temperature but also in some measure upon the shape of the liquid surface and
the pressure of other gases mixed with the vapor.   These secondary effects are
not usually significant in drying technology.

300°F., both in standard atmospheres and in inches equivalent height of a standard mercury column (Marks and Davis 1929; Keenan and Keyes 1936; Goff and Gratch 1945 and 1946; Keyes 1947).

The relative degree of saturation of a vapor space or body of moist air is called the relative humidity. Generally expressed as a percentage, it is defined by Equation (11):

$$r_h = 100 \frac{p_w}{p_s} \qquad (11)$$

where p_s is the vapor pressure of water at the temperature in question. It is also equal to the ratio of the mole fraction of water vapor in the mixture to the mole fraction of water vapor in air saturated at the same temperature and total pressure, expressed in percentage. A relative humidity of zero means that the air contains no water vapor, while a relative humidity of 100 per cent signifies that the air is saturated with water vapor. The average outdoor relative humidity in the United States, winter and summer, is about 65 per cent. On hot afternoons in arid regions it may fall to ten per cent or even lower. Air that is foggy contains suspended droplets in addition to its saturation level of water vapor.

Absolute humidity, which was defined by Equation (4), is likewise an expression of the amount of water vapor in a body of air. Still a third measure is the dew-point temperature, usually referred to simply as the dew point. This is the temperature at which the mixture would just become saturated with water vapor if it were cooled without change in composition or pressure. Thus if the mixture is already saturated, its temperature is the dew-point temperature, while for air that is only partly saturated or has a relative humidity less than 100 per cent the dew point is lower than the temperature of the mixture.

Absolute humidity and per cent relative humidity are related by Equation (12) or Equation (13), which follow from Equations (4) and (11):

$$H = \frac{0.622}{(100 \, P/r_h p_s) - 1} \qquad (12)$$

$$r_h = \frac{100 \, P}{p_s} \left(\frac{H}{H + 0.622} \right) \qquad (13)$$

The interaction between air and water vapor in their mixtures, and the departure from perfect gas laws, make this relation somewhat inexact. True relative humidity will be slightly higher than the computed value. At a temperature of 140° and relative humidity about 40 per cent, the discrepancy is about one-half of one per cent.

The data of Goff and Gratch (1945) allow the difference to be tabulated as a correction factor which can be used in very precise work.

Mean barometric pressure, air temperature, and dew point at selected cities in the United States are given in Table 7.

TABLE 7

MEAN BAROMETRIC PRESSURE, TEMPERATURE, AND DEW POINT AT SELECTED CITIES IN THE UNITED STATES

Place	Elevation Feet	Mean Barometer Inches	January Mean Monthly		April Mean Monthly		July Mean Monthly		October Mean Monthly	
			Temp. (°F.)	Dew Point (°F.)	Temp. (°F.)	Dew Point (°F.)	Temp. (°F.)	Dew Point (°F.)	Temp. (°F.)	Dew Point (°F.)
Portland, Me.	103	29.87	21	13	43	33	68	61	50	42
Buffalo, N. Y.	768	29.18	24	19	45	35	71	61	53	45
Philadelphia, Pa.	114	29.92	33	23	52	38	76	65	58	47
Nashville, Tenn.	546	29.49	39	32	59	46	79	67	61	49
Charleston, S. C.	48	30.03	51	42	65	54	82	73	68	58
Miami, Fla.	25	30.01	68	58	74	65	82	73	78	69
New Orleans, La.	5	30.04	53	43	68	59	82	73	70	61
St. Louis, Mo.	568	29.43	31	23	57	43	80	65	59	47
Minneapolis, Minn.	838	28.99	14	9	46	33	73	60	50	40
Bismarck, N. D.	1,660	28.22	9	6	43	29	71	56	45	33
Omaha, Neb.	1,105	28.83	21	15	51	37	75	63	53	42
Denver, Colo.	5,283	24.70	31	19	48	33	73	52	52	35
San Antonio, Tex.	794	29.17	52	43	69	58	84	72	71	60
Phoenix, Ariz.	1,106	28.74	50	33	69	36	91	56	71	45
Salt Lake City, Utah	4,227	25.73	25	22	50	33	77	36	53	26
Boise, Idaho	2,858	26.96	28	25	49	34	73	45	50	34
Spokane, Wash.	1,900	28.02	9	3	44	27	69	45	44	31
Seattle, Wash.	125	29.92	41	35	51	40	66	52	54	47
Portland, Ore.	154	29.91	39	34	56	46	67	54	54	43
Oakland, Calif.	18	30.01	48	40	56	46	63	54	60	50
Fresno, Calif.	277	29.63	46	42	60	44	81	50	62	47
Los Angeles, Calif.	512	29.35	56	43	60	49	71	59	66	53

Like the absolute humidity, the dew point remains unchanged if the air is heated or cooled. Absolute humidity also remains constant if the pressure of the air is increased or decreased. It is a particularly useful measure of humidity in drier calculations because it is expressed on a weight basis. A pound of dry air entering a drier, for example, still weighs just a pound at any other point in its passage through the system, no matter what changes in temperature or pressure may have taken place or how much water vapor may have been added to it.

Studies of the relation of human comfort to atmospheric conditions have shown that relative humidity correlates closely with comfort. The "feel" of the air, however, is no guide to its usefulness as air supply for a drier. Air that feels very moist on a chilly day, with a temperature of, say, 40°, usually will contain less moisture (*i.e.*, have a lower absolute humidity) than air that feels "dry" and comfortable at 80°. It is almost always a mistake to draw the air supply for a drier from inside the plant building, for that air will usually have a higher absolute humidity than the outside air, even though, being warmer, it may feel much drier. In choosing a location for a dehydration plant, Weather Bureau records of dew point are much more pertinent than the records of relative humidity.

Methods of Measuring Humidity.—Among the numerous ways of measuring the amount of water vapor in air, three are sometimes used for the control of drier operation—observation of the contraction or elongation of a hair or other moisture-sensitive fiber surrounded by the air and held taut by a light spring; determination of the temperature (dew point) at which dew forms on a slowly cooled mirror exposed to the air; and determination of the amount of cooling of a wet object exposed to the rapidly flowing air stream (wet-bulb hygrometry). The third of these is by far the most commonly used. Any instrument used to measure the humidity of air is called a hygrometer.

The hair hygrometer, simple in construction and operation, can be made very sensitive and rapidly responsive. The elongation of the hair is a function of the relative humidity of the air around it, nearly independent of air velocity and not very greatly affected by temperature. Constancy of calibration is very difficult to achieve, and readings are unreliable at very high and very low humidities. The dew point hygrometer can be made very precise. In modern instruments a fine thermocouple is brazed to the back of the wafer-thin mirror, and a light-sensitive cell is used to detect fogging of the artificially cooled mirror, supported in the air stream. The instrument has found particular application for determining a trace of unwanted water vapor in highly compressed industrial gases.

Hygrometry by means of the wet-bulb and dry-bulb thermometers, the combination being known as a "psychrometer," has been extensively investigated. According to Arnold (1933) the technique dates back to Hutton, about 1792. Measurements reported by Ferrel (1886) (see also Brooks 1933; Wexler and Brombacher 1951) became the basis for the "psychrometric formula" which was applied thereafter for reduction of Weather Bureau observations:

$$t_a - t_w = 2{,}730 \, \frac{p_{sw} - p_w}{P \, \{1 + [(t_w - 32)/1{,}571]\}} \tag{14}$$

where

t_a = air temperature (°F.)
t_w = wet-bulb temperature (°F.)
p_{sw} = vapor pressure of water at the wet-bulb temperature (atm.)
p_w = partial pressure of water vapor in the air (atm.)
P = barometric pressure in the vicinity of the wet bulb (atm.)

This is, of course, an empirical correlation which cannot be expected to apply accurately to conditions very far outside of Professor Ferrel's experimental range. We may convert the terms to others more directly useful in drying calculations by replacing p_w by its value in terms of P and H from Equation (4):

$$t_a - t_w = 2{,}730 \, \frac{p_{sw} - [HP/(0.622 + H)]}{P \, \{1 + [(t_w - 32)/1{,}571]\}} \tag{15}$$

or, at a pressure of 1 standard atmosphere,

$$t_a - t_w = 2{,}730 \, \frac{p_{sw} - [H/(0.622 + H)]}{1 + [(t_w - 32)/1{,}571]} \tag{16}$$

Now at any selected value of wet-bulb temperature, t_w, the saturation pressure, p_{sw}, is fixed and known, so that Equation (16) may be used to determine any one of the three quantities (air temperature, wet-bulb temperature, and absolute humidity) if the other two quantities are given.

The Sprung psychrometric formula, quoted by Krischer (1939), omits a small term of the Ferrel formula; in terms of degrees Fahrenheit the expression comparable to Equation (14) above is:

$$t_a - t_w = 2{,}720 \, \frac{p_{sw} - p_w}{P} \tag{17}$$

In careful tests made by Flanigan (1960) the most reliable measurements of humidity for the temperature range of 50° to 62° were obtained with an aspirated psychrometer or a sling psychrometer, neither of which is readily adapted to automatic measurement and control of humidity in industrial operations. Psychrometers in which the wetted wick or sleeve extends into a water-supply reservoir tend to indicate a higher humidity than the true value. The same difficulty is likely to be encountered in carelessly operated psychrometers of any type if the wick is allowed to become coated with dust or crusted from the salts in impure water so that it no longer acts as a true wet bulb. In spite of several elusive sources of error, the psychrometer remains the standard instrument for practical humidity measurement in drying operations. "Wet-bulb depression," the difference between actual air temperature ("dry-bulb temperature") and wet-bulb temperature, is very widely employed as a major factor to be correlated with rate of drying.

Psychrometric Charts.—Calculations required in the design of drying equipment or the correlation and analysis of results from drying experiments can be greatly facilitated, and the complex relationships existing in a drier can be readily visualized, by the use of some form of psychrometric chart. Many different forms have been devised. The one that has been most widely used in the United States for following a drying operation was described by Grosvenor (1908) and Carrier (1911), while the one generally used in Europe (and in the United States for many air conditioning calculations), and often known as the i, x diagram, was proposed by Mollier (1923, 1929). The design and use of such charts has been under study for a number of years by a committee of the American Society of Heating, Refrigerating, and Air Conditioning Engineers, and was the topic of an extensive symposium held by the Society in Dallas in 1960. Precisely graduated charts drawn on a large scale for use in computations have been published by Carrier (1940, 1941); Garber (1943); Goodman (1944); Zimmerman (1945); Lykow (1950, 1955); the American Society of Heating, Refrigerating, and Air Conditioning Engineers (1961); Krischer and Kröll (1956, 1959); Grubenmann (1958); and Eckert and Drake (1959). A Mollier-type chart is included in the back of this book.

Fig. 1 shows the Grosvenor (1908) diagram on a small scale for the purpose of explanation. Co-ordinates are rectangular and graduations are uniform, air temperature usually being shown as the abscissa, absolute humidity as the ordinate. In one form of the i, x diagram (Mollier), Fig. 2, the ordinate is absolute humidity, graduated uniformly, but the other independent co-ordinate is enthalpy (sometimes known as "total heat") of the moist air (see p. 14); the symbols commonly used for enthalpy and absolute humidity in European work are i and x, respectively. Lines of constant enthalpy are parallel and uniformly spaced, but are drawn at an acute angle from the lines of constant humidity, instead of perpendicular to them. The remaining variables, for example temperature, are constructed in the resulting oblique network. Lines of constant temperature are straight, but diverge slightly, fan-wise.

The i, x, or Mollier, diagram has the great advantage that it can be used for the simple graphical solution of mixture problems, because the point representing a mixture of two streams of air differing in

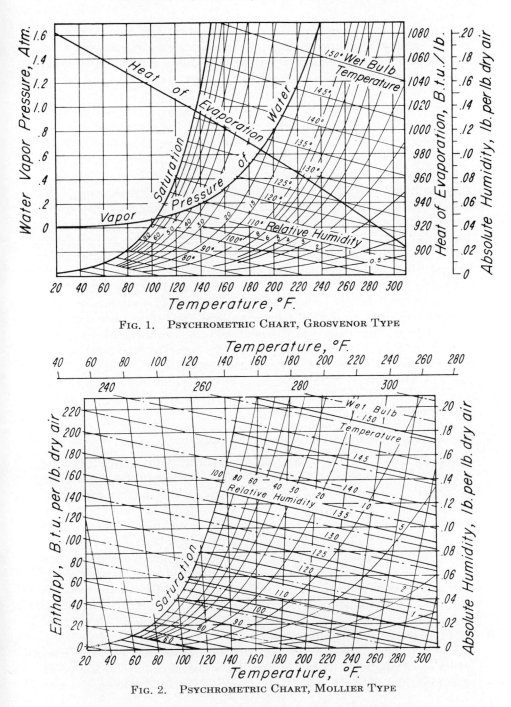

FIG. 1.   PSYCHROMETRIC CHART, GROSVENOR TYPE

FIG. 2.   PSYCHROMETRIC CHART, MOLLIER TYPE

temperature and humidity falls upon a straight line joining the two points on the diagram, dividing it in the same proportion as the masses of dry air contained in the two streams.   For example, if one stream, flowing at a rate of 2,000 lbs. dry air per minute and having $H = 0.080$ lb. water vapor per pound dry air, $E = 120$ B.t.u. per pound dry air, is mixed with a second stream flowing at a rate of 1,000 lbs. dry air per minute, and having $H = 0.020$ lb. per pound dry air, $E = 60$ B.t.u. per pound dry air, the combined flow of 3,000 lbs. dry air per minute will have $H = 0.060$ lb. per pound dry air, $E = 100$ B.t.u. per pound dry air, and the point on the Mollier chart representing this mixture will fall on the straight line between the two points specified, and $^1/_3$ [i.e., $1,000/(1,000 + 2,000)$] of the distance from the first of the points to the second.   To help avoid mistakes, remember that the point representing the mixture always lies *closest* to the point representing the *major* component in the mixture.   The simple mixture rule does not quite hold true in the Grosvenor diagram.

Whichever form of co-ordinate system is used for the basic chart, at least a third family of lines is almost invariably constructed on it, namely the lines of equal "thermodynamic wet-bulb temperature." The latter will be defined in the next section.   Additional curves or families of curves are frequently added in order to facilitate various calculations.   Examples are percentage relative humidity or percentage absolute humidity, humid heat, humid volume, heat of evaporation, and saturated vapor pressure, shown as functions either of temperature or of absolute humidity.

Applications of the Psychrometric Chart

Conditions During Adiabatic Evaporation.—Any process which takes place without transfer of heat to or from the surroundings is termed "adiabatic."   Many drying operations are so conducted that in the section of the equipment where most of the evaporation occurs the heat absorbed by the wet body from the air stream, thus cooling the latter, far outweighs any heat transfer inward by radiation from a furnace or by conduction from the environment; that section of the equipment behaves in a particularly simple way, because of the nearly adiabatic conditions.   The heat abstracted from the sensible heat of the air is practically all transformed to the latent heat of the water vapor formed.   The enthalpy of the air remains almost unchanged, increases very slightly.

The Thermodynamic Wet-Bulb Temperature.—If the condition of adiabatic evaporation just described is carried to the point of equilibrium through effectively infinite contact between the wet body and the air, the temperature of the air falls and its humidity rises until an equilibrium saturation of the air at the new temperature is attained. This *temperature of adiabatic saturation*, designated by the symbol t^*, is approximately the same as the physically observed *wet-bulb temperature* of the same air, designated t_w, provided the velocity of air past the wet-bulb thermometer is relatively high—on the order of 1,000 ft. per min.—and no high-temperature radiating surface is visible from the thermometer. For this reason the former is also known as the *thermodynamic wet-bulb temperature* (designation t^*). Curves of constant t^* are indicated on both psychrometric charts illustrated here (Figs. 1 and 2).

The lines of equal thermodynamic wet-bulb temperature on the psychrometric chart are computed from the hypothetical energy balance. Assume an adiabatic system into which flows air of humidity H and enthalpy E. Saturated air at a humidity of H^* and enthalpy E^* leaves the system, and liquid water at the enthalpy E_w^*, corresponding to the temperature of the saturated air leaving the system, is supplied. Then the adiabatic energy balance is as follows:

$$E^* = E + (H^* - H)E_w^* \tag{18}$$

where the asterisk indicates enthalpy or humidity condition at saturation at the thermodynamic wet-bulb temperature. For any chosen air temperature, t, there is one, and only one, set of values of E^*, H^*, and E_w^*, so all three of these are functions of t alone. Now if Equation (18) is combined with Equation (7) and solved for H, we have:

$$H = \frac{-0.240\ (t - 32) + E^* - H^*E_w^*}{0.440\ (t - 32) - E_w^* + 1,076} \tag{19}$$

This constitutes the relation between H and t which is plotted on the chart as a family of lines of equal thermodynamic wet-bulb temperature.

Example 1.—Air with an absolute humidity of 0.010 and temperature of 80° (point A, Fig. 3) is heated indirectly to a temperature of 190° (point B). The (thermodynamic) wet-bulb temperature, t^*, is then 92°. This air evaporates water adiabatically from a wet material until the temperature of the air falls to 120° (point C, like point B, lies on the 92° thermodynamic wet-bulb line). At that point absolute humidity of the air has risen from 0.010 to 0.026. If 1,000 lbs. of water are to be evaporated per hour $(1,000)/(0.026 - 0.010)$, or 62,500 lbs. of dry air per hour must be passed over the wet material.

The Evaporation Limit and the Drying Potential.—As is immediately apparent upon looking at the psychrometric chart, the process of adiabatic evaporation can continue to the left along a line of constant wet-bulb temperature until the latter intersects the saturation curve, as at D, Fig. 3. In fact, if, as we stipulated in the example, no additional heat is supplied to the air, the fall in temperature from point B to point D represents the maximum amount of heat available for evaporation of water, per pound of dry air circulated.

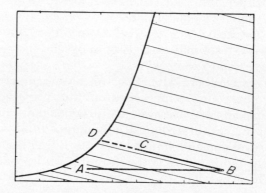

FIG. 3. HEATING AND ADIABATIC COOLING LINES ON PSYCHROMETRIC CHART

The distance BD represents an unspent working balance of available energy; or, to use another metaphor, the distance of a point on the chart from the saturation curve, measured along an adiabatic cooling curve, is one measure of a *drying potential*. As evaporation proceeds, this potential becomes smaller and smaller, approaching zero as saturation is approached.

Example 2.—Assume that 1,000 lbs. of air, having a temperature of 160° and a wet-bulb temperature of 95°F., evaporates adiabatically one pound of water already at the wet-bulb temperature, 95°. The latent heat of evaporation of water at 95° (see curve in Fig. 1) is 1,040 B.t.u. per lb. In addition to this heat of evaporation the air must also supply the smaller amount of heat needed to raise the temperature of the pound of water vapor from 95°F. up to the new temperature of the air-vapor mixture. From the psychrometric chart, initial humidity of the air was 0.021 lb. water vapor per pound dry air; the initial 1,000 lbs. therefore contained 21/1.021, or 20.55 lbs. of water vapor and 979.45 lbs. of dry air. Then 20.55 lbs. of water vapor, with a specific heat of 0.44, cools from 160° to the new temperature, t_n, and 979.45 lbs. of dry air, with a specific heat of 0.24, also cools from 160° to t_n. The quantity of heat thus given up is balanced by the heat absorbed; one pound of liquid water is evaporated at 95°, absorbing 1,040 B.t.u., and the pound of vapor is warmed from 95° to t_n, also at a specific heat of 0.44. The resulting equality can be solved for t_n; t_n = 155.5°. That is, the adiabatic evaporation of a pound of water has cooled 1,000 lbs. of air almost 5°F.

In air having the initial condition assumed for this example, adiabatic saturation would reduce temperature all the way from 160°F. to the wet-bulb temperature, 95°, a temperature fall of 65°, corresponding to an increase in humidity from 0.021 to 0.0365, some 15 times as much as in the example. Thus the drying potential of the air is only slightly decreased. The *evaporative limit* can be taken to mean the maximum number of pounds of water that can be evaporated adiabatically per pound of dry air. In the example this would be 0.0155 lb. of water per pound of dry air.

A rough rule of thumb, useful for quick approximations, is that each 5° of difference between air temperature ("dry bulb") and wet-bulb temperature makes possible a rise of 0.001 in humidity, or the evaporation of a pound of water into 1,000 lbs. of air.

The Cooling Effect of Evaporation.—The high absorption of heat accompanying the evaporation of water (approximately 1,000 B.t.u. per lb. of evaporation) is, of course, a major factor in our ability to dry delicate food materials in high-temperature air without scorching the food. So long as the material is completely wet it will assume a temperature approximately the same as that of a wet-bulb thermometer in the same air stream—perhaps as much as 150°F. lower than the air temperature. When the surface is no longer completely wet the rate of evaporation falls and hence the cooling effect decreases; the material temperature rises. When the rate of drying becomes very low the material temperature rises to near equality with the air temperature. Ede and Hales (1948) give data on the temperature of potato strips during drying in air of 70°C. temperature, 44°C. wet-bulb temperature, from which Fig. 4 is taken. Air velocity was 10 ft. per sec.

Effect of Recirculation on Air Condition.—Many industrial driers are so constructed that a part (sometimes a very large proportion) of the air introduced into the drier is circulated over the moist product again and again before it is exhausted from the equipment. The psychrometric chart enables one to visualize the resulting effect on drying conditions. Fig. 5 represents the situation on a Mollier-type chart. Point A shows the temperature and humidity of the incoming fresh air. Heating of this air to temperature t' when there is no recirculation takes place along line AB, without change in humidity. If this air is now brought into contact with the moist

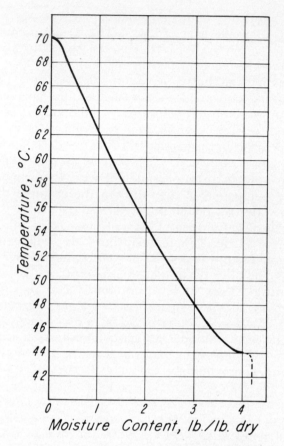

From Ede and Hales 1948

FIG. 4.   TEMPERATURE OF POTATOE STRIP DURING DRYING AT
CONSTANT AIR CONDITION

material adiabatically, its condition will change along some such path
as line BC, and the air will be exhausted at condition C.   All of the
air contacted with the moist material will have been heated from A
to B;   this will have required a quantity of heat proportional to the
rise in enthalpy, and therefore, since the enthalpy scale is uniform, to
the length of the line AB.   But if only a part of the air at the exit is
exhausted, the remainder mixed back with enough fresh air to make
up the loss, and then the mixture heated to the same temperature, t',
and circulated through the drying chamber, the humidity in the
drying chamber will build up until a new equilibrium condition is
reached, at some such condition as point D in the figure.   As evapo-

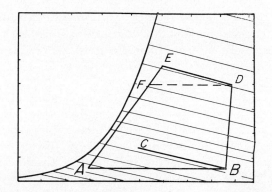

FIG. 5.   EFFECT OF RECIRCULATION ON AIR CONDITION

ration takes place the air temperature will fall and humidity will rise to the condition of point E.   Part of the air at this exit condition will be exhausted and the remainder will be mixed with the make-up fresh air to give condition F.   Now the heat to be supplied is the much smaller amount, proportional to the length of line FD, instead of AB.

A mass balance on the water entering and leaving such a dehydrator system leads to the following simple relation:

$$r_d = \frac{H' - H_0}{H'' - H_0} \tag{20}$$

where

r_d = proportion of the combined air flow that is recirculated
$1 - r_d$ = corresponding proportion of fresh air introduced
H_0 = absolute humidity of the fresh, or make-up air
H' = absolute humidity of the mixture of recirculated air with fresh air
H'' = absolute humidity of the air as it leaves the drying chamber, to be partly discarded, partly returned

For example, suppose that a dehydrator is operating at a wet-bulb temperature of 100°F., air going to the drying chamber has a temperature of 165°, and at the exhaust stack has a temperature of 137.5°. The fresh air drawn in has a temperature of 60° and a wet-bulb temperature of 55°.   What is the proportion of recirculation, and what is the fresh air intake?

From the psychrometric chart, $H_0 = 0.0080$, $H' = 0.0271$, and $H'' = 0.0337$.   Applying the above equation, $r_d = 0.743$, or 74.3 per cent, and $1 - r_d = 0.257$, or 25.7 per cent.   If the total circulation of air in the drying chamber is 2,000 lbs. per min., 514 lbs. per min. of fresh air must be drawn in.

Control of the proportion of recirculation in a dehydrator enables the operator to maintain substantially uniform drying conditions regardless of variations in atmospheric conditions. Automatic control of wet-bulb temperature can be accomplished by making the controller operate recirculation dampers.

The reader must not conclude that a high proportion of recirculation of air—or, indeed, any proportion whatsoever—is to be recommended under all circumstances. We have pointed out that increasing recirculation raises the humidity in the dehydrator; at a given air temperature the drying potential of the air is thereby reduced and, as will be discussed later, the drying rate will usually decrease. Several factors must be balanced against one another to arrive at the optimum proportion of recirculation. In some very important and well-designed installations, no recirculation of air takes place.

Effect of Reheating the Circulating Air.—In some types of dehydrator the heating unit is built in sections within the drying chamber and arranged so that air flows over the moist material, then through a heating section, then through another drying section, then another heating section, and so on, in as many as 6 or 8 reheating stages. The air is therefore successively cooled by evaporation of water, reheated, cooled by evaporation again, and so on. As Fig. 6 illustrates, wet-bulb temperature of the air rises at each reheating, and absolute humidity of the air finally discarded, shown at point B, may be quite high.

Humidity and Temperature in a Direct-Fired Drier.—Some driers are heated solely by mixing the products of combustion of an oil or gas burner directly with the circulating air. Combustion of the hydrogen in the fuel increases the amount of water vapor in the

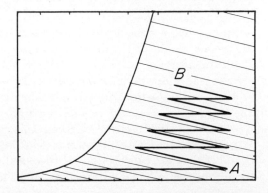

FIG. 6.   EFFECT OF REHEATING THE CIRCULATING AIR

circulating mixture and therefore raises the humidity and wet-bulb temperature. The temperatures, humidities, and proportion of recirculation are then related by the following modification of Equation (20):

$$r_d = \frac{H' - H_0 - f(t' - t_0)}{H'' - H_0 - f(t'' - t_0)} \tag{21}$$

where

t' = temperature of the mixture of recirculated air with fresh air (°F.)
t'' = temperature of the air as it leaves the drying chamber, to be partly discarded, partly returned (°F.)
t_0 = temperature of the fresh, or make-up air (°F.)
f = coefficient depending upon the composition and heating value of the fuel (°F.)$^{-1}$

For natural gas, with a heating value of 1,000 B.t.u. per cu. ft., f will be about 0.000025; for fuel oil, of 15 per cent hydrogen and 18,000 B.t.u. per lb. heating value, f will be about 0.000019. The rise in absolute humidity is not, in fact, great enough to have a serious effect on drier performance under most circumstances. The formula states that in a non-recirculating drier ($r_d = 0$, as in some simple tunnel driers and many spray driers) the incoming fresh air would have to be raised in temperature by about 400°F. to cause a rise in absolute humidity of only 0.01 lb. water vapor per pound dry air due to combustion of the hydrogen in natural gas.

Construction of Psychrometric Chart for Non-Standard Barometric Pressure

Most published psychrometric charts have been constructed for a standard atmospheric pressure, one atmosphere, in most of the charts published in the United States for both air conditioning and drying calculations. Charts in most of the European engineering texts are based on the slightly lower pressure of 750 mm. of mercury. Most published charts are accompanied by instructions for calculating the correction to be applied to the various psychrometric quantities at a different atmospheric pressure.

As a matter of fact, the standard chart would be of only limited value to a person who needed to make numerous calculations that would be valid for, say, Denver, Colo., at an altitude of 5,283 ft. and a mean barometric pressure of 24.70 in. of mercury (0.825 standard atmosphere). Construction of a working chart for any pressure can be accomplished by going back to the numerical relations on which all such charts are based, included among Equations (1), (4), (7), (9), (10), (11), (13), and (19).

The approximate mean barometric pressure at altitudes up to
8,000 ft. is shown in Fig. 7.   In addition to the predictable effect of
altitude, actual barometric pressure at any location fluctuates from
day to day, with a range of as much as two inches of mercury, or
more.   For very precise calculations relating to a specific time and
place, both this variation and the actual pressure within the drier
itself must be taken into account.

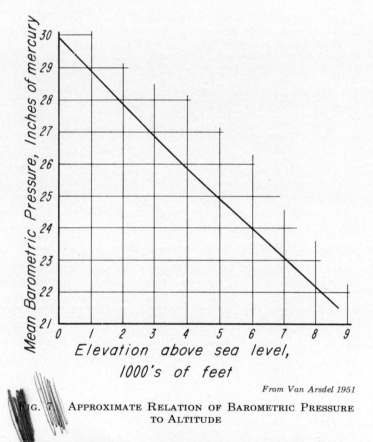

From Van Arsdel 1951

FIG. 7. APPROXIMATE RELATION OF BAROMETRIC PRESSURE
TO ALTITUDE

Effect of External Conditions on Water Vapor Pressure

Capillaries and Drops.—The vapor pressure of a liquid is pre-
dictably affected by surface forces such as those which pull a small
isolated body of liquid into spherical shape (a drop) or produce capillary rise in a fine tube or wick.   Under tension—for example, beneath
the liquid surface in a capillary—the pressure of the vapor decreases
by an amount dependent on the curvature of the liquid surface; a

curvature of one micron radius lowers the vapor pressure by only about 0.1 per cent, but a curvature of one millimicron radius lowers it by about 50 per cent.   Under the convex liquid surface of a drop, on the other hand, the pressure of the vapor increases.   In both cases the fractional change in vapor pressure is inversely proportional to the radius of curvature of the liquid surface.

The surface tension of water in moist air, 51.8×10^{-4} lb. (force) per ft. at 32°F., is somewhat lower at higher temperatures (46.5×10^{-4} lb. per ft. at 122°F., 40.3×10^{-4} lb. per ft. at 212°F.).   The radius of droplets produced by atomization into a spray drier is therefore a function of the temperature of the feed liquid.   The surface tension is also affected to some extent, generally being increased, by the presence of dissolved substances in the liquid.   On the other hand, it can be greatly reduced by the presence of even a small proportion of a surface-active agent such as a soap or other detergent. The effects of such an agent include facilitation of the wetting of a dry surface, the production of foam, and the emulsification of immiscible liquids; a surface-active agent will also increase the rate at which the liquid will penetrate a porous body.   The activity is very sensitive to the specific chemical composition of the surface-active material. Reduction of surface tension is always one effect, but other properties are also involved in high detergency.   Saravacos and Charm (1962) found experimentally that soaking pieces of various fruits and vegetables in solutions of such surface-active agents as Myveral, Myrj, or sodium oleate caused some increase in drying rate during the constant rate phase (see p. 92), but no change in the equilibrium moisture relations or in the shrinkage during drying.

Vapor Pressure of Solutions.—The water vapor pressure of a solution such as the liquid part of food materials is lower than the vapor pressure of pure water, but the difference becomes substantial only when the concentration of solid becomes high, as in the final stages of drying.   This is a reflection of the fact that the molecular weight of substances occurring in solution in foods is generally high. Since vapor pressure lowering is approximately proportional to the number of molecules of solute per unit weight of pure solvent, the relative vapor pressure lowering is small when the molecules are large. Even with a comparatively small molecule, sucrose, having a molecular weight of 342, the vapor pressure of a solution of 10 gm. of sucrose per 100 gm. of water is lower than that of pure water by only about 0.6 per cent.   International Critical Tables (1928) gives the vapor pressure of solutions of gelatin in water at 25°C. as shown in Table 8. At the high concentrations of gelatin we are really dealing with water that is sorbed in a colloidal solid, a subject which is covered more extensively in the next section.

The solute molecules in a solution exert an osmotic pressure within the solution, corresponding to a suction or negative pressure in the solvent—in this case, water. Like the vapor pressure lowering, the osmotic pressure of the dissolved substance in dilute solutions is approximately proportional to the number of molecules of solute per unit weight of solvent.

Vapor Pressure of Adsorbed Water.—Molecular forces at the surface of a solid bind molecules of a surrounding gas or vapor more or less firmly into an adsorbed layer; the escaping tendency of a gas or vapor molecule in this layer, that is to say, its fugacity or vapor pressure, is correspondingly reduced. In the case of water vapor in contact with the organic substances of which most foods are composed, the adsorption of one or a few complete layers of water molecules on the solid surface is so strong that the water vapor pressure becomes very low. This tightly bound water is correspondingly difficult to remove. The terms "bound water" and "free water" are, however,

TABLE 8

VAPOR PRESSURE OF GELATIN SOLUTIONS

Per Cent Gelatin	Vapor Pressure Per Cent of the V. P. of Pure Water
76	82.5
90	24
92.5	14
95	6
97	2
98	0

hard to define sharply, since the binding energy may have any value between zero and the energy of a valence bond (Kuprianoff 1958). Only that water which exerts full vapor pressure should be regarded as truly "free." A rather large proportion of the moisture content of many raw foods substantially meets this requirement.

The consequences of the reduction of water vapor pressure due to capillary forces, presence of dissolved compounds, and binding by adsorption are discussed more fully in sections dealing with the sorption isotherm and equilibrium moisture content, pp. 67–71.

BIBLIOGRAPHY

AMERICAN SOCIETY OF HEATING, REFRIGERATING, AND AIR CONDITIONING ENGINEERS. 1961. ASHRAE Guide and Data Book, *1*. The Society, New York.

ARNOLD, J. H. 1933. The theory of the psychrometer. I. The mechanism of Evaporation. Physics *4*, 255–262. II. The effect of velocity. *Ibid. 4*, 334–340.

BROOKS, D. B. 1933. Psychrometric Charts. U. S. Bureau of Standards. Misc. Publ. *143*.

CARRIER, W. H. 1911. Rational psychrometric formulae. Trans. Am. Soc. Mech. Eng. *33*, 1005–1053.

CARRIER, W. H. 1921. The theory of atmospheric evaporation, with special reference to compartment driers. Ind. Eng. Chem. *13*, 432–438.

CARRIER, W. H. 1940. Low and Normal Temperature Psychrometric Charts. Carrier Corporation, Syracuse, N. Y.

CARRIER, W. H. 1941. Psychrometric Chart for High Temperatures. Carrier Corporation, Syracuse, N. Y.

ECKERT, E. R. G., and DRAKE, R. M., JR. 1959. Heat and Mass Transfer. Second Ed. McGraw-Hill Book Co., New York.

EDE, A. J., and HALES, K. C. 1948. The physics of drying in heated air, with special reference to fruit and vegetables. Dept. Sci. Ind. Research, Food Investigations, Spec. Rept. *53*.

FERREL, W. 1886. Annual Report of Chief Signal Officer U. S., Appendix 24.

FLANIGAN, F. M. 1960. Comparison of the accuracy of humidity measuring instruments. ASHRAE J. *2*, 56–59.

GARBER, H. J. 1943. Humidity Chart for Air and Water. Reinhold Publishing Co., New York. Supplement to Chem. Eng. Catalog.

GOFF, J. A., and GRATCH, S. 1945. Thermodynamic properties of moist air. J. Am. Soc. Heating Ventilating Eng. *51*, 125–139. *Also in* Heating, Piping, Air Conditioning, J. Sec. *17*, 334–348.

GOFF, J. A., and GRATCH, S. 1946. Low-pressure properties of water in the range −160° to 212°F. J. Am. Soc. Heating Ventilating Eng. *52*, 95–121.

GOODMAN, W. 1938. New tables of the psychrometric properties of air-vapor mixtures. Heating, Piping, Air Conditioning *10*, No. 1, 1–4, 119–122.

GOODMAN, W. 1944. Air Conditioning Analysis—With Psychrometric Charts and Tables. Macmillan Co., New York.

GOODMAN, W. 1939, 1940. Properties of mixtures of air and saturated water vapor for barometric pressures from 22 to 32 in. of mercury. Heating, Piping, Air Conditioning *11*, No. 7, 445–446; No. 8, 505–506; No. 9, 567–568; No. 10, 627–628; No. 11, 689–690; No. 12, 755–756; *12*, No. 3, 185–186; No. 4, 253–254; No. 5, 311–312; No. 6, 373–374; No. 7, 435–436.

GROSVENOR, W. M. 1908. Calculations for drier design. Trans. Am. Inst. Chem. Eng. *1*, 184–202.

GRUBENMANN, M. 1958. I-x Diagrams for Humid Air. (In German.) Springer-Verlag, Berlin.

HINCHLEY, J. W., and HIMUS, G. W. 1924. Evaporation in currents of air. Trans. Inst. Chem. Eng. (London) *2*, 57–64.

International Critical Tables. 1928. McGraw-Hill Book Co., New York.

KEENAN, J. H., and KEYES, F. G. 1936. Thermodynamic Properties of Steam. John Wiley and Sons, New York.

KEYES, F. G. 1947. Thermodynamic properties of water substance, 0° to 150°C. J. Chem. Phys. *15*, 602–612.

KRISCHER, O. 1939. Physical problems in the drying of solid porous materials. (In German.) Chem. App. *26*, 17–23.

KRISCHER, O., and KRÖLL, K.   1956, 1959.   Drying Technology.   (Trocknungstechnik).   1.   O. Krischer, The Scientific Fundamentals of Drying Technology.
(Die wissenschaftlichen Grundlagen der Trocknungstechnik.)   (In German.)
Springer-Verlag, Berlin-Göttingen-Heidelberg.   2.   K. Kröll, Driers and Drying Processes.   (Trockner und Trocknungsverfahren.)

KUPRIANOFF, J.   1958.   "Bound water" in foods.   In Fundamental Aspects of
the Dehydration of Foodstuffs.   Soc. Chem. Ind., 14–23.

LYKOW, A. W.   1950, 1955.   Experimental and Theoretical Fundamentals of
Drying.   Moscow, 1950.   (In Russian.)   Veb. Verlag, Berlin, 1955.   (In German.)

MARKS, L. S., and DAVIS, H. N.   1929.   Tables and Diagrams of the Thermal
Properties of Saturated and Superheated Steam.   Longmans, Green and Co.,
New York.

MARVIN, C. F.   1941.   Psychrometric tables for vapor pressure, relative humidity, and temperature of the dew point.   U. S. Weather Bureau, Pub. 235,
Washington.

MOLLIER, R.   1923.   A new diagram for water vapor—air mixtures.   (In German.)   Z. Ver. deut. Ing. 67, 869–872.

MOLLIER, R.   1929.   The i-x diagram for water vapor—air mixtures.   (In German.)   Z. Ver. deut. Ing. 73, 1009–1013.

POWELL, R. W.   1940.   Further experiments on the evaporation of water from
saturated surfaces.   Trans. Inst. Chem. Eng. (London) 18, 36–55.

POWELL, R. W., and GRIFFITHS, E.   1935.   The evaporation of water from plane
and cylindrical surfaces.   Trans. Inst. Chem. Eng. (London) 13, 175–198.

SARAVACOS, G. D., and CHARM, S. E.   1962.   Effect of surface-active agents on
dehydration of fruits and vegetables.   Food Technol. 16, No. 1, 91–93.

SCOTT, A. W.   1958.   Some properties of air in relation to dehydration.   In
Fundamental Aspects of the Dehydration of Foodstuffs.   Soc. Chem. Ind.
33–36.

SHEPHERD, C. B., HADLOCK, C., and BREWER, R. C.   1938.   Drying materials in
trays—evaporation of surface moisture.   Ind. Eng. Chem. 30, 388–397.

SHERWOOD, T. K., and COMINGS, W. E.   1932.   An experimental study of the
wet-bulb hygrometer.   Trans. Am. Inst. Chem. Eng. 28, 88–117.

SMITH, A. J. M.   1943.   Note on physical aspects of drying and some drying
characteristics of foods.   Dehydration.   U. K. Progress Reports, D. S. I. R.,
Ministry of Food, Sec. X, Part 3.

VAN ARSDEL, W. B.   1951.   Principles of the drying process, with special reference to vegetable dehydration.   U. S. Dept. Agr. Bur. Circ. AIC-300.

WEXLER, A., and BROMBACHER, W. G.   1951.   Methods of measuring humidity
and testing hygrometers.   National Bureau of Standards Circ. 512.

ZIMMERMAN, O. T.   1945.   Psychrometric Tables and Charts.   Industrial Research Service, Dover, N. H.

CHAPTER 3

Phenomena of Heat and Mass Transfer

HEAT TRANSFER BY CONDUCTION, CONVECTION, AND RADIATION

One definition of "drying" is the removal of a liquid from a solid by thermal means (Marshall and Friedman 1950). The definition emphasizes the basic fact that the evaporation of a liquid (or a decrease in the moisture content at any point in a body) is invariably linked with a corresponding flow of heat. Transfer of heat inward from the surroundings is accompanied by the transfer of mass in the form of water vapor outward from the wet body to its surroundings. In large measure the rate at which a body can be dried is limited by the rate at which heat can be supplied to the point where the decrease in moisture content is occurring.

Heat transfer by conduction, radiation, or convection is extensively treated in engineering handbooks (for example, Perry 1950; Marks 1951) and texts on chemical engineering such as Badger and Banchero (1955), and Coulson and Richardson (1955), and in numerous other publications. All of these modes of heat transfer may be involved in the processes going on in a practical drier. Only a brief mention of the main characteristics of each can be made here.

Heat Transfer by Conduction

Transfer of heat by conduction through a solid, liquid, or gas is defined by the following equation:

$$q = \frac{dQ_h}{d\theta} = -kA \frac{dt}{dl} \qquad (21)$$

where

q = rate of heat flow (B.t.u.)/(hr.)
Q_h = quantity of heat transferred (B.t.u.)
θ = time (hr.)
A = area normal to heat flow (ft.²)
k = thermal conductivity (B.t.u.)/(hr.)(ft.)(°F.)
t = temperature (°F.)
l = distance in direction of heat flow (ft.)

The negative sign in the equation signifies that the flow of heat is in the direction of decreasing temperature.

Transfer of energy in heat conduction takes place by the exchange of momentum of random thermal motion of the molecules with neighboring molecules; it is passed along hand to hand, as it were. Thermal conductivity is a property of the matter of which the body is composed, being low in gases and vapors (from Table 1, 0.016 (B.t.u.)/(hr.)(ft.) (°F.) for dry air at 100°F.) higher in liquids (0.363 (B.t.u.)/(hr.)(ft.) (°F.) for water at 100°F.) and ranging in solids from quite low in insulating materials like corkboard (approximately 0.025 (B.t.u.)/ (hr.)(ft.)(°F.)), through a range averaging approximately ten times as great in solid organic materials like celluloid and rubber, up to several thousand times as great in many metals. The conductivity of water is somewhat greater than the conductivity of the dry solid substance of most food materials. In fresh fruits and vegetables, whose moisture content is very high, the conductivity is not far from that of pure water. As drying takes place, however, conductivity falls. If shrinkage is complete, so that the dry product is free from internal voids, the decrease in conductivity is only minor, but if the body becomes highly porous as it dries the low conductivity of the air in the open spaces reduces the over-all conductivity markedly. The conductivity of water vapor is slightly less than the conductivity of dry air at the same temperature.

The equation of heat conduction takes the following generalized form for unsteady one-dimensional flow of heat in a body whose thermal conductivity, density, and specific heat may vary both with temperature and with position within the body:

$$\frac{\partial^2 t}{\partial \theta^2} = \frac{\partial}{\partial l}\left(\alpha\,\frac{\partial t}{\partial l}\right) \tag{22}$$

$$\alpha = \frac{k}{\rho c} \tag{23}$$

where

α = thermal diffusivity of the material (sq. ft.)/(hr.)
θ = time (hr.)
ρ = density of the material (lb.)/(cu. ft.)
c = specific heat of the material (B.t.u.)/(lb.)(°F.)

If a heat source is present in the body, as in radio-frequency heating, an appropriate term is added to Equation (22). Analytical solutions of Equation (22) have been obtained for numerous specific cases, see Carslaw and Jaeger (1959), but not for the general non-linear case. Numerical methods of solution, suitable for programming on automatic computers, have been described by Dusinberre (1949), Milne (1953), and Scarborough (1950).

Heat Transfer by Convection

Heat is transferred within an opaque solid body by the process of conduction only. In a liquid or gas, however, heat conduction will

often be small in comparison with heat transfer by the bodily movement of some portions of the fluid with respect to the containing walls
or other portions of the fluid, or with transfer by means of radiant
energy.   In many practical processes all three modes of heat transfer
occur simultaneously.   In microporous bodies whose internal voids
are filled with liquid or vapor the internal heat transfer takes place
essentially by conduction only; if the internal voids are large, however, convection within each of the fluid-filled holes can increase the
heat transfer within the body markedly.   If the air pressure around
the body is reduced, as in vacuum drying, both the conduction and the
convection modes of heat transfer diminish.   Radiative transfer then
becomes a major means of supplying heat required for drying.   A
mass of powder under vacuum, or a microporous freeze-dried body, is
an excellent heat insulator.

The Film, or Boundary Layer Concept.—The main resistance to
transfer of heat to or from a solid body by convection of a fluid in
which it is immersed resides in a thin layer of the fluid adjacent to the
solid surface.   Fluid actually in contact with the wall is visualized as
remaining stationary (but note the "slip-flow" phenomenon discussed
under Freeze Drying, p. 161), while fluid at successively greater dis-
tances from the wall moves at successively higher velocities.   A
velocity gradient therefore exists, as sketched in Fig. 8.   Heat is
transferred through the stationary film by pure conduction.   Layers
of liquid at greater distance from the wall move in orderly streamlines,
in what is known as "laminar" flow.   Up to a certain velocity, known
as the critical velocity, the film remains in laminar flow, but beyond

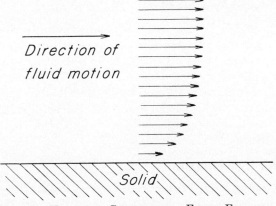

Direction of
fluid motion

Solid

FIG. 8.   VELOCITY GRADIENT IN FLUID FLOWING
PAST A SOLID

that point the flow breaks up into twisted and rapidly fluctuating flow
lines.   This "turbulent" flow characterizes all higher velocities.   The
critical velocity is a function of the kinematic viscosity of the fluid and
the dimensions and shape of the surface.   Physical data are usually
correlated with a dimensionless quantity, the Reynolds number,
which is defined as follows:

$$\mathbf{Re} = \frac{uD}{\nu} \tag{24}$$

where

u = velocity of flow (ft.)/(hr.)
D = diameter or other characteristic linear dimension (ft.)
ν = kinematic viscosity (sq. ft.)/(hr.)

For flow of a fluid in a tube, for example, flow is usually turbulent if
Re exceeds about 2,300.

Heat Transfer Coefficient.—In turbulent flow, heat which has
passed through the laminar film is rapidly mixed with the main body
of the fluid.   Over-all heat transfer therefore is the combined effect of
several different transport mechanisms.   It is greatly affected by even
minute details such as surface roughness and geometric shape.   For
many purposes, however, convectional heat transfer is conveniently
correlated by a simple Ohm's law type of expression, namely:

$$q = hA \ (t - t_s) \tag{25}$$

where

q = rate of heat transfer (B.t.u.)/(hr.)
h = heat transfer coefficient (B.t.u.)/(hr.)(sq. ft.)(°F.)
t = temperature of the body of the fluid (°F.)
t_s = temperature of the surface (°F.)

That is to say, rate of heat transfer is proportional to the temperature
difference, which may be thought of as a driving potential.   The
engineering literature on heat transfer embraces results from thousands
of determinations of the coefficient h under different conditions of
temperature, temperature difference, fluid velocity, the geometry of
the system, and the nature of the fluids and the solid wall; Eckert and
Drake (1959); Bosworth (1956); McCabe and Smith (1956); Jacob
(1949, 1957); Kern (1950); McAdams (1954).

Heat Transfer by Radiation

Transfer of energy by thermal radiation is ordinarily a minor fraction of the total energy supplied in a drying process, but under conditions that hinder transfer by conduction and convection radiant

energy may become the principal source of the necessary heat.   This may be the case in vacuum drying and especially in freeze drying. Radiative transfer is appreciable, however, even under the usual conditions of tray drying or spray drying.

According to the Stefan-Boltzmann law, radiative transfer of energy between two bodies takes place proportionally to the difference of the fourth powers of their absolute temperatures.   Radiative heat exchange therefore increases very rapidly with temperature difference. If a body with absolute surface temperature T_1 and area A is completely enclosed by the other body, which has a surface temperature of T_2, the following relation can be written:

$$q_R = CA (T_1{}^4 - T_2{}^4) \qquad (26)$$

where the constant C has the value 0.173×10^{-8} (B.t.u.)/(hr.)(sq. ft.)($°R^4$).   The actual energy transferred in any specific case will depend, however, upon the exact geometry of the situation and the physical nature of the emitting and absorbing surfaces.   The emissivity is a decimal fraction, very low for a polished metal such as silver, ranging upward toward 0.6 to 0.95 for most rough or matte structural materials.   The somewhat awkward fourth-power computation is sometimes replaced by the combination of a simple first-power temperature difference with a table or set of curves giving a "radiative transfer coefficient," h_R:

$$q_R = \epsilon h_R (t_1 - t_2) \qquad (27)$$

where ϵ is the emissivity.   If ϵ is taken as 1, the coefficient h_R has the following value:

$$h_R = 0.173 \frac{(T_1/100)^4 - (T_2/100)^4}{t_1 - t_2} \qquad (28)$$

Fig. 9 gives numerical values of this coefficient in the usual range of temperatures likely to be encountered in steam heated food dehydrators.

Marshall and Friedman (1950) compute as an example the probable temperature of the wet surface of a trayload of material exposed to the 300°F. radiation from the bottom of the tray above it, and held in a 300°F. air stream flowing at 400 ft./min.   If the wet-bulb temperature of the air is 113°, the radiated heat raises the actual temperature of the wet material 7° above wet-bulb temperature, or to 120°.

MASS TRANSFER

External and Internal Factors

The drying of a moist substance always involves the movement of a quantity of water away from a dry substance.   The separation is

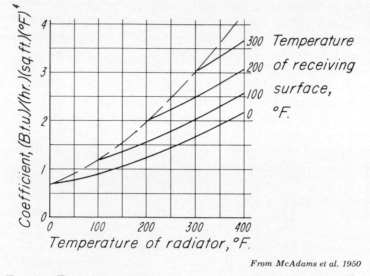

From McAdams et al. 1950

FIG. 9.   EQUIVALENT RADIATIVE HEAT TRANSFER COEFFICIENT

usually regarded for purposes of analysis as the result of two successive phenomena: (1) migration of water within the moist body to its surface; and (2) conveyance of the vaporized water away from the body.   The factors controlling the rate of transfer of water vapor from the moist body to its surroundings, whether accomplished in a stream of hot air or in a vacuum chamber, can be regarded as determined by the physical characteristics of the body's environment, especially temperature, pressure, humidity, and velocity, and not by conditions within the moist body; on the other hand, the factors that determine the rate of movement of water within the body can be regarded as independent of the external conditions.   A useful analysis of the process can be made on the basis of this simplified picture, even though in some cases it may become evident that vaporization is in fact occurring in an ill-defined zone within the moist body instead of only at its geometrical surface.   In the case of freeze drying, the transfer of water vapor through the fine pores in a shell of already dry material surrounding a solid icy core is one of the most important limiting factors in the whole process.   This important special case is discussed at greater length on p. 160.

Water Movement Within the Wet Body

Modes of Water Movement.—We have already referred to the change in character of a fluid flow as the velocity increases and finally exceeds a critical value, laminar flow changing at that moment abruptly to turbulent flow. When water is moving from one place to another within a wet body that is being dried, the nature of the flow can become far more complex. Quantitative descriptions of the phenomenon by various investigators historically emphasized either one or the other of two quite distinct physical mechanisms, namely molecular diffusion and capillary flow. The former, as first developed especially by Sherwood and his associates (1929–1936, see below) at the Massachusetts Institute of Technology, assumed that diffusion laws can account completely for the observed phenomena of drying. Fisher (1923, 1935), however, found that account must be taken of surface forces in the drying of fibrous or granular materials, and Lykow (1933) pointed out major disagreements with observed behavior of several materials. Ceaglske and Hougen (1937) vigorously attacked the diffusional analysis as leading to an entirely erroneous idea of the moisture distribution in a body during drying; they based a theory upon the capillary behavior alone. Later writers have tended to accept parts of both mechanisms, but to emphasize one or the other according to whether the materials of principal interest to them are definitely granular like wet sand or clay (Krischer 1938 A, B), fibrous like wood (Bateman *et al.* 1939), or more or less structureless wet gels. Lykow (1948, 1950) and numerous other investigators picture practical drying operations as nearly always involving a progression from an initial phase, in which water moves within the wet body readily under the control mainly of surface forces in pores and capillaries, to a final stage in which tightly bound hygroscopic moisture must diffuse through nearly dry solid.

Görling (1958) pictures five distinct physical mechanisms as being involved to some extent in the drying of such materials as potato, wood, or macaroni: (1) liquid movement under capillary forces; (2) diffusion of liquid caused by a difference in concentration; (3) surface diffusion in liquid layers adsorbed at solid interfaces; (4) water vapor diffusion in air-filled pores, caused by a difference in partial pressures; and (5) water vapor flow under differences in total pressure, as for example in vacuum drying under radiation. Marshall and Friedman (1950) recognize the first two of these, and add the following three: (6) flow caused by shrinkage and pressure gradients; (7) flow caused by gravity; and (8) flow caused by a vaporization-condensation sequence. The latter is, of course, related to Görling's number (4); flow would certainly occur, for example, if a temperature gradient existed in the moist body. Lykow (1935) described experiments on thermal diffusion of moisture in colloidal clays, that is, a molecular motion of water in the direction of a temperature gradient, analogous to thermal diffusion in a gas or solution.   In his development of drying theory he finds this mechanism is especially significant in determining the extent of transport of soluble materials along with the moisture in a body, as in the drying of dyed sheet leather.

Jason (1958) concluded that the most likely mechanism for molecular diffusion of water through a continuous gel is a surface migration of the higher-energy molecules along molecular fibrils of protein.   The computed activation energy, about 9,000 calories per mole, is not far from that found by Fish (1957, 1958), for diffusion of water in starch gel.

To the early investigators of drying as a "unit operation" the well developed theory of heat conduction seemed to offer a straightforward approach to practical design procedures through application of the obvious analogy between the diffusion of heat and the diffusion of moisture.   A moist body suspended in an air stream gradually approaches moisture equilibrium with that air in a way that seems entirely analogous to the gradual temperature equilibration of a warm body suspended in a cool air stream.   Analytical solutions for the differential equations describing temperature distribution within such a body at any subsequent time were already available—provided the thermal properties of the material were independent of temperature. Lewis (1921, 1922), Sherwood (1929, 1930, 1931, 1932, 1936), Sherwood and Comings (1932, 1933), Gilliland and Sherwood (1933), Comings and Sherwood (1934), Newman (1931), and McCready and McCabe (1933), developed many consequences of a drying theory based on this analogy.   No particular effort was made to scrutinize the intimate physical mechanisms of moisture transfer; moisture movement within the wet body was assumed to take place at a rate proportional to the moisture concentration gradient at any point, just as internal heat flow is proportional to the temperature gradient:

$$G = - \mathbf{D} \frac{dC}{dl} \tag{29}$$

where

G = mass-velocity of water diffusing (lb.)/(hr.)(sq. ft.)
$\mathbf{D}$ = diffusivity of water in this material (sq. ft.)/(hr.)
C = instantaneous water concentration at any point within the material (lb.)/(cu. ft.)
l = distance measured in the direction of the diffusion movement (ft.)
dC/dl = concentration gradient (lb.)/(cu. ft.)(ft.)

The minus sign signifies that water moves in the direction of decreasing concentration of water—*i.e.*, from a wetter toward a drier place

In terms of moisture content rather than concentration,

$$G = \mathbf{D}\rho_d \frac{dW}{dl} \tag{30}$$

where

ρ_d = density of the moisture-free material (lb.)/(cu. ft.)
W = moisture content (lb.)/(lb. dry)

Tests of this concept with a variety of materials were only moderately successful, for reasons that will be discussed later. Perhaps the closest approach to confirmation was the work of Jason (1958), which will be described at some length in connection with the phenomena observed in the drying of an isolated piece of wet colloidal material (fish muscle). See pp. 95–97.

Saravacos and Charm (1962) have recently reported experiments on the air drying of potato dice or slices which also appear to be consistent with the molecular diffusion mechanism.

The food materials with which we are dealing in this work are almost without exception hygroscopic and colloidal, and many of them dry to gel-like or glassy solids of poorly defined geometrical shape, frequently "honeycombed," and both coarsely and finely porous. The actual physical systems are so complex as to defy accurate description; and yet, surprisingly enough, investigators have been able to devise comparatively simple mathematical models which simulate observed moisture transfer rates and moisture distributions reasonably well.

Movement of Liquid Water Under Surface Forces.—*The Capillary Flow Mechanism.*—The flow and distribution of water in granular solids were first investigated by Slichter (1898), Buckingham (1907), Gardner (1919), and Haines (1927), and other soil scientists in studies of the flow of ground waters. The physical unbalance of forces at an interface between a liquid and a gas or vapor produces the effect of a suction on the liquid, familiar in the rise of a liquid in a capillary tube or wick dipping beneath its surface. If a single such capillary be pictured, as in Fig. 10, the maximum capillary rise is determined by Equation (31):

$$h = \frac{2\sigma\cos\varpi}{rg\rho} \tag{31}$$

where

h = rise (ft.)
σ = surface tension (lb.)/(sec.^{2})
ϖ = wettability of the solid; cos ϖ is substantially unity for hydrophilic solids in water
r = radius of the capillary (ft.)

g = acceleration of gravity (ft.)/(sec.²)
ρ = density of the liquid (lb.)/(cu. ft.)

The maximum rise, it will be seen, varies inversely as the radius of the capillary. At a radius of 0.01 micron, ($= 10^{-6}$ cm.), the maximum suction would be almost a mile of water, corresponding to a negative pressure of more than a ton per square inch. Capillary pores of this order of size exist in silica gel and doubtless in many solid organic gels as well.

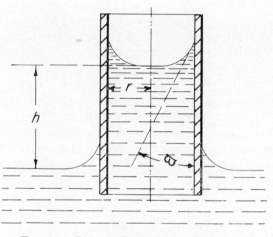

FIG. 10. RISE OF LIQUID IN A CAPILLARY

If instead of an open capillary tube a tube full of sand be held with the bottom end dipping below the surface of a container of water, the water will rise through the sand and come to an equilibrium level above the level in the container. Just as in the capillary, surface forces in the curved spaces between sand grains exert a suction on the water; very fine, closely packed grains can exert a high suction. Equation (31) can represent this situation as well as that of a single capillary tube, even if the granular material is a mixture of a wide range of different sizes and shapes of particles; the factor then represents an equivalent mean radius of the open pore spaces. Lykow (1948) gives data, abstracted in Table 9, on pore sizes in certain porous materials.

The simplest model to illustrate this mechanism in action during drying would consist of a flat layer of glass beads in a horizontal pan, with water filling the interstices between beads, and a current of air flowing across the surface of the layer. As water is evaporated there, the "water table" within the layer of beads must fall, air being drawn

TABLE 9

POROSITY OF SELECTED MATERIALS

Material	Volume of Voids per Unit Total Volume (cm.^{3}/cm.^{3})	Proportion of Pores with Radius Less Than 10^{-6} cm. (Per Cent)
Birch charcoal	0.936	70.0
Activated carbon	0.870	98.6
Porcelain	0.031	10.9

in between surface beads, leaving wet surfaces but no continuous column of water capable of maintaining a suction.

In most wet granular food materials, soft and easily deformed when wet, the picture would not be so simple. Water keeps the wet body distended, but its interior is under compression because of the surface forces. When any water is removed at the surface of a flat layer of such a substance, these forces draw the weak solid constituents into closer packing, by folding and crumpling them so that they occupy less volume; that is, the layer shrinks. Water at all levels within the layer moves through the gradually narrowing channels between solid structures at velocities dependent on the forces producing the flow and the viscous resistance to this motion; the latter, in turn, is a function of the effective radius of the open channels and the viscosity of the liquid. So long as the shrinkage can occur with little opposition, all the pores and interstices will remain completely full of water. When the solid structure begins to resist further distortion strongly, water in the surface layer of material will begin to be drawn down into the interstices, exerting stronger and stronger suction as the curvature of the liquid surfaces becomes sharper. Eventually air will be drawn all the way to the bottom of the layer, and capillary suction can then no longer be a force producing flow of the remaining water.

Krischer (1938 B, 1940, 1942, 1956) regards the early, or high-moisture, stages of drying as being controlled by capillary-flow relationships. He uses the following expression for correlating experimental data on transfer of moisture across unit cross-section area within the body during the stage of pure capillary-flow mechanism:

$$G = -k_w \, \rho_d \, \frac{dW}{dl} \tag{32}$$

where

G	= mass-velocity of water being transferred (lb.)/(hr.)(sq. ft.)
k_w	= "moisture conductivity" (sq. ft.)/(hr.)
ρ_d	= density of the moisture-free solid (lb. dry)/(cu. ft.)

dW/dl = moisture gradient, $1/$(ft.)
W = moisture content (lb.)/(lb. dry)
l = distance perpendicular to the cross-section through which the flow is occurring (ft.)

This Ohm's law type of expression, completely analogous to the simple diffusion law, Equation (30), simply states that rate of flow is proportional to a potential gradient, here identified as the change in moisture content of the wet body per unit of distance from the surface where evaporation is occurring. The conductivity factor, k_w, lumps together the effects of the distribution of pore diameters within the material and

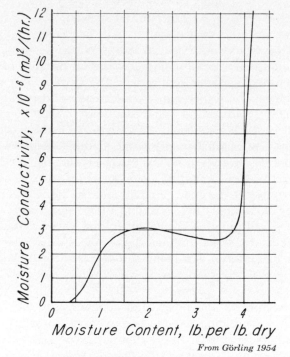

From Görling 1954

FIG. 11. MOISTURE CONDUCTIVITY AS A FUNCTION OF MOISTURE CONTENT IN POTATO

the surface tension and viscosity of the liquid. Experimentally, in any particular solid body, k_w is always found to be strongly dependent on the water content of the material. The relationship may be quite complex, but at high levels of moisture content the resistance to internal flow of water is low and the conductivity is correspondingly high. Görling (1956, 1958) found that moisture conductivity of potato varies with moisture content as shown in Fig. 11. While the value remains about constant in the middle range of moisture contents, it falls rapidly toward zero as moisture falls below about 0.3 lb./lb. of dry matter.

Experimental studies of moisture conductivity have been made by determining the amount of water removed from various wet bodies by applying a graded series of pressures (Macey 1942); centrifuging (Krischer 1956); or drying under especially simple conditions (Görling 1956). As might be expected, even slight changes in the internal structure of a material, such as those accompanying shrinkage, can change the moisture conductivity by several orders of magnitude.

Diffusional Transfer of Water.—Whether or not the early phases of the drying of a wet body are considered to be governed by capillary flow phenomena, the late phases are indisputably governed by diffusional phenomena. These take place both within the solid fine structure of the moist body and within the capillaries, pores, and small voids, filled with vapor which diffuses outward until, at the open end of a capillary, it is carried away in the rapidly moving air stream. It will be convenient to discuss first the relatively simple case of vapor diffusion through open capillaries. In the view of McCready and McCabe (1933), Krischer (1938, 1942, 1956), Lykow (1948), and some other workers, this represents one of the two major flow mechanisms, capillary liquid movement being the other.

Diffusion of Water Vapor Through Open Spaces.—Krischer (1938) pictures the air within open pores as remaining stationary while diffusing water molecules, which are being continuously supplied by evaporation of liquid water into the pores, make their way through that air from a region of higher water vapor pressure toward the nearest region of lower vapor pressure. The following equation describes the rate of movement:

$$G = - \frac{\mathbf{d}}{\phi} \cdot \frac{1}{R_w T} \cdot \frac{P}{P - p_v} \cdot \frac{dp_v}{dl} \tag{33}$$

where

G	= mass-velocity of water being transferred (lb.)/(hr.)(sq. ft.)
ϕ	= a "diffusion resistance factor," dimensionless
$\mathbf{d}$	= diffusivity of water vapor in air (sq. ft.)/(hr.)
R_w	= gas constant for water vapor, 0.0405 (atm.)(cu. ft.)/(lb.)(°R.)
T	= absolute temperature (°R.)
P	= atmospheric pressure (atm.)
p_v	= partial pressure of water vapor (atm.)
l	= distance perpendicular to the cross-section through which flow is occurring (ft.)
dp_v/dl	= vapor pressure gradient (atm.)/(ft.)

The diffusion resistance factor, ϕ, like the moisture conductivity through water-filled pores, k_w, is dependent not only on the geometrical fine structure of the solid material, but also, in hygroscopic materials, very strongly on the moisture content. Görling's (1958) results on potatoes show an exceedingly steep increase in the diffusional resistance as moisture content falls below about 0.20 lb./lb. dry matter (Fig. 12). This resistance also increases quite sharply from one level to another at a temperature of about 140°F. It is not clear from the publications whether Görling's experimental samples were always scalded, or blanched, before drying; if they were not, this change of resistance in the neighborhood of 140° may have been due to the gelatinization of starch at about that temperature.

Krischer (1956) lists diffusion resistance factors determined by various workers for a large number of building materials, and also tabulates (see Table 10) this factor for certain food products, as measured by the Institut für Lebensmitteltechnologie und Verpackung, Munich. The practical usefulness of these figures seems doubt-

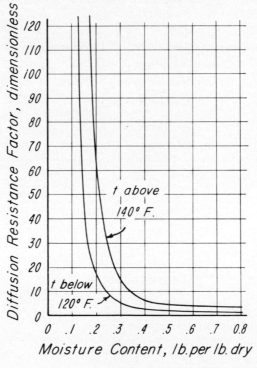

From Görling 1954

FIG. 12. DIFFUSION RESISTANCE FACTOR AS A FUNCTION OF MOISTURE CONTENT IN POTATO

TABLE 10

DIFFUSION RESISTANCE FACTOR FOR CERTAIN FOOD PRODUCTS[1]

Substance	Density ρ, (lb.)/ (cu. ft.)	Porosity ψ^2	Diffusion Resistance Factor, ϕ^2
"Malt coffee"	27	0.725	1.6
"Alete" milk powder	38	0.61	2.5
"Alete" milk powder	53	0.454	3.0
Spray dried non-fat milk	50	0.482	3.3
Dried vegetables	9	0.907	1.7
Egg powder	20	0.80	2.6
Egg powder	21	0.79	2.4
Flour	30	0.69	3.7
Chocolate pudding powder	49	0.5	6.8
Pea sausage, compressed	66	0.322	15.2

[1] From Krischer (1956).
[2] Dimensionless.

ful if, as is likely, the true values of the factor are radically dependent on moisture content of the materials, as Görling's curve shows potato flesh is.

Equations (32) and (33) can be combined to give the total moisture transfer by both of the major mechanisms, Krischer (1938, 1956):

$$G = -k_w \rho_d \frac{\delta W}{\delta l} - \frac{d}{\phi} \cdot \frac{1}{R_w T} \cdot \frac{P}{P - p_v} \cdot \left(\frac{\delta p_v}{\delta W} \cdot \frac{\delta W}{\delta l} \right) \qquad (34)$$

Diffusional Migration of Water Within the Body.—Marshall and Friedman (1950) regard diffusion of liquid water within the body as important only in single-phase solid systems in which the liquid and solid components are mutually soluble, such as soaps and glues, and to transfer of equilibrium moisture in wood, starch, textiles, and the like. The problem is discussed at some length on pp. 43–44. All writers on drying theory have evidently had difficulty in dealing with the liquid diffusion concept in terms of mechanism. Krischer dispenses with it altogether. If such materials as soap, glue, or gelatinized potato flesh were actually homogeneous solid solutions of the components in one another, one might deal with molecular diffusion of the water component through the other component (or vice versa) with some degree of confidence; the conceptual model would seem simple. However, the supposed simplicity vanishes in the light of actual electron micrographs, which show the complex network or lamellar structure that exists in a soap gel, individual muscle fibers, plant cell walls, and the like.

Migration of water within the hypothetical "structureless" wet material can be described in terms of the diffusivity of water in that material and the gradient of water concentration or water content, as stated in Equations (29) and (30) above.   Even in his earliest publications, however Sherwood (1929, 1930) noted that the data on drying of soap give a computed diffusion coefficient whose value must decrease markedly at low levels of moisture content;   *i.e.*, diffusivity is not constant.   Unfortunately, if this were to turn out to be the case also for other important systems, much of the attractiveness of the simple diffusional model would disappear, because the ready-made analytical solutions of the differential equation, borrowed from heat-flow theory, would no longer be applicable.   One line of attack on the difficulty which has met with some success has been to develop the mathematical methods, either analytical or numerical, for obtaining solutions of the differential equation with variable coefficients (Scarborough 1950; Milne 1953; Philip 1955, 1960 A, B, 1961; Carslaw and Jaeger 1959).   Crank (1956, 1958), in particular, has made extensive investigations of the mathematical procedures that can be used to derive drying rates from known values of the variable diffusivity, and conversely, to find the diffusivity and its moisture-dependence from measurements of drying rate.

Other Mechanisms of Water Movement.—At relatively low moisture contents (*i.e.*, below about 10 to 15 per cent moisture in many food materials) the water is all adsorbed on the immense internal surface of the high-molecular-weight solid.   As will be discussed more fully below, although water molecules are strongly attracted to the solid surfaces, any molecule that by chance experiences an unusually strong thermal vibration may escape that captivity briefly, move at random in a short free path, and come to rest again at a different adsorption site.   If there is a gradient of moisture concentration, the process will result in a gradual net transfer of water molecules downhill on this gradient.   This is, in fact, the mechanism of "activated" diffusional movement of water within such a body.   It has been thoroughly analyzed by Jason (1958).   "Flow" seems hardly an appropriate term to describe what happens;   even though the forces that determine flow of liquid or vapor through an open channel are still operative even on the molecular scale, they are far overbalanced by the adsorptive force.   The essentially discontinuous activity in this model—individual molecules alternating between long periods of rest and short jumps to new positions—bears little resemblance to the usual picture of flow, and the terms "liquid" and "vapor" both become essentially meaningless.   The rise in water vapor pressure of moist material as temperature is increased is largely a measure of the rise in number of water molecules possessing more than the threshold activation energy required to break free for a short jump to a new position.

Flow of moisture within a body due to a temperature gradient has already been mentioned. It has been studied especially by investigators of the translocation of moisture through building materials, where it may assume great importance. Lykow (1950) found that in capillary-porous bodies such as clay, moisture diffuses *with* the temperature gradient (*i.e.*, moves from a high-temperature region toward a low-temperature region) at high moisture levels, but below a certain moisture level the movement is in the opposite direction. He attributes this to the greater effect of temperature gradient on the heavier molecules of air in the pores than on the lighter molecules of water vapor. The part played by thermal diffusion during the late stages of vacuum drying of a body heated on one side by radiation (so that a large temperature gradient exists in the body) seems not to have been determined.

Expression of Flow Potential in Concentration or Activity Terms.—As Sherwood and Comings (1932, 1933) had themselves pointed out, the rate of moisture movement through a solid body had not been shown experimentally to be proportional to the moisture gradient. That it actually could not be was deduced by Hougen *et al.* (1940) from the data of Kamei and Shiomi (1937) on the drying of soap, clay, and wood pulp. The distribution of moisture within a body under uniform drying conditions was far different from anything predicted by the diffusional theory as originally presented. Distribution of moisture in $^3/_4$-in. scalded slices of potato dried in a stream of air at 158°F. was reported by Ede and Hales (1948) and gave an especially clear picture of the kind of results to be found experimentally (Fig. 13). The broken curve on the same figure is the theoretical distribution predicted by the classical diffusion theory, with diffusivity of moisture assumed constant; the total moisture content of the sample and moisture content at the face are the same for both of these curves.

One especially significant characteristic of the Ede and Hales data, as well as some of the other reported results, is the double curvature and inflection of the plotted moisture distribution curves. Hougen *et al.* (1940) showed that such doubly inflected curves always appeared if there was obviously a capillary flow mechanism; they presented illustrative data taken from experiments on the drying of sand. Indeed, Marshall and Friedman (1950) consider the occurrence of a doubly inflected moisture distribution curve as the infallible criterion for capillary flow mechanism. It was thought that the portion of such a curve that was concave upward must signify an absurd *negative* diffusivity. Van Arsdel (1947) showed, however, that the diffusional

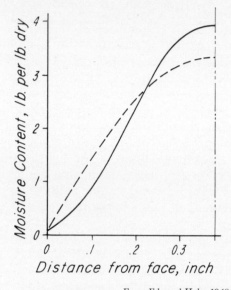

From Ede and Hales 1948

Fig. 13. Distribution of Moisture in Potato Slice
During Drying

flow mechanism could lead to a doubly inflected distribution if diffusivity is markedly lower at low moisture contents than at high, and pointed out that distribution curves similar to those observed were exactly what would be expected if diffusion theory were stated in terms of vapor pressure gradient rather than moisture content or concentration gradient.

Babbitt had, in fact, reported (1940) the results of experiments with fiberboard in which an imposed temperature gradient through the board produced a vapor pressure gradient opposite to the moisture content gradient; water then moved from the warmer, but drier, face to the cooler but wetter face—in other words, *against* the concentration gradient. He concluded that at a moisture content lower than that corresponding to a relative humidity of 75 per cent the vapor pressure gradient controls the rate of moisture movement. At higher levels of relative humidity and moisture content the rate of moisture transfer is no longer proportional to vapor pressure gradient, but is determined by the surface forces acting on liquid in capillaries and pores.

The concept of a pressure gradient as driving force for diffusion of moisture in solids has been much further developed during the intervening years, particularly in conjunction with better pictures of the adsorption phenomena which play the leading role in the relations between water and the hydrophilic polymers which constitute most of our foods. Brunauer *et al.* (1938) had published the now-classic "B-E-T" theory of adsorption of gases in multimolecular layers on solid surfaces. Babbitt (1950, 1951 A, B) furnished a definitive description of the diffusional movement of adsorbed layers of a mobile substance like water in and through a solid which can have a large internal surface. These internal surfaces are pictured as accessible to adsorbed water molecules, but not to mass flow of either liquid or air. The water molecules are in strongly damped thermal vibration. Occasional molecules have high enough energy to leap the potential barrier between adsorption sites and migrate to new sites. There is thus a net movement of water toward the low-pressure side of the solid. The adsorbed layer of water molecules has the thermodynamic properties of a two-dimensional gas under pressure; it exerts a spreading force which is related to the Gibbs free energy of the adsorbed film by the relation:

$$\Pi = - \frac{\delta g_{ads}}{\delta A} \tag{35}$$

where

Π = spreading potential
g_{ads} = Gibbs free energy of spreading
A = area of the film

According to this picture, the space gradient of the spreading potential, $\delta \Pi / \delta l$, is the appropriate term to be equated to the rate of transfer of water through the solid. The potential, in turn, is a function of the number of adsorbed molecules per unit volume, as expressed in the vapor adsorption isotherm.

Similar conclusions were reached by Thomas (1951) in a study of moisture permeability, diffusion, and sorption in organic film-forming materials. Fick's diffusion law is found to be applicable only in the region of low relative humidity, and the rate of permeation depends directly on the vapor pressure difference.

This analysis provides a connecting link with the concept of water vapor pressure gradient as the driving force for diffusion, and answers an objection sometimes raised about the latter, namely that one cannot picture vapor *as such* diffusing through a gelatinous or glassy solid; the spreading pressure of an adsorbed film, however, has been physically familiar ever since Langmuir's classic demonstrations—and the gradient of this pressure varies with temperature and composition in the same way as vapor pressure gradient would.

Van Arsdel's analysis (1947) had shown, through computation of a number of selected hypothetical diffusing systems, that drying rate curves similar to the peculiar rate curves observed in drying carrot and potato pieces to low moisture levels can be duplicated by making relatively simple assumptions about the moisture content-permeability relationship. "Permeability" he defined in terms of rate of water transfer through unit cross-section under unit vapor pressure gradient:

$$G = -\mathbf{P} \frac{dp}{dl} \tag{36}$$

where

G = mass-velocity of water diffusing (lb.)/(hr.)(sq. ft.)
$\mathbf{P}$ = permeability (lb.)/(hr.)(ft.)(atm.)
p = vapor pressure at the point in question (atm.)
l = distance measured in the direction of water movement (ft.)
dp/dl = vapor pressure gradient (atm.)/(ft.)

Then the permeability and the diffusivity for water at the point in question are related as follows:

$$\mathbf{P} \frac{dp}{dW} = \rho_d \mathbf{D} \tag{37}$$

where

W = moisture content (lb.)(lb. dry)
ρ_d = density of the dry substance (lb. dry)/(cu. ft.)
$\mathbf{D}$ = diffusivity (sq. ft.)/(hr.)
dp/dW = slope of the water vapor pressure isotherm

It was also pointed out that in the absence of an internal temperature gradient, the predicted moisture distribution and rate of internal moisture movement will both be exactly the same whether computed from concentration gradient or from vapor pressure gradient, provided the diffusivity and the permeability are related as shown in Equation (37). The relation between vapor pressure and moisture content is strongly curved (see Equilibrium Moisture Content, pp. 67–68) so either the diffusivity or the permeability or both must vary with moisture content; they cannot both remain constant.

The most detailed study of the behavior of water in a colloidal food material, especially from the standpoint of theoretical interpretation, is the investigation by Fish (1957) of the diffusion and equilibrium properties of water in a clear gel prepared from pure potato starch. This system has the great experimental advantages of good reproducibility, ease of preparation in a solid piece of known shape and dimensions, and a good degree of isotropy; besides, it is not too distant a representative of a large class of food products. Stitt (1958) has also analyzed and commented on the data obtained by Fish in these experiments.   Fish also obtained data (1958) on the diffusivity of water in the flesh of scalded potatoes at 1, 25, and 35°C.   Fig. 14 presents his results at 25°, expressed in engineering units, square feet per hour.   The diffusivity is only slightly different from that of water in pure starch gel; this fact indicates that the cell walls and other non-starch constituents of potato have only a minor influence on the transport of water through the scalded material.   The hundred-fold decrease in diffusivity as moisture content falls from $W = 0.15$ to $W = 0.03$ helps to explain the difficulty experienced in drying potato to really low moisture levels.

The only other published data on diffusivity of water in scalded potato, those of Saravacos and Charm (1962), were derived only as a mean over the moisture range 1.0 to 0.1, and for temperatures of 130°F.   ($D_m = 1.0 \times 10^{-5}$ ft.²/hr.), 140°, 150°, and 156°F.   ($D_m = 2.4 \times 10^{-5}$ ft.²/hr.); from an Arrhenius-type plot of log D against $1/T$, the activation energy for this diffusion was estimated to be 12,500 cal. per gram mole of water transferred in this moisture range.

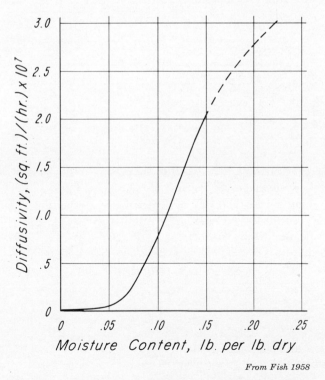

From Fish 1958

FIG. 14.   DIFFUSIVITY OF WATER IN POTATO AT 25°C.

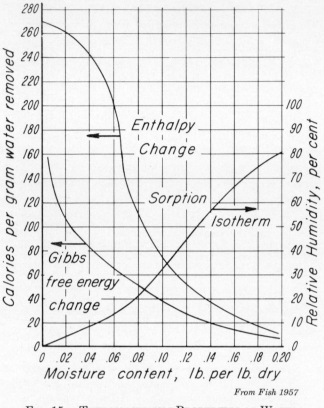

From Fish 1957

FIG. 15. THERMODYNAMIC PROPERTIES OF WATER
IN POTATO STARCH GEL

Fig. 15 gives the values of other thermodynamic properties of pure starch gel, as derived by Fish (1957). The figure shows both the enthalpy change and the Gibbs free energy change per gram of water removed from an indefinitely large quantity of starch gel at moisture contents between 0.20 and zero. The free energy change, identified with the chemical potential, is derived from the expression,

$$\Delta g = \frac{RT}{M} \ln \frac{p_1}{p_s} \tag{38}$$

where

Δg = free energy change (cal.)/(mole)
R = gas constant, 1.989 (cal.)/(mole)(°K.)
T = absolute temperature (°K.)
M = molecular weight—in this case, 18
p_1 = water vapor pressure in equilibrium with the sorbed water
p_s = saturation pressure at the same temperature

This extended discussion of the factors which control the internal movement of water in the wet body might be summed up by saying that while this massive and difficult research has succeeded in deepening our understanding of the phenomena of drying, it has accomplished much less of immediate practical usefulness than systematic empirical studies of the effects of external or environmental factors on drying rates. The next generation of research workers may discover how to extend and perfect the theory and use it to make radical improvements on all of our present drying procedures.

Effect of External Factors on Water Vapor Transfer From Wet Body to Surrounding Air

As we have pointed out in an earlier section, the convective transfer of heat to the evaporating surface has its counterpart in the convective transfer of mass in the form of water vapor away from the body. Just as in heat transfer, the principal resistance to the mass transfer resides in the thin stationary film of gas and vapor in the near vicinity of the solid surface.

As an approximation, we frequently assume that water vapor at the surface of the moist body mixes immediately and completely with the main air stream, so that the actual environment of the body has exactly the same humidity, temperature, and pressure as that air. This cannot be quite true in any case, and it may be far from exact if velocities and pressures are low and radiative heat transfer is significant; the stagnant film of mixed water vapor and air has a higher water vapor content than the main stream of air. The effective thickness of the film decreases, and the vapor content approaches that of the main stream, as the relative velocity increases. The exact relationships, especially the effects of relative velocity and radiation, have been studied by a number of investigators. See especially Arnold (1933). Experimental results are often correlated by use of the Chilton-Colburn (1934) dimensionless "*j*-factor," which is based on the analogies between heat- , mass- , and momentum-transfer.

During early stages of the drying of very wet bodies the rate at which evaporation can occur is completely determined by the rate at which water vapor can be transferred through the stagnant gas film just outside the water surface and be mixed with the main air stream. For a time the rate of evaporation is even independent of the kind of material being dried. As will be more fully discussed in a later section (pp. 92–93) this early phase of the drying is known as the "constant rate" phase.

Marshall and Hougen (1942) concluded that the constant rate of drying can be expressed by the following equation:

$$\left(\frac{dW}{d\theta}\right)_c = k_G \left(\frac{D_p G}{\mu}\right)^n \left(\frac{\mu}{\rho_a \mathbf{D}}\right)^m \left(\frac{P}{p_{am}}\right) \Delta p_w \tag{39}$$

where

k_G = mass transfer coefficient (lb.)/(hr.)(sq. ft.)(atm.)
D_p = particle diameter (ft.)
G = mass velocity (lb.)/(hr.)(sq. ft.)
μ = dynamic viscosity of the gas film (lb.)/(hr.)(ft.), and the group $(D_p G/\mu)$ is a modified Reynolds number
ρ_a = density of the gas film (lb.)/(cu. ft.)
$\mathbf{D}$ = diffusivity of water vapor through air (sq. ft.)/(hr.), and the group $(\mu/\rho_a \mathbf{D})$ is a Schmidt number
P = total pressure (atm.)
p_{am} = logarithmic mean partial pressure of dry air in the gas film

$$\Delta p_w = p_{wp} - p_{wa}$$

where

p_{wp} = partial pressure of water vapor at the surface of the particle (atm.)
p_{wa} = partial pressure of water vapor in the main air stream (atm.)

This relation is materially simplified if we take into account the facts that the Schmidt number for air is nearly independent of temperature, the particle diameter is nearly constant, and the ratio (P/p_{am}) is nearly unity;

$$\left(\frac{dW}{d\theta}\right)_c = k_G{}' \, G^n \, \Delta p_w \tag{40}$$

At low partial pressures of water vapor, by Equation (5), $p_w = H/0.622$, hence

$$\left(\frac{dW}{d\theta}\right)_c = k_G{}'' G^n \Delta H \tag{41}$$

Experiments by many investigators have shown that the exponent n in these expressions is approximately 0.80; that is, in the constant-rate phase the drying rate increases as the 0.8 power of the mass air velocity.

Krischer (1956), enlarging upon several of his earlier publications (1938 A, B, 1940, 1942), analyzed mass transfer conditions in the boundary layer around solids in terms of Reynolds number, Lewis number, and modified Schmidt, Nusselt, Grashof, and Peclet numbers, and derived a similar defining equation for the mass transfer coefficient, taking "driving force" as the difference between partial pressures of water vapor at the solid surface and in the air stream at a distance.

Removal of water vapor from the vicinity of the evaporating surface is a major factor in successful vacuum drying, and is especially critical in freeze drying.   Experimental and theoretical conditions have been discussed by Carman (1948, 1956), Ede (1949), Cooke and Sherwood (1955), and Kramers (1958), among others.

RELATION BETWEEN HEAT AND MASS TRANSFER OCCURRING SIMULTANEOUSLY

In most of the foregoing discussion the tacit assumption has been made that mass transfer and heat transfer can be analyzed separately and the effects simply added to produce a measure of the over-all effect. Ever since the investigations of Ackerman and Gnam (1937), Krischer (1942), and especially the derivation of the "phenomenological flow equations" by Onsager (1945), it has been known that this simple additivity is only approximately true.   The flow of heat affects the transfer of mass, and vice versa.   The principle is stated as follows by Hearon (1950): "when two or more irreversible transport processes, e.g., heat conduction, electrical conduction, or diffusion, take place in a given system, there is mutual interaction between the individual transports."   Hall (1953) developed the theory further in a study of "non-equilibrium thermodynamics."   So far as our subject is concerned, available evidence indicates that the practical design and operation of dehydrators can be based confidently on the transport relations considered independently of one another.   Significant departures would be expected only where large potential differences are involved.

BIBLIOGRAPHY

ACKERMAN, G., and GNAM, E.   1937.   Heat transfer and molecular mass transfer in the same field under large temperature and partial pressure differences.   (In German.)   VDI. Forschungsh. 382, Suppl. to Forsch. Gebiete Ingenieurw., Publ. B. 8, Jan.-Feb.

ARNOLD, J. H.   1933.   The theory of the psychrometer. I.   The mechanism of evaporation.   Physics 4, 255–262.   II.   The effect of velocity.   Ibid. 4, 334–340.

BABBITT, J. D.   1940.   Observations on the permeability of hygroscopic materials to water vapor.   Can. J. Research 18(A), 105–121.   NRC No. 907.

BABBITT, J. D.   1950.   On the differential equations of diffusion.   Can. J. Research 28(A), 449–474.

BABBITT, J. D.   1951 A.   A unified picture of diffusion.   Can. J. Phys. 29, 427–436.

BABBITT, J. D.   1951 B.   On the diffusion of adsorbed gases through solids.   Can. J. Phys. 29, 437–446.

BADGER, W. L., and BANCHERO, J. T.   1955.   Introduction to Chemical Engineering.   McGraw-Hill Book Co., New York.

BATEMAN, E., HOHF, J. P., and STAMM, A. J.   1939.   Unidirectional drying of wood.   Ind. Eng. Chem. 11, 1150–1154.

BOSWORTH, R. C. L.   1956.   Transport Processes in Applied Chemistry.   John Wiley and Sons, New York.

BRUNAUER, S., EMMETT, P. H., and TELLER, E. 1938. Adsorption of gases in multimolecular layers. J. Am. Chem. Soc. *60*, 309–319.

BUCKINGHAM, E. 1907. Studies on the movement of soil moisture. U. S. Dept. Agr. Bureau of Soils, Bull. *37*.

CARMAN, P. C. 1948. Molecular distillation and sublimation. Trans. Faraday Soc. *44*, 529–536.

CARMAN, P. C. 1956. Flow of Gases Through Porous Media. Butterworth's Scientific Publications, London; Academic Press, New York.

CARSLAW, H. S., and JAEGER, J. C. 1959. Conduction of Heat in Solids. Second Ed. Oxford University Press, London.

CEAGLSKE, N. H., and HOUGEN, O. A. 1937. The drying of granular solids. Trans. Am. Inst. Chem. Eng. *33*, 283–312.

CHILTON, T. H., and COLBURN, A. P. 1934. Mass transfer (absorption) coefficients—prediction from data on heat transfer and fluid friction. Ind. Eng. Chem. *26*, 1183–1187.

COMINGS, W. E., and SHERWOOD, T. K. 1934. The drying of solids. VII. Moisture movement by capillarity in drying granular materials. Ind. Eng. Chem. *26*, 1096–1098.

COOKE, N. E., and SHERWOOD, T. K. 1955. The effect of pressure on the rate of sublimation. Proc. 9th Int. Congress of Refrigeration, Rept. 2.79, *1*, No. 2, 133–141.

COULSON, J. M., and RICHARDSON, J. F. 1955. Chemical Engineering, Vol. 2. Unit Operations. McGraw-Hill Book Co., New York.

CRANK, J. 1956. The Mathematics of Diffusion. Clarendon Press, Oxford.

CRANK, J. 1958. Some mathematical diffusion studies relevant to dehydration. *In* Fundamental Aspects of the Dehydration of Foodstuffs. Soc. Chem. Ind. 37–41.

DUSINBERRE, G. M. 1949. Numerical Analysis of Heat Flow. McGraw-Hill Book Co., New York.

DUSINBERRE, G. M. 1961. Heat Transfer Calculations by Finite Differences. International Textbook Co., Scranton, Pa.

ECKERT, E. R. G., and DRAKE, R. M., JR. 1959. Heat and Mass Transfer. Second Ed. McGraw-Hill Book Co., New York.

EDE, A. J. 1949. Physics of the low-temperature vacuum drying process. J. Soc. Chem. Ind. *68*, 330–332, 336–340.

EDE, A. J., and HALES, K. C. 1948. The physics of drying in heated air, with special reference to fruit and vegetables. Dept. Sci. Ind. Research, Food Investigations Spec. Rept. *53*.

FISH, B. P. 1957. Diffusion and equilibrium properties of water in starch. Dept. Sci. Ind. Research, Food Investigations Tech. Paper *5*.

FISH, B. P. 1958. Diffusion and thermodynamics of water in potato starch gel. *In* Fundamental Aspects of the Dehydration of Foodstuffs. Soc. Chem. Ind. 143–157.

FISHER, E. A. 1923. Some moisture relations of colloids. I. A comparative study of rates of evaporation from wool, sand, and clay. Proc. Roy. Soc. (London) A *103*, 139–161. II. Further observations on the evaporation of water from clay and wool. *Ibid.* A *103*, 664–675.

FISHER, E. A. 1935. Some fundamental principles of drying. J. Soc. Chem. Ind. *54*, 343–348.

GARDNER, W. 1919. The movement of moisture in soil by capillarity. Soil Science *7*, 313–317.

GARDNER, W. 1920. A capillary transmission constant and methods of determining it experimentally. Soil Science *10*, 103–126.

GARDNER, W. 1921. The movement of soil moisture. Soil Science *11*, 215–232.

GARDNER, W. 1921. Notes on the dynamics of capillary flow. Phys. Rev. (Ser. 2) *18*, 206–209.

GILLILAND, E. R., and SHERWOOD, T. K. 1933. The drying of solids. VI. Diffusion equations for the period of constant drying rate. Ind. Eng. Chem. 25, 1134–1136.

GÖRLING, P. 1954, 1956. Investigations to elucidate the drying behavior of vegetable materials, especially potato pieces. (In German.) Diss. T. H. Darmstadt. Also in VDI-Forschungsheft 458, Düsseldorf 1956.

GÖRLING, P. 1958. Physical phenomena during the drying of foodstuffs. In Fundamental Aspects of the Dehydration of Foodstuffs. Soc. Chem. Ind. 42–53.

HAINES, W. B. 1927. Studies in the physical properties of soils. IV. A further contribution to the capillary phenomena in soils. J. Agr. Sci. 17, 264–290.

HAINES, W. B. 1930. Studies in the physical properties of soils. V. The hysteresis effect in capillary properties and the modes of moisture distribution associated therewith. J. Agr. Sci. 20, 97–116.

HALL, N. A. 1953. Non-equilibrium thermodynamics. J. Appl. Phys. 24, 819–825.

HEARON, J. Z. 1950. Some cellular diffusion problems based on Onsager's generalization of Fick's law. Bull. Math. Biophys. 12, 135–159.

HOUGEN, O. A., McCAULEY, H. J., and MARSHALL, W. R., JR. 1940. Limitations of diffusion equations. Trans. Am. Inst. Chem. Eng. 36, 183–206.

JACOB, MAX. 1949, 1957. Heat Transfer. Vol. 1, 1949; Vol. 2, 1957. John Wiley and Sons, New York.

JASON, A. C. 1958. A study of evaporation and diffusion processes in the drying of fish muscle. In Fundamental Aspects of the Dehydration of Foodstuffs. Soc. Chem. Ind. 103–135.

KAMEI, S., and SHIOMI, S. 1937. A study of the drying of solids. XIX. Moisture distribution in the course of drying. J. Soc. Chem. Ind. (Japan) Suppl. Binding 40, 257–263.

KERN, D. Q. 1950. Process Heat Transfer. McGraw-Hill Book Co., New York.

KRAMERS, H. 1958. Rate-controlling factors in freeze-drying. In Fundamental Aspects of the Dehydration of Foodstuffs. Soc. Chem. Ind. 57–66.

KRISCHER, O. 1938 A. Fundamental laws of the movement of moisture in bodies being dried; capillary water movement and water vapor diffusion. (In German.) Z. Ver. deut. Ing. 82, 373–378.

KRISCHER, O. 1938 B. The drying of solid substances, as a problem in the movement of capillary moisture and the diffusion of vapor. (In German.) Z. Ver. deut. Ing. Verfahrenstechnik Beih. 4, 104–110.

KRISCHER, O. 1940. Heat, liquid, and vapor movement in the drying of porous materials. (In German.) Z. Ver. deut. Ing. Suppl. 1, 17–25.

KRISCHER, O. 1942. Heat- and mass-transfer in a material being dried; the analytic and graphic treatment of the drying of porous hygroscopic materials. (In German.) VDI Forschungsheft 415, Publ. B 13, July-Aug.

KRISCHER, O. 1956. The Scientific Fundamentals of Drying Technology. (In German.) Volume I of O. Krischer and K. Kröll, Drying Technology (Trocknungstechnik.) Springer-Verlag, Berlin-Göttingen-Heidelberg.

KRISCHER, O., and KRÖLL, K. 1956, 1959. Drying Technology. (Trocknungs-technik.) 1, O. Krischer, The Scientific Fundamentals of Drying Technology. (Die wissenschaftlichen Grundlagen der Trockungstechnik.) (In German.) Springer-Verlag, Berlin-Göttingen-Heidelberg. 2, K. Kröll, Driers and Drying Processes. (Trockner und Trocknungsverfahren.)

LEBEDEV, P. D. 1961 A. Heat and mass transfer during the drying of moist materials. Int. J. Heat. Mass Transfer 1, 294–301.

LEBEDEV, P. D. 1961 B. Heat and mass transfer between moist solids and air. Int. J. Heat. Mass Transfer 1, 302–305.

LEWIS, W. K. 1921. The rate of drying of solid materials. Ind. Eng. Chem. 13, 427–432.

LEWIS, W. K.   1922.   The evaporation of a liquid into a gas.   Trans. Am. Soc. Mech. Eng. *44*, 445–446.

LYKOW, A. W.   (Also transliterated Luikov, A. V.)   1933.   Investigation of the dynamics of drying; equation of the diffusion of humidity during the process of drying of solids.   (In Russian.)   Izvest. Teplotekh. Inst. *8*, 1354–1359.

LYKOW, A. W.   (Also transliterated Luikov, A. V.)   1935.   The thermal diffusion of moisture.   (In Russian.)   Zhur. Priklad. Khim. *8*, 1354–1359.

LYKOW, A. W.   (Also transliterated Luikov, A. V.)   1948.   Theory of the kinetics of the process of drying of colloidal capillary-porous bodies.   (In Russian.)   Kolloid. Zhur. *10*, 289–304.

LYKOW, A. W.   1950, 1955.   Experimental and Theoretical Fundamentals of Drying.   Moscow, 1950.   (In Russian.)   Veb. Verlag, Berlin, 1955.   (In German.)

McADAMS, W. H.   1954.   Heat Transmission.   Third Ed.   McGraw-Hill Book Co., New York.

McADAMS, W. H., HOTTEL, H. C., COLBURN, A. P., and BERGELIN, O. P.   1950.   Heat Transmission.   *In* Perry, J. H., Ed.   Chemical Engineers Handbook.   Third Ed.   McGraw-Hill Book Co., New York.

McCABE, W. L., and SMITH, J. C.   1956.   Unit Operations of Chemical Engineering.   McGraw-Hill Book Co., New York.

McCREADY, D. W., and McCABE, W. L.   1933.   The adiabatic air drying of hygroscopic solids.   Trans. Am. Inst. Chem. Eng. *29*, 131–160.

MACEY, H. H.   1942.   Clay-water relationships and the internal mechanism of drying.   Trans. Brit. Ceram. Soc. *41*, 73–121.

MARKS, L. S.   1951.   Mechanical Engineers Handbook.   Fifth Ed.   McGraw-Hill Book Co., New York.

MARSHALL, W. R., JR., and FRIEDMAN, S. J.   1950.   Drying.   *In* Chemical Engineers Handbook, J. H. Perry, Ed., Third Ed.   McGraw-Hill Book Co., New York. 799–884.

MARSHALL, W. R., JR., and HOUGEN, O. A.   1942.   Drying of solids by through-circulation.   Trans. Am. Inst. Chem. Eng. *38*, 91–121.

MILNE, W. E.   1953.   Numerical Solution of Differential Equations.   John Wiley and Sons, New York.

NEWMAN, A. B.   1931.   Drying of porous solids.   Trans. Am. Inst. Chem. Eng. *27*, 203–216, 310–333.

ONSAGER, L.   1931.   Reciprocal relations in irreversible processes.   Phys. Rev. *37*, 495–526; *38*, 2265–2279.

ONSAGER, L.   1945.   Theories and problems of liquid diffusion.   Ann. N. Y. Acad. Sci. *46*, 241–265.

PERRY, J. H., Editor.   1950.   Chemical Engineers Handbook.   Third Ed.   McGraw-Hill Book Co., New York.

PHILIP, J. R.   1955.   Numerical solution of equations of the diffusion type, with diffusivity concentration-dependent.   Trans. Faraday Soc. *51*, 885–892.

PHILIP, J. R.   1960 A.   A very general class of exact solutions in concentration-dependent diffusion.   Nature *185*, No. 4708, 233.

PHILIP, J. R.   1960 B.   General method of exact solution of the concentration-dependent diffusion equation.   Australian J. Phys. *13*, 1–12.

PHILIP, J. R.   1961.   n-Diffusion.   Australian J. Phys. *14*, 1–13.

SARAVACOS, G. D., and CHARM, S. E.   1962.   A study of the mechanism of fruit and vegetable dehydration.   Food Technol. *16*, No. 1, 78–81.

SCARBOROUGH, J. B.   1950.   Numerical Mathematical Analysis.   Johns Hopkins Press, Baltimore.

SHERWOOD, T. K.   1929.   The drying of solids.   Ind. Eng. Chem. *21*, I, 12–16; II, 976–980.

SHERWOOD, T. K.   1930.   The drying of solids.   III.   Mechanism of the drying of pulp and paper.   Ind. Eng. Chem. *22*, 132–136.

SHERWOOD, T. K. 1931. Application of theoretical diffusion equations to the drying of solids. Trans. Am. Inst. Chem. Eng. 27, 190–200.

SHERWOOD, T. K. 1932. The drying of solids. IV. Application of diffusion equations. Ind. Eng. Chem. 24, 307–310.

SHERWOOD, T. K. 1936. The air drying of solids. Trans. Am. Inst. Chem. Eng. 32, 150–168.

SHERWOOD, T. K., and COMINGS, E. W. 1932. The drying of solids. Trans. Am. Inst. Chem. Eng. 28, 118–133.

SHERWOOD, T. K., and COMINGS, E. W. 1933. The drying of solids. V. Mechanism of drying of clays. Ind. Eng. Chem. 25, 311–316.

SLICHTER, C. S. 1898. Theoretical investigations of the motion of ground water. U. S. Geological Survey, 19th Ann. Rpt., Part 2, 301–384.

SMITH, A. J. M. 1943. Note on physical aspects of drying and some drying characteristics of foods. In Dehydration, Section X. (Physical Data for Dried Foods) Part 3. U. K. Progress Reports, D.S.I.R., Ministry of Food, London.

STITT, F. 1958. Moisture equilibrium and the determination of water content of dehydrated foods. In Fundamental Aspects of the Dehydration of Foodstuffs. Soc. Chem. Ind. 67–88.

THOMAS, A. M. 1951. Moisture permeability, diffusion, and sorption in organic film-forming materials. J. Appl. Chem. 1, 141–158.

VAN ARSDEL, W. B. 1947. Approximate diffusion calculations for the falling-rate phase of drying. Chem. Eng. Progr. 43, 13–24. Also issued as U. S. Dept. Agr. Bur. Circ. AIC-152.

CHAPTER 4

Characteristics of Food Substances
Related to Drying Behavior

STRUCTURE AND CHEMICAL COMPOSITION

The subject matter of this work being a class of food products, our interest lies in the drying of organic plant or animal materials. These are all characterized by great complexity and heterogeneity of physical structure, and water is a ubiquitous and fundamental part of the structure. Each is an assemblage of strongly hydrated high-molecular-weight compounds, mostly belonging to the classes we call proteins, carbohydrates, and lipids. Complete quantitative description of even a single one of these systems is out of the question. We always deal, in practice, with the average or combined behavior of a large number of individual units or pieces, or, in the case of fluids, the churned or homogenized material. We speak of the water content of a piece of potato flesh, knowing full well that microscopic regions within the sample may, because they comprise local concentrations of a lipid component, contain much less water than neighboring regions containing protein constituents of the cytoplasm; we can at least feel sure that the diverse kinds of constituent are in equilibrium with one another with respect to chemical potential, osmotic pressure, or vapor pressure. A related problem, discussed by Salwin and Slawson (1959), is the interchange of moisture between the different components of a dehydrated composite ration enclosed in an impermeable container; vapor pressure will eventually be equalized throughout at any steady temperature, but the moisture contents of the different constituents may differ widely at equilibrium.

Both plant and animal tissues in their natural state are cellular. The differences in composition and properties of cell walls and cytoplasm are responsible for marked differences in drying behavior; cell wall permeability, in particular, is usually increased markedly and irreversibly by scalding or blanching. In the course of drying, with an accompanying strong shrinkage of volume, even though the distance through which water must travel to reach the surface is steadily decreasing, the number of cell walls through which it must pass is not changing. Stamm (1946) based a procedure for correlating data on the drying of wood upon the cellular nature of the substance; cell walls, pit membranes, pores, and capillaries act as individual elements of resistance to water movement, combined in a piece of wood into a multiplicity of series and parallel connections.   In the case of wood, in particular, the properties in the longitudinal, tangential, and transverse directions are completely different.   Kamei (1937), Bateman *et al.* (1939), Schauss (1940), and Stamm (1946, 1948) have reported studies of the drying of wood which have added greatly to practical knowledge of this most complex art.

CHANGES IN PROPERTIES AS AFFECTED BY MOISTURE CONTENT AND TEMPERATURE

The Sorption Isotherm

As is evident from the foregoing discussion, the behavior of water in a moist substance during drying is intimately related to changes in the water vapor pressure of the substance.   In general, a moist organic material held at constant temperature in a small evacuated chamber connected to a sensitive pressure gage displays a vapor pressure which approaches a steady equilibrium value characteristic of the material, its moisture content, and the temperature.   The experimentally determined relation between water vapor pressure and moisture content at equilibrium is sometimes known as equilibrium vapor pressure (or equilibrium relative humidity), or more often as "equilibrium moisture content."   The quantitative relation between vapor pressure and moisture content at constant temperature constitutes a vapor pressure isotherm.

Moisture Sorption Isotherms of Representative Food Materials.—Extensive measurements of moisture sorption have been reported by Gane (1941, 1943, 1950); Bate-Smith *et al.* (1943); Makower and Dehority (1943); Benson and Richardson (1955); Karel *et al.* (1955); Görling (1954, 1956); Fish (1957); and Notter *et al.* (1959). Curves showing the relation between moisture content (dry basis) and percentage relative humidity for several food products at approximately room temperature are shown in Fig. 16, and a family of curves giving the relation for potatoes at temperatures from 20° to 100°C. is shown in Fig. 17 (Görling 1958).   Data for other commodities have been published for wheat by Gane (1941), egg by Makower (1945), garlic by Pruthi *et al.* (1959), egg albumin and gelatin by Benson and Richardson (1955), and carrot, cabbage, and a number of other vegetables, fruits, and miscellaneous products by Gane (1950).

Two pecularities of observed sorption isotherms which have attracted the attention of investigators are their striking S-shape and the phenomenon of hysteresis, the latter signifying a difference in the

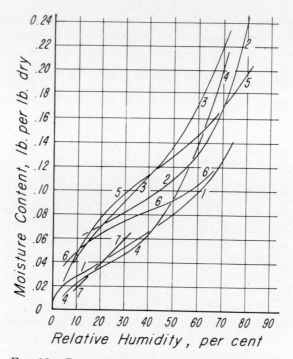

FIG. 16.   SELECTED WATER SORPTION ISOTHERMS

(1)   Egg solids, 10°C. *From Gane 1943A*
(2)   Beef, 10°C.   *From Bate-Smith et al. 1943*
(3)   Fish (cod), 30°C.   *From Jason 1958*
(4)   Coffee, 10°C. *From Gane 1950*
(5)   Starch gel, 25°C. *From Fish 1957*
(6)   Potato, 28°C.   *From Gane 1950*
(7)   Orange juice, 20°C. *From Notter et al. 1959*

equilibrium moisture content at a given vapor pressure according to whether the equilibrium point is approached from the higher moisture or the lower moisture direction.   In fact, considerable advances in knowledge of the internal architecture of proteins and other natural polymers have resulted from these studies.

The "B-E-T" theory of the adsorption of gases in multimolecular layers (Brunauer *et al.* 1938), already referred to, predicts the S-shape but does not agree closely with experiment at relative humidities higher than about 50 or 60 per cent.   Henderson (1952) proposed the following empirical relationship:

$$W^n = \frac{\log (1 - r_h)}{-KT} \qquad (42)$$

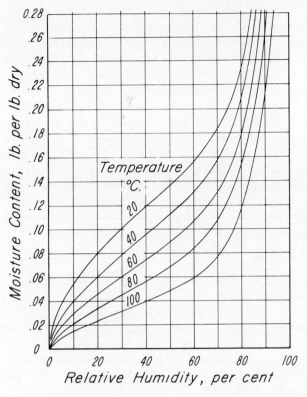

From Görling 1958

FIG. 17. WATER SORPTION ISOTHERMS, POTATO

where

n and K	= empirical constants
W	= moisture content, dry basis
r_h	= relative humidity
T	= absolute temperature

When the constants were determined by fitting the data at 20 and 75 per cent humidity, good agreement was obtained except near the ends of the curves. Rockland (1957) correlated sorption data by use of the following modification of the Henderson equation:

$$n \log W + Y = \log \log \frac{1}{1 - r_h} \tag{43}$$

where n and Y are the empirical constants. If the right-hand member of this expression is plotted against $\log W$ for a material, two or more intersecting straight lines can be drawn through the points with good accuracy. This is interpreted as corresponding to two or three successive steps in the process of adsorbing water molecules on the polymeric solids, probably because the mechanism of adsorption changes. Kuprianoff (1958) also noted that there must be a definite discontinuity in the isotherm because of the large difference in binding energy as water content is increased. However, he believes the discontinuity is usually obscured by the overlapping of the stages. In general, up to about 20 per cent humidity, the adsorption is monomolecular and is accompanied by a high heat of adsorption or desorption. Between 20 per cent and saturation, a colloidal material shows only a small heat of sorption, and the effective binding energy consists principally of the latent heat of water vapor condensation. A capillary-porous product behaves differently from the colloidal material between about 80 per cent humidity and saturation; water condenses in the larger capillaries with no heat of sorption at all. Such a substance may exhibit a more complex isotherm, containing two points of inflection.

Hysteresis in Moisture Sorption.—The phenomenon of hysteresis in sorption is only imperfectly understood. A well characterized substance like bovine serum albumin, a soluble protein which has been studied extensively by Benson and his associates (see especially Seehof *et al.* 1953), reaches an equilibrium moisture content of about ten per cent in air of 34 per cent relative humidity at 25°C. if it is being dried down from a higher moisture content (*i.e.*, if we are dealing with an instance of desorption), but if it is initially drier and is taking up (*i.e.*, adsorbing) moisture from air of 34 per cent relative humidity, its moisture content will come up to a limiting value of only seven per cent. These two distinct equilibrium values can be reproduced again and again if the sample is alternately moistened and redried. Obviously we are usually concerned with the *desorption* equilibrium, which is always the higher of the two. In preceding paragraphs, and in Figs. 16 and 17, the values given for various substances either refer to the desorption isotherm or the extent of hysteresis is negligible.

"Free Moisture."—The term "free moisture," meaning the moisture content in excess of equilibrium moisture content at the given temperature and humidity, has come into rather general use, unfortunately, because it erroneously conveys the impression that this moisture is not bound to the solid by any adsorptive force whatever. The German term "die entfernbaren Feuchtigkeit," "the removable moisture," would express the meaning less ambiguously. Drying rates are often correlated with this quantity, which will be represented by the expression $W - W_e$, where W_e is the equilibrium moisture content.

The Definition of "Moisture Content."—In view of the complex relationships discussed in the last several paragraphs it is apparent that the term "moisture content" must be defined operationally— *i.e.*, in terms of the exact procedure used physically to determine the quantity. In the absence of a precise definition the meaning is seriously ambiguous. Worse yet, a number of different moisture determination methods are being used, both routinely and for research purposes, and reports of the work frequently fail to identify the method used. Significant differences are possible, especially in the low-moisture region which is especially important for food dehydration. Stitt (1958) has recently reviewed this entire question and made a critical evaluation of eight methods. The one generally used by workers in the Western Regional Research Laboratory for referee determinations is the vacuum oven method of Makower *et al.* (1946), calling for 40 hrs. of drying at 70°C. for potatoes and carrots, 30 hrs. at 60°C. for cabbage and onions. This method gives a moisture content in dehydrated potatoes about two per cent higher than the 6-hr. vacuum oven method described in many purchase specifications—*e.g.*, eight per cent moisture in a sample of potatoes reported by the 6-hr. method to contain only six per cent (see Appendix B, p. 173).

Changes Due to Migration of Soluble Constituents

Water is not the only substance which changes its location within a body as drying occurs. The water in living tissues exists as a solution of scores or hundreds of constituents, some of which are small molecules like simple sugars, while others are very large and highly hydrated molecules. The press juice from fresh carrots, for example, contains about six per cent of sugars in solution. During the drying some of the dissolved substances must migrate within pieces.

In the living tissue only the water and small molecules in solution will diffuse readily through cell walls; the latter act as highly selective semipermeable membranes. Scalding, or any other way of killing the tissue, changes its characteristics so as to make it more readily permeable, not only to water but also to rather large molecules in solution. When a piece of scalded tissue is dried in an air stream a moisture gradient is very quickly set up within it, each succeeding layer from the center outward being a little drier than the layer below it. At the same time, shrinkage in the drying surface layers puts the deeper layers under compression. The resulting complex state of affairs can only be described qualitatively.

Reduction of moisture content at an internal location in a piece of material undergoing drying must reflect a *radial outward* motion of water; *i.e.*, away from the center and toward the surface of the piece—because, after all, whatever water leaves the surface must have come originally from within. As was pointed out in the discussion of theories of water transfer, this motion may be the result of any of several different physical mechanisms, some of which picture the movement as a liquid flow, while others think of it as the streaming of water vapor under a pressure gradient or the diffusion of individual free water molecules. Now the migration of a dissolved non-volatile substance can take place only in liquid solution, not by either of the other mechanisms. Therefore the behavior of the dissolved substances in any particular case will depend in part on the nature and physical structure of the wet material and in part on the conditions of drying which determine material temperature and the distribution of moisture within the piece.

Lykow (1950, 1955), for example, says that the drying of leather after tanning must be conducted in such a way as to hold the soluble tannins in the body of the leather and prevent their migration to the surface, where they would oxidize and cause undesirable darkening. To accomplish this the moisture transport within the sheet must be made to take place mainly as a streaming of water vapor, so that the non-volatile solutes will be left in place inside the leather.

If the water movement occurs as a liquid flow, the dissolved substances will tend to accompany the water toward the surface of the piece, although there may be some separation of low-molecular weight substances from colloidal or suspended ones if the solution must pass through cell walls. In addition, shrinkage of the surface layers of the material puts the interior of the piece under compression which may cause extrusion of juice through pores, capillaries, or cracks, and this also results in movement of solutes toward the surface. The extent of this action will depend on the steepness of the moisture gradient near the surface of the piece, the size and arrangement of cracks, intergranular spaces, or pores, and the structural stiffness of the underlying wet substance; if it is soft and weak the solid structure can readily fold or crumple under stress so as to reduce the volume it occupies by an amount equal to the volume of liquid extruded. Soft fruits, meat, and fish not infrequently ooze liquid during early stages of dehydration; the resulting gummy "taffy" on trays and the bottom of drier bodies may be a decided nuisance to the drier operator.

As was pointed out by Van Arsdel (1951), a physical mechanism comes into action when drying begins that can produce transfer of dissolved substances in the opposite direction—that is, a buildup of solutes at the *centers* of pieces. As soon as a moisture gradient is established within a piece of material, solutes must begin to diffuse from the region of high solute concentration at the surface toward the region where the solution is more dilute, namely, in the interior. This concentration difference will continue as long as the drying continues, but transfer of solute molecules will slow down when the concentration gradient diminishes and will cease entirely when there is no longer a continuous liquid phase throughout the body.

These oppositely directed tendencies are, of course, both exerting their influences simultaneously, and the net movement of solute in any particular case will depend on the preponderance of one or the other effect. It is easily conceivable that in the absence of gross extrusion of solution to the surfaces, accumulation of solutes at the centers of pieces might predominate at one stage of a single drying experiment, and accumulation at the surfaces in another stage. The actual existence of both mechanisms of solute transport has been demonstrated experimentally by Duckworth and Smith (1961) by soaking carrot and potato strips in solutions of labeled glucose, then securing autoradiographs of sections taken at various intervals during drying. In scalded potato and carrot there is a net inward movement and accumulation of labeled glucose at the centers of the strips, slow at first but very marked by the time most of the volume shrinkage has occurred. In unscalded potato there is a peripheral accumulation during the early stages of drying, then little further change.

One type of "heat damage" sometimes observed in dehydrated potatoes is a strikingly distinct brown center in the dried dice or strips. The appearance suggests strongly that migration of sugars toward the center has increased the amount of browning there above what it would normally be after the same history of changing moisture content and temperature in a low-sugar potato. Exaggeration of the effect might be expected from a combination of high material temperature at early stages of drying (favored by high wet-bulb temperature) and early creation of a steep moisture gradient within each piece of product (favored by high wet-bulb *depression*, light tray loading, and high air velocity).

"Case Hardening."—Migration of solutes to the surface of drying pieces may be responsible for an operational difficulty sometimes experienced, which has come to be known by the picturesque expression "case hardening." The term, probably borrowed from the metallurgical technique of forming a hard steel "case" on an iron object by heating it in contact with charcoal, was picked up by driers of macaroni and operators of lumber kilns and used to signify trouble, rather than a desired effect. Experience with the drying of green lumber had shown that in order to produce sound dry product, free from checking and warping, it was necessary to control temperature and rate of drying very carefully. If external conditions were such as to favor immediate rapid drying, the outer layers tended to shrink down so strongly onto the nearly incompressible wet core that the elastic limit of the surface layers would be exceeded and they would stretch plastically. Then when the inner portions finally dried and shrank, these stretched outer layers would no longer shrink down tightly upon the center, but would open up in shrinkage cracks along planes of weakness. The resulting defect would be blamed upon the creation of too steep a moisture gradient within the pieces and the premature hardening and setting of the outer "case."

Operators of fruit dehydrators, as well as many experimenters who had worked on the drying of soap, meat, fish, leather, and other colloidal materials, sometimes found that a dehydration run would begin normally but then after a time come almost to a standstill while the centers of the pieces were still very wet. This condition was frequently called "case hardening," and the opinion was sometimes expressed that too-rapid initial drying was responsible; it was said that "water had been removed from the surface layers faster than it could be replenished by diffusion from the deeper layers." Several writers spoke of the formation of a gummy, glassy, or leathery surface layer, substantially impermeable to water (Pierce 1953).

The latter phenomenon is known to take place in some materials under some conditions, as has been discussed above in connection with the migration of solutes. Sugar solutions from juicy fruits or serum from meat or fish could unquestionably form a gummy or glassy non-porous surface layer through which water would diffuse only very slowly. The conditions which lead to serious trouble on this account have not been thoroughly investigated. Qualitatively, it has usually been concluded that, just as in the case of wood or macaroni drying, the initial drying rate must be limited and the temperature of the material must be kept relatively high so as to increase the rate of internal diffusion of moisture.

On the other hand, in the dehydration of cut vegetables (with the possible exception of moist-type sweet potatoes) the condition that might appropriately be called "case hardening" apparently does not occur. Consequently, instead of controlling drying conditions so as to reduce the initial rate of drying, operators purposely use drastic conditions (high air temperature, low humidity, high air velocity) from the very beginning. This ordinarily leads to the formation of internal shrinkage checks or voids (see following section) and an actual acceleration of the drying rate in the late stages of drying. The phenomenon might therefore almost be called a "reverse case hardening" with respect to the effect on drying rate.

We have already sketched the overwhelming evidence that resistance to internal movement of moisture in colloidal organic materials is greater by several orders of magnitude at low levels of moisture content than at levels of, say, 20 to 25 per cent or higher. This fact is responsible for the drastic fall in drying rate usually observed at some stage of a drying run, even while the total weight of the material indicates that the mean moisture content is still relatively high; any additional moisture evaporated must be transferred to the outer air through the relatively dry external "skin" of the pieces, which by reason of its dryness is almost impermeable to moisture. Many people were led to believe that total drying time might be shortened if such a "skin" were prevented from forming, for example by maintaining a higher relative humidity in the drying air. This is, of course, the "case hardening" argument again. Crank (1950, 1958), Crank and Henry (1949 A, B, C), and Crank and Park (1951) investigated this whole question, both mathematically and experimentally, and conclusively disproved the supposition. The rate of drying into an atmosphere containing some water vapor is always less than the rate in a completely dry atmosphere. The moisture in a body being dried always distributes itself through the solid in such a way that a low diffusivity in a zone of low-moisture content is compensated by a steeper moisture gradient in that zone. The existence of "wet centers" in pieces of a vegetable during drying, far from being a sign of trouble, actually is the very condition of high internal moisture gradient which favors the most rapid further drying. The argument is not valid, however, if migration of solutes occurs or a chemical reaction which changes the character of the surface as it dries. This is undoubtedly the reason why measures to prevent "case hardening" have been efficacious in some cases.

Irreversible Changes of the Tissue

Many dehydrated foods are being manufactured on a large scale under drying conditions that cause little or no damage to the important quality factors, but for various reasons this has still not been successfully accomplished for some other important types of food material. The crisp tenderness of lettuce, for example, or the firm juiciness of a ripe tomato, has not been captured in even the most carefully dried and carefully rehydrated product.   Oxidative destruction of some of the original ascorbic acid content of vegetables inevitably occurs, according to Diemair (1941), the proportion of loss varying in different raw materials from as little as 15 per cent (leek leaves and Savoy-type cabbage) to more than 90 per cent (potato strips) for reasons as yet unknown.   Some other types of oxidative damage are discussed below under the heading of "Browning."   In a general way, it seems that characteristic texture is the most difficult of all properties to preserve unchanged.   True natural flavor is almost as hard to save.

Structural Damage Due to Shrinkage Stresses.—A portion of cellular animal or vegetable tissue in its living state exhibits the property of "turgor," meaning that each cell is distended by its liquid contents and consequently has taken on a structural stiffness or solidity, like an inflated toy balloon.   Cell walls are under tension, cell contents under compression.   The cell wall structures possess strength and elasticity, but if the unit tensile stress is increased beyond a quite modest value the structure yields, in part irreversibly.   Upon removal of the stress the stretched structure does not retract all the way to its original no-load dimensions.

This kind of plastic deformation takes place to some extent in any kind of drying of animal or vegetable tissue except, perhaps, in freeze drying, where the original dimensions of the quickly frozen tissue are maintained unchanged.   In ordinary drying the permanent deformation may be marked, and various kinds of damage, including tearing, shearing, and crushing, may be found in the dried tissue.

Structural damage arising from shrinkage stresses during drying was discussed earlier, in the section on "case hardening."   Significant experimental and theoretical work on the drying of macaroni and similar food products without checking has been reported by Earle and Ceaglske (1949), Lykow (1950, 1955), Beuschel (1955), and Görling (1958).

During earlier stages of the drying of a colloidal substance like macaroni dough, at not too rapid a rate so that internal moisture gradients remain small, the shrinkage of any linear dimension of the piece is a linear function of the moisture content,

$$L = L_0(1 + aW) \tag{44}$$

where a is a linear shrinkage coefficient.   As drying is continued, further shrinkage is hindered more and more and the dimensions of the piece become substantially fixed while some moisture still remains. Lykow (1950, 1955) gives the following one-dimensional coefficients for a few substances of interest to us: wheat dough, $a = 0.47$; macaroni, $a = 0.91$; rye bread, $a = 0.56$. The shrinkage in volume is also a linear function of moisture content, the coefficient being approximately three times the one-dimensional coefficient.

Lykow carefully measured and weighed cubes of peat at frequent intervals during drying. Fig. 18, taken from his Fig. 143, (1955), shows the remarkably linear course of volume shrinkage all the way from an initial moisture content of about 8.20 lbs. per pound of dry solids

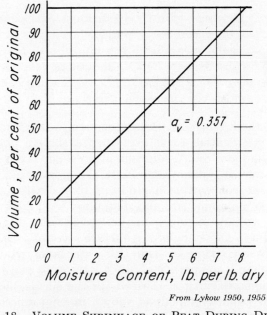

From Lykow 1950, 1955

FIG. 18. VOLUME SHRINKAGE OF PEAT DURING DRYING

down to about 0.35 lb. per pound, or approximately 25 per cent moisture. The reduction in volume taking place between any two levels of mean moisture content remains substantially constant at about 92 to 94 per cent of the volume of water lost by evaporation. This approximate equality between volume shrinkage and volume of water removed has also been noted in early stages of the dehydration of vegetables (Van Arsdel 1951). It is unusual for the shrinkage to continue unchecked to so low a mean moisture content as 25 per cent, especially if moisture removal has been so rapid as to set up a large moisture gradient in each piece.

Changes in dimensions and shape of vegetable pieces during drying can be described qualitatively as follows: A piece of such a vegetable as carrot, cut, for example, into a cube like (*a*) in Fig. 19, is in a condition of turgor, even if the tissue has been killed by scalding; the fluid or gelled contents of intact cells are under some pressure, and the cell membranes are under some tension. The surface of the piece is wet with carrot juice, which may have been somewhat diluted in the scalding operation. If the carrot cube is now exposed to a current of

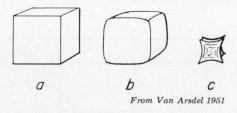

a   *b*   *c*

From Van Arsdel 1951

Fig. 19.   Change of Shape of Vegetable Dice
During Drying

warm dry air, the first effect is evaporation of water from the wet surface. The concentration of solutes in the surface liquid increases. Water from the more dilute solution in a deeper layer of tissue then immediately moves outward through the permeable cell walls in obedience to the concentration gradient thus created. Any surface cell, even while remaining full and distended with fluid, flattens so as to diminish in volume in step with the loss of fluid. The first step in shrinkage is thus a flattening of the surface layer of cells, coupled with the appearance of a tensile stress in this outer layer, which is trying to shrink down upon a comparatively incompressible and fully wet core. As drying progresses further, the cells in the surface layers are completely flattened and stretched, as shown in photomicrographs made by Reeve (1942), Fig. 20. The piece of carrot will now have partly lost its eight square corners and been pulled into a "pillow" shape, like (*b*) in Fig. 19.

As drying progresses still further so that shrinkage is occurring throughout the entire piece, the eight corners of the cube will have become dry, hard, and almost unchanging while the center is still wet and plastic. Final stages of shrinkage thus take place mainly in the center, with the result that the shape eventually looks something like sketch (*c*) in Fig. 19, although usually more irregularly distorted. Reeve's photograph of a sectioned carrot cube after drying, Fig. 21 (1942), pictures the extreme distortion that accompanies shrinkage of a high-moisture material; in this case at least ten volumes of water were evaporated for every one volume of dry solid remaining.

From Reeve 1942

FIG. 20.   CROSS-SECTION OF OUTER PART OF CARROT
CYLINDER AFTER $1/2$ HR. OF DRYING, $\times$ 150

If drying conditions during the entire time that any portion of the piece remains moist and plastic are so gentle that the surfaces are never much drier than the center, the piece will shrink down with only a minimum distortion of shape.   However, if initial drying conditions are rigorous, the outer layers will become dry enough to be quite rigid and have considerable mechanical strength while the inside of the piece must still undergo much further shrinkage and will have very little tensile strength.   Under these circumstances the final volume of the piece is substantially fixed while the average moisture content of the piece is still high; the result is that the tissue splits or ruptures internally at one or several places and shrinks out toward the already set outer faces.   The internal splits open up wider and wider.   If the finally dry piece is cut open it will be found to contain voids, or a hollow center; it is sometimes said to be "honeycombed."

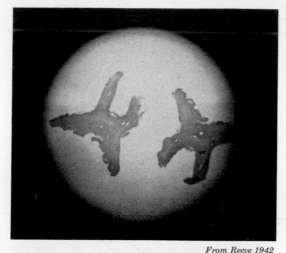

From Reeve 1942

FIG. 21.   CROSS-SECTION OF A CARROT CUBE
AFTER COMPLETE DRYING, × 4

One consequence of this effect is that the "bulk density" (measured in pounds per gross cubic foot) of a dehydrated product is likely to be strongly influenced by the conditions of dehydration.   Fig. 22, from Van Arsdel (1951), illustrates the effect with two beakers side by side, each containing 250 gm. of dehydrated $^3/_8$-in. potato dice.   Those on the left had been quickly dried by P. W. Kilpatrick (Western Regional Research Laboratory) in air at 150°F., wet-bulb temperature 85°, $3^3/_4$ hr. to $W = 0.11$.   Product in the right-hand picture was very slowly dried at 125°, wet-bulb temperature 120°, $10^1/_2$ hr. to $W = 0.61$, then $4^1/_2$ hr. at 150°, wet-bulb temperature 85°, to a final moisture content of $W = 0.11$.   The bulk density of the former is only about half that of the latter.

This difference in bulk density is paralleled by other differences. The pieces of the rapidly dried product have maintained their cubical shape with little outward distortion, but the dice are full of small air bubbles or voids, representing breaks in the potato tissue.   These breaks may lead to an undesirable degree of sloughing during rehydration, but they also greatly accelerate the rehydration as well as the late stages of the drying itself.   The most obvious effect is the substantial difference in size of container required to hold a specified net weight, and the corresponding difference in proportion of space saved by dehydration.   The advantages of a highly compact, dense, concentrated product must be weighed against its very real drawbacks, particularly in terms of product quality.

From Van Arsdel 1951

FIG. 22.   RELATIVE BULK OF RAPIDLY DRIED AND SLOWLY DRIED
POTATO DICE

Loss of Ability to Rehydrate Completely.—The rehydration of
a dehydrated food product is too often taken for granted; not infrequently it turns out to be difficult or even quite unsatisfactory.
One could probably assert flatly that no animal or vegetable tissue has
ever been dried completely without irreversibly losing some of its
original properties.   Practical conditions of dehydration are to a large
extent governed by the necessity for minimizing this damage.   Indeed, the principal reason why freeze drying is currently such an
important development is that freeze-dried products rehydrate
quickly and assume something like their initial moisture content and
physical properties.

Davis and Howard (1943) found that exposure of carrot slices to
conditions in which the product reached a temperature of 200°F.
reduced both the rate and the maximum extent of rehydration, and
the longer the high-temperature exposure was continued the lower a
rehydration ratio was observed.

Gane and Wager (1958) point out that in vegetable tissue both the
elasticity of cell walls and the swelling power of starch gel are important for good rehydration;   both are reduced by any substantial
amount of heat treatment.   Heating coagulates the protoplasmic
proteins and destroys the osmotic properties of cell walls.   The
original turgor of a vegetable tissue is mostly lost.

Brooks (1958) found that the changes in the properties of egg upon
spray drying or freeze drying are related to an irreversible change in

the protein characteristics. Freeze-dried meat has a drier and tougher texture than the frozen control with which it is compared. The ability of muscle to hold water resides in its possession of a system of membranes and structural proteins which are capable of forming gels by enclosing water in a three-dimensional network of protein chains. Dried meat which will absorb only a fraction of the water it formerly contained has obviously been damaged by the drying; however, even complete regain of original weight does not necessarily mean that the meat has recovered its former structure. The rehydrated product is generally reported to be less juicy, more crumbly, than the original meat.

A study of rehydration described in the U. S. Department of Agriculture's Dehydration Manual (1944) was designed primarily to standardize the procedure for testing the rehydration properties of dehydrated vegetables. Great variability between supposed replicates was usual, with respect both to the maximum amount of water that would be taken up on long soaking or boiling and to the rate at which this uptake would proceed.

Careful attention to definitions is necessary to avoid possible confusion. A rehydration test always comprises determination of the drained weight of a rehydrated sample, using specified procedures both for the rehydration by soaking or boiling and for the drained weight determination. The "rehydration ratio" is defined simply as the ratio of the drained weight after this treatment to the weight of sample taken. Ordinarily the weight of sugars and other solubles leached out during the soaking is disregarded, although it may be appreciable. A comprehensive test will, of course, involve making a careful mass-balance in which leaching losses will be accounted for. A "coefficient of restoration of weight" may be calculated directly if both the initial weight of a sample before dehydration and the weight of the same sample after it has been dehydrated and then rehydrated are known. It is simply M_R/M_0, where M_R is the weight of the rehydrated sample and M_0 the weight before drying. But, of course, we usually do not know what the original weight M_0 was. The coefficient can be estimated from the moisture content of the rehydrated sample, W_R, and the average or usual moisture content of that fresh commodity, W_0, if we assume that no solid matter is leached out in the rehydration process:

$$\text{Coefficient of restoration} = \frac{M_R}{M_0} = \frac{W_R + 1}{W_0 + 1} \tag{45}$$

The coefficient observed will, of course, be lower if some of the solid is dissolved and discarded with the excess rehydration water.

Much more experimental work could profitably be done to throw light on the factors which cause slow or incomplete rehydration and excessive leaching of solutes, and on the relations between these factors and the pretreatment and dehydration conditions. It has been said that reduction of the final moisture content of dehydrated vegetables much below the customary four to six per cent greatly increases the difficulty of rehydration, but there is also evidence contrary to this view.

Loss of Volatile Constituents.—When water is evaporated from a food product the water vapor leaving the drier invariably carries with it at least traces of every other volatile constituent of the fresh food. Ordinarily the consequence is an unwanted, disadvantageous, and irreversible loss of characteristic flavor. Little has been accomplished in the way of applying physical principles to reduction of this loss. Various proposals have been made, and some industrial development carried out, to recapture volatile constituents from the air exhausted from a dehydrator, with a view either to returning the recovered substance in order to improve the character of the dry product or to disposing of it acceptably if it is obnoxious, as it is in the case of onion or garlic dehydration.

Little more can be said here than that the relative volatilities of the different odorous components may be quite differently affected by changes in temperature or system pressure. The amounts of any of them that volatilize along with a given weight of water will depend on their mutual solubilities even more than on their vapor pressures in the pure state. The fact is that some constituents undoubtedly contribute so powerfully to flavor that the vapor pressure needed to produce the sensation is vanishingly low. One cannot say on the basis of known physical properties whether the true aroma of orange juice, for example, or chicken meat, will be better retained in the residual dry solids if the water is all evaporated in the course of many hours from ice at a temperature of no more than 20°F. than if it is all evaporated within a few minutes at a temperature of 100°F., or higher.

Browning, or "Heat Damage."—The most obvious, and in some respects the most troublesome of the irreversible changes that may accompany the dehydration of a food product is the color change variously called "browning," "scorching," "burning," or simply "heat damage." As some of these names suggest, it is commonly associated with overheating. Familiar in daily life in the cooking of all kinds of food, it is sometimes highly desired—for example, in the brown crust formed on a loaf of bread during baking—but in food dehydration it is generally a most serious quality defect. If the degree of browning is not great, the off-color may be the only noticeable effect, but when the change proceeds further the flavor and the rehydration capacity may also be adversely affected.

Hodge (1953), Lea (1958), and Ellis (1959) have reviewed the extensive literature on the chemistry of the several kinds of reaction which cause this phenomenon. They include not only the carbonyl-amino group of reactions described by Maillard (1912) and typified by the reactions between amino acids and sugars, but also non-amino and oxidative reactions. Similar changes take place more slowly in the long-time storage of dehydrated foods at ordinary temperatures. For example, Burton (1945) found that mashed potato powder at a moisture content of twelve per cent browned perceptibly in ten months at 25°C. The reaction was anaerobic and it involved a loss of hexose sugars and aspartic acid and a production of CO_2. The time required to produce perceptible browning increased about 3.5-fold if the temperature was lowered by 10°C. Legault et al. (1947) measured the rate of formation of water-soluble brown color in unsulfited dried vegetables, the moisture contents and temperatures being in the range of practical conditions of storage. They found a considerably higher temperature quotient (Q_{10}) than 3.5 at their lower level of moisture content; in carrots Q_{10} rose from 6.7 to 7.3 as moisture content was lowered from 8.0 to 5.4 per cent; in potatoes Q_{10} rose from 6.8 to 7.6 as moisture was lowered from 8.0 to 5.3 per cent; in onions, Q_{10} was 8.4 at 3.5 per cent moisture; and in sweet potatoes Q_{10} was 5.0 at 7.4 per cent moisture. The rate of formation of soluble brown substances was much more rapid in carrots than in potatoes, but of course color change in the dry materials is much more readily observable in the potato.

Mangels and Gore (1921) had noted that perceptible browning of a number of different dehydrated vegetables heated in air occurred at a somewhat lower temperature if the air was relatively moist (64 per cent relative humidity at 50°C., 49 per cent at 60°C.) than if it was very dry. They found onions and cabbage to be damaged much more quickly at a given temperature than potatoes or carrots. Hendel et al. (1955) and Hendel (1956) made a careful study of the effects of temperature and moisture content (as well as various raw material characteristics) on the rate of browning of potato dice. When the samples were heated in closed containers so that moisture content remained constant, the rate of browning (determined by measuring optical density of a dilute acetic acid-acetone extract) increased exponentially with temperature, with an apparent activation energy of about 25 kcal. per mole remaining constant down to a moisture content of about 0.20 lb. per lb. dry, and then gradually rising to 37 kcal. per mole at a moisture content of 0.05 lb. per lb. dry. The rate of browning reached a decided maximum at a moisture content of about 0.20 lb. per lb. dry. For example, at 65 °C. the relative rates of browning at moisture contents of 0.05, 0.09, 0.15, 0.32, 1.00, and 3.50 lb. per lb. dry were 180, 450, 650, 450, 200, and 85, respectively. However, the authors were unable to confirm expected results very well when they attempted to use these isolated browning rates to predict the amount of browning in regular cabinet drying experiments, probably because of the complication introduced by high internal moisture gradients and possible migration of solutes during the experimental runs. Additional careful experimental work will be necessary before it will become possible to attain Hendel's objective of devising an optimum bin-drying procedure by combining these browning-rate data with known drying rates in the low-moisture range.

Use of Sulfur Dioxide to Retard Browning.—The origin of the practice of exposing cut fruits to the fumes of burning sulfur before drying them for storage and subsequent consumption seems to be lost in antiquity. As our forefathers well knew, thoroughly "sulfured" apple rings and apricot, peach, and pear halves can be sun dried without darkening or loss of their attractive color. Some sulfuring of cut potatoes and other vegetables intended for drying seems to have been traditional. Use of sulfur dioxide or a sulfite solution to inhibit the browning which may take place during drying and subsequent storage finally received thorough investigation, beginning intensively during World War II. First it was aimed especially at preventing the browning of dehydrated cabbage, but studies were broadened later to include some other vegetables. See especially the publications by Allen et al. (1943); Mackinney and Howard (1944); Beavens and Bourne (1945); and Legault et al. (1949, 1951). It is not our purpose to go into the chemical and technological aspects of sulfite treatment beyond their direct bearing on the drying itself.

Higher drying temperatures can be used in the presence of a small amount of sulfite (specifications of government procurement agencies call for SO_2 content ranging from 200 to 400 parts per million for potato granules and from 1,500 to 2,500 parts per million for cabbage, dry basis, even higher for dried fruits) than without it, thus making it possible to shorten the drying time and correspondingly increase the drier capacity, without exceeding the tolerable small degree of heat damage.

The quantitative relationship has not been worked out, but plant operators believe the finishing temperature in tunnels drying potato half-dice can safely be from 5° to 10°F. higher in the presence of an allowable level of SO_2 than in its absence.

When a drier is heated directly by the products of combustion of gas or oil, as is very common practice, some "sulfuring" of the product occurs during drying if the fuel contains more than a trace of sulfur. The amount of SO_2 that can be thus incorporated into the product may not be by any means negligible. Operators of potato dehydrators, for example, have found it necessary to restrict their purchases of fuel oil to known low-sulfur sources in order to avoid exceeding the SO_2 tolerance in the dry product. The quantitative relationship has, no doubt, been determined from experience by these operators, but we are not aware of any published information.

BIBLIOGRAPHY

ALLEN, R. J. L., BARKER, J., and MAPSON, L. W. 1943. The drying of vegetables. I. Cabbage. J. Soc. Chem. Ind. *62* T, 145–160.

BARKER, J., BURTON, W. G., and GANE, R. 1943. Mashed potato powder. I. Properties and methods of production. Great Brit. Dept. Sci. and Indus. Research and Ministry of Food. U. K. Progress Report VI, Part 6, London.

BATEMAN, E., HOHF, J. P., and STAMM, A. J. 1939. Unidirectional drying of wood. Ind. Eng. Chem. *31*, 1150–1154.

BATE-SMITH, E. C., LEA, C. H., and SHARP, J. G. 1943. Dried meat. I. J. Soc. Chem. Ind. *62* T, 100–104.

BEAVENS, E. A., and BOURNE, J. A. 1945. Commercial sulfiting practices. Food Inds. *17*, 1044–1045.

BENSON, S. W., and RICHARDSON, R. L. 1955. A study of hysteresis in the sorption of polar gases by native and denatured proteins. J. Am. Chem. Soc. *77*, 2585–2590.

BEUSCHEL, H. 1955. Dissertation, Technische Hochschule, München. (Concerns mechanical stresses in macaroni during drying.)

BROOKS, J. 1958. Structure of animal tissues and dehydration. *In* Fundamental Aspects of the Dehydration of Foodstuffs. Soc. Chem. Ind. 8–13.

BRUNAUER, S., EMMETT, P. H., and TELLER, E. 1938. Adsorption of gases in multimolecular layers. J. Am. Chem. Soc. *60*, 309–319.

BURTON, W. G. 1944. Mashed potato powder. II. Spray drying method. J. Soc. Chem. Ind. *63*, 213–215.

BURTON, W. G. 1945. Mashed potato powder. III. High-temperature browning of mashed-potato powder. J. Soc. Chem. Ind. *64*, 215–218.

CRANK, J. 1950. The influence of concentration-dependent diffusion on rate of evaporation. Proc. Phys. Soc. (London) *63* B, Pt. 7, No. 367, 484–491.

CRANK, J. 1951. Diffusion in media with variable properties. III. Diffusion coefficients which vary discontinuously with concentration. Trans. Faraday Soc. *47*, 450–461.

CRANK, J. 1958. Some mathematical diffusion studies relevant to dehydration. *In* Fundamental Aspects of the Dehydration of Foodstuffs. Soc. Chem. Ind., 37–41.

CRANK, J., and HENRY, M. E. 1949 A. A comparison of rates of conditioning by different methods. Proc. Phys. Soc. (London) *42* B, 257–269.

CRANK, J., and HENRY, M. E. 1949 B. Diffusion in media with variable properties. I. The effect of a variable diffusion coefficient on the rates of absorption and desorption. Trans. Faraday Soc. *40*, 636–650.

CRANK, J., and HENRY, M. E. 1949 C. Diffusion in media with variable properties. II. The effect of a variable diffusion coefficient on the concentra tion-distance relationship in the non-steady state. Trans. Faraday Soc. *40*, 1119–1130.

CRANK, J., and PARK, G. S. 1951. Diffusion in high polymers; some anomalies and their significance. Trans. Faraday Soc. *47*, 1072–1084.

DAVIS, M. E., and HOWARD, L. B. 1943. Effects of varying conditions on the reconstitution of dehydrated vegetables. Proc. Inst. Food Technologists 1943, 143–155.

DIEMAIR, W. 1941. The Preservation of Foodstuffs. (In German.) F. Enke Verlag, Stuttgart.

DUCKWORTH, R. B., and SMITH, G. M. 1961. The diffusion of glucose during vegetable dehydration. J. Sci. Food Agr. *12*, 490–492.

EARLE, P. L., and CEAGLSKE, N. H. 1949. Factors causing the checking of macaroni. Cereal Chem. *26*, 267–286.

EARLE, P. L., and ROGERS, M. C. 1941. Drying macaroni. Ind. Eng. Chem. *33*, 642–647.

ELLIS, G. P. 1959. The Maillard reaction. Advances in Carbohydrate Chemistry *14*, 63–134.

FISH, B. P. 1957. Diffusion and equilibrium properties of water in starch, Dept. Sci. and Ind. Research Food Investigations Tech. Paper 5.

GANE, R. 1941. The water content of wheats as a function of temperature and humidity. Soc. Chem. Ind. Trans. *60*, 44–46.

GANE, R. 1943 A. The activity of water in dried foodstuffs; water content as a function of humidity and temperature. Dehydration—U. K. Progress Reports (London) Sec. X, Part 1.

GANE, R. 1943 B. Dried meat. III. Water relations of air dried precooked beef and pork. J. Soc. Chem. Ind. *62* T, 139–140.

GANE, R. 1950. The water relations of some dried fruits, vegetables, and plant products. J. Soc. Food Agr. *1*, 42–46.

GANE, R., and WAGER, H. G. 1958. Plant structure and dehydration. *In* Fundamental Aspects of the Dehydration of Foodstuffs. Soc. Chem. Ind. 3–7.

GÖRLING, P. 1954, 1956. Investigations to elucidate the drying behavior of vegetable materials, especially potato pieces. (In German.) Diss. T. H. Darmstadt. Also in VDI-Forschungsheft 458, Düsseldorf 1956.

GÖRLING, P. 1958. Physical phenomena during the drying of foodstuffs. *In* Fundamental Aspects of the Dehydration of Foodstuffs. Soc. Chem. Ind. 42–53.

HENDEL, C. E. 1956. Browning rates and equilibrium vapor pressures of white potatoes in later stages of dehydration. Diss. Univ. Calif., Berkeley.

HENDEL, C. E., SILVEIRA, V. G., and HARRINGTON, W. O. 1955. Rates of non-enzymatic browning of white potato during dehydration. Food Technol. *9*, 433-438.

HENDERSON, S. M. 1952. A basic concept of equilibrium moisture. Agr. Eng. *33*, 29–32.

HODGE, J. E. 1953. Dehydrated food: Chemistry of browning reactions in model systems. J. Agr. Food Chem. *1*, 928–943.

JASON A. C. 1958. A study of evaporation and diffusion processes in the drying of fish muscle. *In* Fundamental Aspects of the Dehyration of Foodstuffs. Soc. Chem. Ind. 103–135.

KAMEI, S. 1937. A study of the drying of solids. XVI–XVIII. Theoretical investigations of drying. J. Soc. Chem. Ind. (Japan) Suppl. Binding *40*, 251–257.

KAREL, M., AIKAWA, Y., and PROCTOR, B. E. 1955. A new approach to humidity equilibrium data. Modern Packaging 29, No. 2, 153–156, 237–238, 240.

KRISCHER, O. 1938 A. Fundamental laws of the movement of moisture in bodies being dried; capillary water movement and water vapor diffusion. (In German.) Z. Ver. deut. Ing. 82, 373–378.

KRISCHER, O. 1938 B. The drying of solid substances, as a problem in the movement of capillary moisture and the diffusion of vapor. (In German.) Z. Ver. deut. Ing. Verfahrenstechnik Beih. No. 4, 104–110.

KRISCHER, O. 1940. Heat, liquid, and vapor movement in the drying of porous materials. (In German.) Z. Ver. deut. Ing. Suppl. 1, 17–25.

KRISCHER, O. 1942. Heat- and mass-transfer in a material being dried; the analytic and graphic treatment of the drying of porous hygroscopic materials. (In German.) VDI Forschungsheft 415, Publ. B. 13, July-Aug.

KRISCHER, O., and KRÖLL, K. 1956, 1959. Drying Technology. (Trocknungstechnik.) 1, O. Krischer, The Scientific Fundamentals of Drying Technology. (Die wissenschaftlichen Grundlagen der Trocknungstechnik.) (In German.) Springer-Verlag, Berlin-Göttingen-Heidelberg. 2, K. Kröll, Driers and Drying Processes. (Trockner und Trocknungsverfahren.)

KUPRIANOFF, J. 1958. "Bound water" in foods. In Fundamental Aspects of the Dehydration of Foodstuffs. Soc. Chem. Ind., 14–23.

LEA, C. H. 1958. Chemical changes in the preparation and storage of dehydrated foods. In Fundamental Aspects of the Dehydration of Foodstuffs. Soc. Chem. Ind., 178–196.

LEGAULT, R. R., HENDEL, C. E., TALBURT, W. F., and POOL, M. F. 1951. Browning of dehydrated sulfited vegetables during storage. Food Technol. 5, 417–423.

LEGAULT, R. R., HENDEL, C. E., TALBURT, W. F., and RASMUSSEN, C. L. 1949. Sulfite disappearance in dehydrated vegetables during storage. Ind. Eng. Chem. 41, 1447–1451.

LEGAULT, R. R., TALBURT, W. F., MYLNE, A., and BRYAN, L. 1947. Browning of dehydrated vegetables during storage. Ind. Eng. Chem. 39, 1294–1299.

LYKOW, A. W. 1950, 1955. Experimental and Theoretical Fundamentals of Drying. Moscow, 1950. (In Russian.) Veb. Verlag, Berlin, 1955. (In German.)

MACKINNEY, G., and HOWARD, L. B. 1944. Sulfite retards deterioration of dehydrated cabbage shred. Food Inds. 16, 355–356.

MAILLARD, J. C. 1912. Action of amino acids on sugars. (In French.) Compt. rend. 154, 66.

MAKOWER, B. 1945. Vapor pressure of water adsorbed on dehydrated eggs. Ind. Eng. Chem. 37, 1018–1022.

MAKOWER, B., CHASTAIN, S. M., and NIELSEN, E. 1946. Moisture determination in dehydrated vegetables: Vacuum oven method. Ind. Eng. Chem. 38, 725–731.

MAKOWER, B., and DEHORITY, G. L. 1943. Equilibrium moisture content of dehydrated vegetables. Ind. Eng. Chem. 35, 193–197.

MANGELS, C. E., and GORE, H. C. 1921. Effect of heat on different dehydrated vegetables. Ind. Eng. Chem. 13, 525–526.

NOTTER, G. K., TAYLOR, D. H., and DOWNES, N. J. 1959. Orange juice powder: Factors affecting storage stability. Food Technol. 13, 113–118.

ONSAGER, L. 1931. Reciprocal relations in irreversible processes. Phys. Rev. 37, 495–526; Ibid., 38, 2265–2279.

PIERCE, D. E. 1953. Products that are inclined to develop "skins" may be best dried with wet air. Ind. Eng. Chem. 45, 83A–86A.

PRUTHI, J. S., SINGH, L. J., and GIRDHARI, L. 1959. The equilibrium relative humidity of garlic powder. J. Sci. Food Agr. 10, 359–361.

REEVE, R. M.   1942.   Facts of vegetable dehydration revealed by microscope. Food Inds. *14*, No. 12, 51–54.

ROCKLAND, L. B.   1957.   A new treatment of hygroscopic equilibrium: Application to walnuts (Juglans regia) and other foods.   Food Research *22*, 604–628.

SALWIN, H., and SLAWSON, V.   1959.   Moisture transfer in combinations of dehydrated foods.   Food Technol. *13*, 715–718.

SCHAUSS, H.   1940.   Physical processes of moisture movement and their effects in the various procedures of wood drying.   (In German.)   Diss. T. H. Darmstadt. D87.

SEEHOF, J. M., KEILIN, B., and BENSON, S. W.   1953.   The surface areas of proteins.   V.   The mechanism of water sorption.   J. Am. Chem. Soc. *75*, 2427–2430.

STAMM, A. J.   1946.   Passage of liquids, vapors, and dissolved materials through softwoods.   U. S. Dept. Agr. Tech. Bull. *929*.

STAMM, A. J.   1948.   The passage of water through the capillary structure of wood.   Discussions Faraday Soc. 1948, No. 3, 264–273.

STITT, F.   1958.   Moisture equilibrium and the determination of water content of dehydrated foods.   *In* Fundamental Aspects of the Dehydration of Foodstuffs.   Soc. Chem. Ind. 67–88.

TAYLOR, A. A.   1961.   Determination of moisture equilibria in dehydrated foods.   Food Technol. *15*, 536–540.

UNITED STATES DEPARTMENT OF AGRICULTURE.   1944.   Vegetable and Fruit Dehydration—a Manual for Plant Operators.   Misc. Pub. *540*.

VAN ARSDEL, W. B.   1951.   Principles of the drying process, with special reference to vegetable dehydration.   U. S. Dept. Agr. Bur. Cir. AIC-300.

CHAPTER 5

Drying Phenomena

EXPERIMENTAL METHODS

Much of the following discussion will concern primarily the phenomena observed in the air drying of piece-form wet solids. This is, of course, only one of several important types of drying operation for food products; spray drying, drum drying ("roller drying"), vacuum drying (including freeze drying), belt-trough drying, air suspension drying, and other methods find important applications, but will not be analyzed in detail here. Spray drying, undoubtedly the most important process of all as measured by dollar value of products, has been studied by many able workers, see pp. 151–154. Nevertheless, it is inherently so complex a dynamic system that its operation must still be described as in large measure an art. The air drying of wet pieces has complexities of its own, as will become apparent in the following discussion, but it does lend itself to relatively simple physical and mathematical analysis. For that reason the classic early analyses of the drying operation, those of Lewis and Sherwood, previously referred to, were directed primarily to the tray drying of pieces, and much of the later theoretical development has continued in that line.

Drying Under Simulated Practical Conditions

Experimental study of piece drying should employ a carefully designed drier equipped for precise control of the temperature, humidity, and velocity of the air stream in which the wet body is supported. Fig. 23 is a diagrammatic sketch of such a drier, designed specifically for study of the air drying of cut pieces of fruits or vegetables, uniformly spread on shallow mesh-bottom trays. Fresh air drawn in past the adjustable recirculation damper B is pulled through multiple fin-coil steam heaters C by the centrifugal fan D. The fan discharges through a set of turning vanes E and perforated screens F intended to straighten out and equalize the air flow through the tray section G. Exhaust air leaves the drier at H. In some designs the entire tray section is supported on a balance arm so that its gross weight can be followed continuously during the drying. Usually, however, individual trays are easily removable for quick weighing on separate scales.

90

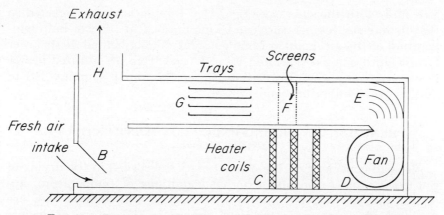

FIG. 23.   DIAGRAM OF EXPERIMENTAL TRAY DRIER (ELEVATION)

Drying of Isolated Moist Bodies

Only a few investigators have reported studies of the air drying of isolated pieces of wet food material, experiments being planned and executed in such a way as to separate the effects of all the important variables.   One of the most significant is Jason (1958), who has described his specially designed equipment for studying the mechanism of drying of lean fish flesh, cut into carefully measured parallelopipeds of appreciable size.   The drying apparatus automatically recorded drying conditions and sample weight, and was operated continuously over long periods of time.   The frequent measurements made it possible to analyze drying rates in great detail.

Ede and Hales (1948) used a cabinet-type experimental drier of fairly conventional design in their study of the drying of potato and carrot strips.   They first tried a procedure in which the individual weighed pieces were carried on small hooks suspended by threads in the air stream, but abandoned it in favor of a method utilizing 24 measured pieces at once on a wire-bottom tray, with air flowing down through the almost unobstructed tray; the results agreed well with those obtained by the more arduous thread-suspension method.

Krischer and Kröll (1956, 1959) describe an experimental drier intended to isolate the individual variables as completely as possible.   A steady stream of air of known temperature, humidity, and velocity is passed through a rectangular duct, 800 mm. long, 80 mm. wide, and 50 mm. high; at intervals in the bottom of this duct are four circular openings 37.5 mm. in diameter.   One test sample, carried on a sensitive balance, is supported at each of these openings with its upper face flush with the duct opening. One sample is water jacketed so that its internal temperature can be maintained at the wet-bulb temperature of the air, another sample is controllably heated at its lower face, a third sample is heated by radiation from an infrared heater positioned over a window in the duct, and the fourth sample is left to find its own equilibrium temperature.

PHENOMENA IN DRYING UNDER CONSTANT EXTERNAL CONDITIONS

We shall consider first the characteristics observed in the drying of wet bodies under constant external conditions of temperature, humidity, and air velocity, and in later sections will see how they are modified when external conditions change in the course of drying. We shall also consider first the relatively simple drying behavior of non-hygroscopic granular solids, typified by sand.

Drying of Non-Hygroscopic Solids

If a tray full of wet sand is exposed to the air stream the temperature in the sand will quickly reach an equilibrium, heat absorbed by evaporation of water at the moist surface being balanced by heat flow from the warm air stream into the cooler wet body. This equilibrium temperature will approximate the wet-bulb temperature of the air if the air velocity is high and no extra radiation energy is supplied. So long as the capillary forces in the sand are great enough to bring water from within the body of sand to its surface at the same rate as it evaporates there, the surface evaporation rate must remain constant. This is called the "constant drying rate" phase of drying. Moisture content at 0.1-hr. intervals of time and at different levels in the sand shows a gradation as indicated by the curves marked from 0 to 1.0 hr. in Fig. 24. At 0.6 hr. the moisture content at the surface falls to zero. From that moment the rate of evaporation from the body of sand decreases, as seen in Fig. 25. The experiment has entered the "falling-rate" phase. The zone of evaporation then retreats deeper and deeper into the sand, and the rate continues to decrease as the length of path through which the water vapor must diffuse through the voids between grains increases. The rate remains finite, however (point A in Fig. 25), until the last moisture is evaporated from the bottom of the sand.

Some substances (wood pulp, textiles, etc.) show hygroscopic behavior at very low moisture contents, but when dried from high initial moisture content behave like the non-hygroscopic materials

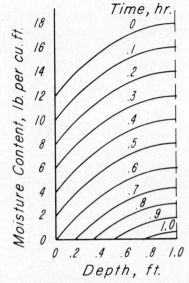

FIG. 24. MOISTURE GRADIENTS IN GRANULAR
MATERIAL DURING DRYING

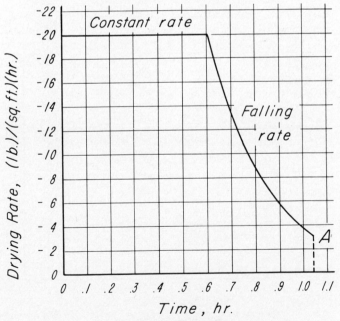

FIG. 25. TYPICAL CHANGE IN DRYING RATE OF
GRANULAR MATERIAL

except that the final drying rate in the falling-rate phase approaches zero instead of a finite value.

Drying of Hygroscopic Solids

The phenomena are, in general, more complex. Careful drying experiments may bring out a short period of constant-rate drying (when the appropriate corrections for decreasing surface area due to shrinkage are made) but often the rate begins to decrease at once.

Drying of An Isolated Piece.—If the drying of a single piece of the wet substance supported in an air stream is followed by means of precise weighings, the rate of weight loss typically falls off as drying progresses, not in a single smooth curve, but rather in two or three distinguishable segments separated by one or two distinct breaks in slope. Görling (1958) gives the curve shown in Fig. 26 for the drying rate of a single potato slice dried from one side only in a current of air at 140°F. The loss in weight is multiplied by the measured thickness of the slice in order to compensate for shrinkage. Two distinct "break-points" are indicated. The first break is interpreted to signify the beginning of evaporation at a zone within the porous body of the sample piece.

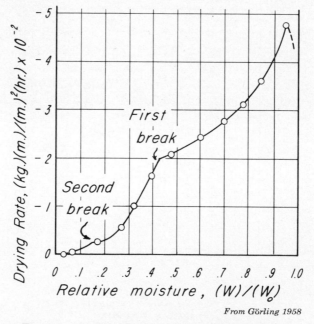

From Görling 1958

FIG. 26.   DRYING RATE OF SINGLE POTATO SLICE

Krischer (1938) had found that in the drying of non-hygroscopic solids of several different thicknesses and at a series of different temperatures and air velocities, if the drying rate were plotted against "relative moisture content," W/W_0, the break-points for samples all dried at the same temperature fell on a smooth curve, the "break-point curve." The break-point curves at a series of different temperatures formed a family of more or less parallel curves, with higher values of the drying rates at the higher temperatures. Furthermore, he found a good correlation between the spacing of these curves from one another and values of the quantity $\sigma\rho/\mu$ for water—that is, the product of surface tension and density, divided by the viscosity. This would be expected if the flow through the solid were determined by the capillary properties of the material. Görling's break-point curves for the first phase of drying of his potato slices similarly were spaced as predicted by that relation. He therefore concludes that "with vegetable products, the moisture transfer during the first drying stage takes place only by means of capillary movement toward the surface." The second break-point occurs when no part of the sample piece contains more moisture than the hygroscopic limit, W = about 1.2 lbs. per pound dry solid.

Jason (1958) takes a very different approach to analysis of the phenomena observed in the drying of an isolated piece of moist material. He made an elaborate study of the characteristics of air drying of cut pieces of 14 kinds of lean fish, with emphasis on the drying of measured rectangular pieces cut from cod fillets. Typical drying experiments under constant conditions disclosed at least two brief constant-rate periods after the initial warm-up, and then a long falling-rate period which could always be analyzed into two distinct phases. The transition from the first of these phases to the second occurred in the moisture content region of about 10 to 15 per cent at temperatures between 60° and 140°F. Fig. 27, adapted from Jason's paper, shows that when the logarithm of the free moisture content is plotted against time, the data (after the short constant-rate phase) can be very well represented by two straight lines, with a short curved transition between the two. The equations of such lines are as follows:

For the upper segment,

$$\ln (W - W_e) = [\ln (W - W_e)]' - \frac{\theta}{\tau_1} \tag{46}$$

and for the lower segment,

$$\ln (W - W_e) = [\ln (W - W_e)]'' - \frac{\theta}{\tau_2} \tag{47}$$

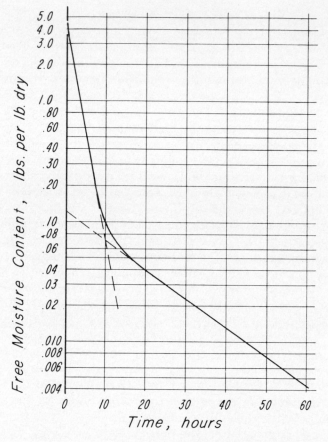

Adapted from Jason 1958

FIG. 27.   TYPICAL DRYING CURVE FOR RECTANGULAR
PIECE OF FISH MUSCLE

where $\ln (W - W_e)'$ and $\ln (W - W_e)''$ are the intercepts of the lines
on the axis of zero time and τ_1 and τ_2 are constants having the dimensions of time and hence called "time constants."   Much of Jason's
work is analyzed in terms of the effects of various conditions upon the
values of the time constants.   Jason found that the analytical solution
to a Fick's law diffusion equation for moisture transfer within the wet
body (equivalent to the equation for heat flow, Equation (22)) takes
a form which also corresponds to the straight-line relation between
logarithm of free moisture content and time.   Then in the first falling-
rate phase,

$$\mathbf{D}_1 = 4/\pi^2 \; \tau_1(a^{-2} + b^{-2} + c^{-2}) \qquad\qquad (48)$$

and in the second phase,

$$\mathbf{D}_2 = 4/\pi^2\, \tau_2(a^{-2} + b^{-2} + c^{-2}) \qquad (49)$$

where $\mathbf{D}$ is the diffusivity (cm.)^2/(sec.), a, b, and c are the half-lengths of the edges of the piece (cm.), and the equation has been simplified by assuming that diffusion in fish muscle is isotropic—i.e., the same in all three dimensions.

Jason determined by statistical analysis of a large body of data the effect on the first time-constant of variations in the shape of the piece, the validity of the assumption that diffusion is isotropic, the effect of air velocity (no effect in the falling-rate period), the effect of higher relative humidity in the air (a slight increase in the time constant), and the effect of higher material temperature. The latter is complicated by the gradual denaturation of fish protein at temperatures above about 90°F., but this turned out to have no appreciable effect on the moisture diffusivity. The dependence on temperature is well expressed by a straight line in an Arrhenius-type plot of $1/T$ against the logarithm of $\mathbf{D}$:

$$\mathbf{D} = \mathbf{D}_0 e^{-\mathbf{E}/RT} \qquad (50)$$

where

$\mathbf{D}_0$ = constant (cm.)^2/(sec.)
$\mathbf{E}$ = energy of activation (cal.)/(mole)
R = gas constant 1.989 (cal.)/(mole) (°K.)
T = absolute temperature (°K)

The computed value of $\mathbf{D}_0$ for the first phase was 0.54, for the second phase about 0.75; $\mathbf{E}$ for the first phase averaged 7190 ± 200 (cal.)/ (mole), for the second phase about 8,500 (cal.)/(mole), with quite a high degree of uncertainty. The higher energy of activation in the second phase of course corresponds with the tighter binding of water molecules in the protein structure at moisture levels below about 15 per cent. Fish (1958), it will be recalled, had observed an activation energy of 9800 (cal.)/(mole) for the diffusion of water in starch gel at 0.8 per cent moisture content, 8,100 (cal.)/(mole) at 6.3 per cent moisture content, and 6,300 (cal.)/(mole) at 14.1 per cent moisture content. The main diffusion mechanism in the cod muscle appears to be migration of adsorbed water molecules on the surfaces of the protein molecules. The transition from the first to the second falling-rate phase corresponds with the uncovering of the monomolecular inner layer of water molecules after the multiple-molecule outer layer is removed.

Jason's analysis is by far the most thorough published study in which the theoretical framework is that of diffusion theory. On the whole, it appears to give a basis for firmly grounded technological application to both equipment design and operational problems in the air drying of fish. One theoretical question seems to the writer to be left in somewhat unsatisfactory state, namely the justification for accepting the analytical solution of the diffusion equation for a constant diffusivity, but nevertheless deciding that in fact the material goes through a transition from one constant diffusivity to a second very much lower one part-way through the drying. The question remains whether the exact solution for such a system would uphold the procedure described. It must also be noted that when drying data for potato strips reported by Ede and Hales (1948) and numerous data on potatoes and other vegetables obtained by the Western Regional Research Laboratory are analyzed in this same way, the low-moisture "tail" of the drying curves is well represented by a straight line when log $(W - W_e)$ is plotted against time, but the whole medium-moisture segment (*i.e.*, above $W = 0.15$) is strongly curved. It would seem that this is what might be expected on theoretical grounds, because even well up in the high-moisture range (of mean moisture content) at least the surface layers of the piece will normally be well down into the low-moisture range; the low diffusivity of moisture in the surface layers must very greatly affect the drying rate of the whole piece, essentially from the very beginning of the drying, and not just in a short transition zone.

Very recently Saravacos and Charm (1962) have reported drying experiments on single layers of onion and garlic slices, peach halves, apple dice, whole lye-dipped seedless grapes, and blanched potato and carrot dice. Gross drying rates (*i.e.*, rates uncorrected for shrinkage of drying area) always showed a short phase of constant rate and a fairly sharp break at a "critical moisture content," W_c. Values of W_c observed were: potatoes 3.5, apples 6.0, carrots 5.0, garlic 2.4, onions 6.0, peaches 7.7, grapes 4.75, pears 6.5. A somewhat irregular falling-rate phase then followed. In the region between $W = 1.0$ and $W = 0.1$ the rate was nearly proportional to the remaining "free moisture" content, $W - W_e$. Then if s is the slope of the nearly straight portion of the plot of log $(W - W_e)/(W_c - W_e)$ against W, a "drying constant," m, is defined as $-2.303\ s$. Measured values of m in these experiments were 1.30–1.53 for potatoes, 2.12 for apples, 2.12 for carrots, 0.42 for garlic, 0.37 for onions, 0.35 for peaches, 0.34 for grapes, and 0.95 for pears.

Drying Under Simulated Practical Loading Conditions.— An entirely different approach to the experimental study, abandoning any effort to separate all factors of the drying phenomenon in com-

plete detail for an isolated piece of the raw material, attempts rather
to simulate the behavior of a mass of pieces of the material such as
would be used in a practical dehydration operation; in other words,
to experiment with a practical load of the material in a prototype
drier, designed so as to behave in operation as nearly as possible like
the full-scale drier.   Nearly all of the author's experimental work in
vegetable dehydration has been done with such a drier, designed to
follow the drying of a tray-load of cut vegetable pieces.   At any time
during the experiment the load of pieces will comprise some that have
been fully exposed to the air stream and have consequently dried
rapidly, and some that have been at the bottom of the layer of product
and have therefore remained relatively wet.   Little information
bearing on the mechanism of drying can be extracted from study of
this mean or average drying rate.   However, the procedure does
lend itself readily to the calculations required for scaling up to practical drier operation.   The procedure will be described in a later
section.

A typical experiment under practical tray-drying conditions is
pictured in the drying rate curve of Fig. 28.   In the experiment, which

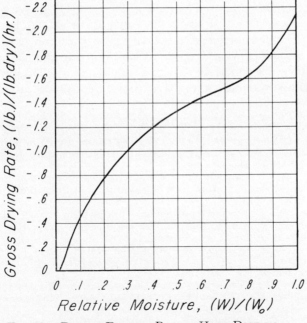

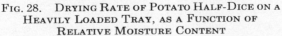

FIG. 28.   DRYING RATE OF POTATO HALF-DICE ON A
HEAVILY LOADED TRAY, AS A FUNCTION OF
RELATIVE MOISTURE CONTENT

was conducted in the Western Regional Research Laboratory by M. E. Lazar, Klamath Russet potato half-dice, $^3/_8$ x $^3/_8$ x $^3/_{16}$ in., blanched 4 min. in steam at atmospheric pressure, loaded on metal mesh-bottom trays at a rate of 3.0 lbs. per sq. ft., were dried in air at a temperature of 150°F., wet-bulb temperature 90°F., and constant air velocity horizontally both above and below the 2-ft. wide tray, 420 ft. per min. The run continued for 22 hr., 42 accurate weighings of the tray being made; the last three weighings had shown no perceptible change in weight. The moisture content of a composite sample of the final product was determined to be 0.042 lb. per pound dry solids. The mean moisture content of the original tray load of material was then computed from the final dry weight and the loss of weight during the experiment.

Drying rate is, of course, properly defined in terms of pounds water evaporated per pound of dry solids per hour *per square foot* of evaporating surface. The evaporating area of a trayload of cut pieces is not easily measured or defined, however. What might be called a "gross drying rate" is therefore often reported instead. This is simply the number of pounds of water evaporated per pound of dry solids per hour.

Fig. 28 may be compared with Fig. 26 (p. 94), showing Görling's results on the drying of a single slice of potato at 140°F. Görling's first break-point occurred at a relative moisture content, W/W_0, of about 0.45. The curve of Fig. 28 exhibits no marked change in slope near that moisture content. There is no sign of a second break-point, which Görling found at a relative moisture content of about 0.15.

BIBLIOGRAPHY

EDE, A. J., and HALES, K. C. 1948. The physics of drying in heated air, with special reference to fruit and vegetables. Dept. Sci. Ind. Research, Food Investigations Spec. Rept. 53.

FISH, B. P. 1958. Diffusion and thermodynamics of water in potato starch gel. *In* Fundamental Aspects of the Dehydration of Foodstuffs. Soc. Chem. Ind., 143–157.

GÖRLING, P. 1958. Physical phenomena during the drying of foodstuffs. *In* Fundamental Aspects of the Dehydration of Foodstuffs. Soc. Chem. Ind. 42–53.

JASON, A. C. 1958. A study of evaporation and diffusion processes in the drying of fish muscle. *In* Fundamental Aspects of the Dehydration of Foodstuffs. Soc. Chem. Ind., 103–135.

KRISCHER, O. 1938. The drying of solid substances, as a problem in the movement of capillary moisture and the diffusion of vapor. (In German.) Z. Ver. deut. Ing. Verfahrenstechnik Beih. No. 4, 104–110.

KRISCHER, O. 1956. The Scientific Fundamentals of Drying Technology. (In German.) Volume I of O. Krischer and K. Kröll, Drying Technology (Trocknungstechnik). Springer-Verlag, Berlin-Göttengen-Heidelberg.

Krischer, O., and Kröll, K.   1956, 1959.   Drying Technology.   (Trocknungs-technik.)   1, O. Krischer, The Scientific Fundamentals of Drying Technology. (Die wissenschaftlichen Grundlagen der Trocknungstechnik.)   (In German.) Springer-Verlag, Berlin-Göttingen-Heidelberg.   2, K. Kröll, Driers and Drying Processes.   (Trockner und Trocknungsverfahren.)

Saravacos, G. D., and Charm, S. E.   1962.   A study of the mechanism of fruit and vegetable dehydration.   Food Technol. *16*, No. 1, 78–81.

Van Arsdel, W. B.   1947.   Approximate diffusion calculations for the falling-rate phase of drying.   Chem. Eng. Progr. *43*, 13–24.   Also issued as U. S. Dept. Agr. Bur. Circ. AIC-152.

Van Arsdel, W. B.   1951 A.   Principles of the drying process, with special reference to vegetable dehydration.   U. S. Dept. Agr. Bur. Circ. AIC-300.

Van Arsdel, W. B.   1951 B.   Tunnel-and-Truck Dehydrators, as used in vegetable dehydration.   U. S. Dept. Agr. Bur. Circ. AIC-308.

CHAPTER 6

Factors Influencing Rate of Drying
Under Constant External Conditions

INTRODUCTION

The following discussion is organized around conditions for the tray drying of a load of fairly uniform pieces of the wet material. Many of the observations also apply, at least qualitatively, to the behavior of food materials in other kinds of driers. Experimental data of this kind on food commodities are fragmentary up to the publication by Culpepper and Moon (1937) on the drying of Kieffer pears cut into pieces of various sizes. Dehydration activity during and following World War II gave rise to publications on drying rates of vegetables by Van Arsdel (1942, 1943 A, B), Brown and Kilpatrick (1943), the U. S. Department of Agriculture Dehydration Manual (1944), the British Ministry of Food (1946), and Ede and Hales (1948); on meat by Ede and Partridge (1943); and on fruits by Perry (1944) and Perry *et al.* (1946). Later (1951) Van Arsdel discussed the application to vegetables more completely.

The illustrative comparisons which follow are sketched to show change in moisture content as a function of time, moisture content always being shown on a logarithmic scale so as to open out the curves in the region of low-moisture content. Most of the drying curves shown were computed, rather than directly observed, by means of the correlations established by the Western Regional Research Laboratory, U. S. Department of Agriculture, and published in a series of nomographs denoted AIC-31, which are described in a later paragraph (pp. 128–130).

NATURE OF THE MATERIAL BEING DRIED

Of all the factors which influence the rate of drying, the individual nature of the raw material (comprehended in its chemical constitution and physical structure) is far and away the most important. However, direct comparison of the drying rates of different materials is not easy, partly because of the different forms and sizes in which they are usually prepared (dice or half-dice, strips, shreds, slices, flakes, rings, eighths, halves, etc.), and partly because of their very different initial moisture contents. With regard to the latter, if carrot dice and potato dice of exactly the same initial dimensions are compared, there is only about half as much solid matter in the carrot piece as in the potato piece; as drying nears completion the potato pieces will be much thicker than the carrot pieces and the transfer of moisture from the interior to the surface of a piece would be slower for that reason alone, even if the composition and properties were otherwise identical. Materials like blanched potato consist mainly of gelatinized starch, strongly adsorbing water at low-moisture levels, while unblanched onion is an example of material consisting in large part of simple sugars and an ungelatinized structural framework.

Fig. 29 compares the drying behavior of potato pieces and carrot pieces of nearly the same size, under the same external conditions. The carrot pieces were $1/4$-in. thick, the potatoes $3/16$-in.; both were

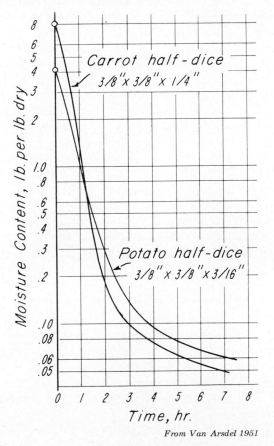

From Van Arsdel 1951

FIG. 29.   DRYING CURVES FOR CARROT AND
POTATO HALF-DICE

$^3/_8$-in. square.   Drying was on metal mesh-bottom trays in air at
160°F., wet-bulb temperature 100°F., tray loading 1.5 lbs. per sq.
ft., air velocity 800 ft. per min.   The carrot pieces reached a final
moisture content of 0.06 in 5 hr., as against 7 hr. for the potato pieces.

The higher initial drying rate of the carrot pieces is probably no
more than a direct reflection of the higher moisture content.   If a
carrot piece and a potato piece had the same surface area, the weight
of moisture lost per hour during the initial phase would be substantially the same from each; but the weight of moisture lost per hour
per pound of dry solids would be almost twice as high from the carrot
piece as from the potato piece.

Differences in the composition of the material are known to have
an effect on the drying rate.   Blanched (scalded) material dries more
rapidly than unblanched, at least in the high-moisture range, probably
because the scalding kills the tissue and makes cell membranes more
freely permeable to water.   A. H. Brown (unpublished report, No-
vember 10, 1943) and his associates at the Western Regional Research
Laboratory compared the drying rates of potato pieces varying widely
in sugar content (the difference was produced by varying the temperature at which the potatoes were stored) and found that while
the drying rate was unaffected by sugar content down to a moisture
content of about 0.30 lb. moisture per pound dry solids, the drying
time from $W = 0.30$ to $W = 0.075$ was longer the higher the sugar
content.   For the material he was using, Brown determined that the
drying time in this low-moisture range was approximately proportional
to either one of the following two expressions: [1 + 0.059 (per cent
total sugar)], or [1 + 0.12 (per cent reducing sugar)].   The sugar
content is expressed as percentage of the weight of dry solids.   The
experimental data were not extensive enough to determine which of
these expressions is the more accurate.

SHAPE, SIZE, AND ARRANGEMENT OF THE MATERIAL PIECES

Classical drying theory (Lewis 1921) predicts that if the surface
film resistance to moisture transfer away from the wet piece is negligible in comparison with internal diffusional resistance, the drying
rate will vary inversely as the square of the piece thickness.   Van
Arsdel (1947) showed that this relation should remain true even if the
internal diffusional resistance is not constant, but a function of moisture content.

The influence of piece size on the course of drying is illustrated by
the data of Ede and Hales (1948).   Fig. 30, taken from their bulletin,
shows drying curves for julienne strips of potato of three different

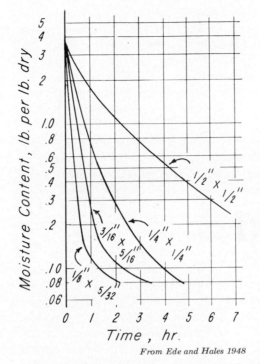

From Ede and Hales 1948

FIG. 30.   EFFECT OF PIECE SIZE ON COURSE OF DRYING OF
POTATO STRIPS

sizes.   The drying was carried out on large trays, the back edges of
which dried materially slower than the front edges; the curves are for
the material near the front edges of the trays.   Trays were loaded at
1.5 lbs. per sq. ft., air velocity was 960 ft. per min., the temperature
was 158°F., and the wet-bulb temperature 95°F.

From this illustration it is plain that a small difference in the thickness of vegetable pieces can cause an altogether disproportionate
change in the drying time.   A difference is evident at all stages of
drying, but is far more marked in the low-moisture range than near
the beginning.   This is what would be expected.   During the initial
phases the rate of evaporation per unit of surface changes but little.
Now suppose that we compare a single cube with two half-cubes cut
from a similar cube.   The weight of dry solids in the two halves will
be the same as in the whole cube, but their combined surface will be
33 per cent greater.   Their initial gross drying rate should be greater
than that of the cube in about the same proportion.   Next, assume
that we compare six separate cubes with six similar cubes put together

to form a strip six times as long as it is thick.   By the same kind of reasoning we can infer that the initial drying rate of the cubes will be some 38 per cent greater than that of the strip.

In the later phases of drying the thickness of solid substance through which water must diffuse will become the controlling factor.   If the rate varies inversely as the square of the thickness, nine times as long will be required for a given amount of drying if the piece is three times as thick.

Drying times may actually be reduced to the order of a second if the piece size is reduced far enough.   This is the secret of the great success of spray drying, in which the individual particles may be only a few microns in diameter and their time of contact with the hot air only a few seconds.

In the opposite direction, the reason why whole carrots or quartered potatoes are not commercially dehydrated is that the drying time would be so long as to be completely impractical, even if a reasonably good final product could be made, which is doubtful.   The sizes into which vegetables are cut for commercial dehydration represent a compromise between the need for rapid drying and the desire to serve the consumer large pieces of the products.   Dehydrated whole fruits, such as prunes, represent a special case in that dehydration is continued only to about 22 per cent moisture, thus avoiding the low-moisture phase completely, and the quality of the fruit remains acceptable even with so long a drying time as 24 to 36 hr. and a material temperature which may rise as high as 165°F. for a period of many hours.

Disposition of the Material with Respect to the Drying Air

The traditional tray drying arrangement successfully exposes a very large area of drying surface per unit of total space occupied, but must be carefully designed and properly operated or it will experience serious trouble with uneven drying.   In commercial dehydrators the trays are stacked one above another to a height of 6 or 7 ft., leaving clear air passages a few inches high between successive trays (Van Arsdel 1951; Kilpatrick et al. 1955).   Tray bottoms are perforated or slotted in various ways.   The main air stream, passing horizontally between trays at a velocity of up to 1,000 or 1,200 ft. per min., is intensely turbulent and creates localized pressure differences which in turn produce more or less flow of air *through* the layer of wet material. Special tray designs are sometimes employed deliberately in order to increase the amount of through-flow; an increase in the drying rate, especially for heavily loaded trays, would be expected (Eidt 1938).

Irregularities in loading the material on the trays may have the doubly evil effect of locally increasing the thickness of the wet layer and diminishing the free space left open for air flow.   The quantitative effect of all these variables is a highly individual consequence of the dehydrator design and operating conditions.

Load of Wet Material Per Unit Tray Area

Cut vegetable pieces are commonly loaded on trays in a reasonably uniform layer from less than $1/2$ in. to more than an inch deep; whole prunes may form roughly a double layer, approximately 2 in. deep. Loading per square foot of tray area is commonly from something less than 1 lb. to as much as 3 lbs. or more.   In a well conducted operation careful attention is given to maintaining a very uniform spread of the cut material on the trays and very uniform and predetermined total weight on each tray.

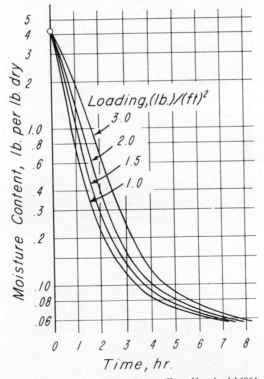

From Van Arsdel 1951

FIG. 31.   EFFECT OF TRAY LOADING ON COURSE OF DRYING
OF POTATO HALF-DICE

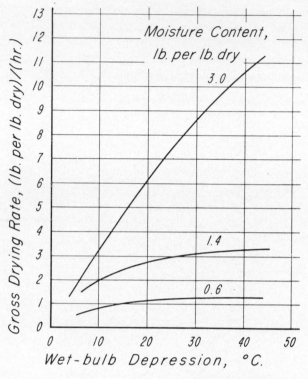

From Ede and Hales 1948

FIG. 32.   EFFECT OF WET-BULB DEPRESSION ON DRYING
RATE OF POTATO STRIPS

Fig. 31 illustrates the effect of varying the weight of potato half-dice spread on a metal-mesh tray at the unit rates of 1.0, 1.5, 2.0, and 3.0 lbs. per sq. ft. of tray surface.   Constant drying conditions of 160°F. temperature, 100°F. wet-bulb temperature, and an air velocity of 800 ft. per min. were assumed.

Increasing the tray loading reduces the rate of drying materially during the early stages, but as the drying progresses the rates become more and more nearly equal; at a final moisture content of $W = 0.06$ in these potato pieces there was only 17 per cent difference in drying times between the two extreme loadings which differ in a ratio of 3 to 1.   After the moisture content falls to about 0.20 no further effect of the initial loading density can be seen.   In the low-moisture range shrinkage of the pieces has reduced even a 3-lb. layer to a very open structure, through which the air can circulate almost as freely as it does through the still lighter layer remaining from a 1-lb. initial loading.   If the original load had been much heavier than 3 lbs. we can surmise that an effect on drying rate would be seen even at the lowest moisture level.   A reduction in final rate would be especially likely to occur if the material were cut into thin slices instead of dice, because the slices would tend to stick together, making, in effect, a much thicker body of material through which the moisture must diffuse.   A similar adverse effect on rate would occur if the prepared material were so soft that pieces would mash together during the spreading operation or that the bottom layers would crush together under their own weight.

M. E. Lazar, of the Western Regional Research Laboratory, showed in an unpublished report dated June 9, 1945 (Van Arsdel 1951) that the initial rate of drying of a trayload of $3/8$ x $3/8$ x $3/16$ in. carrot half-dice corresponds approximately with the rate of evaporation from 3 to 4 sq. ft. of free water surface per square foot of tray surface.   The evaporation takes place almost exclusively from the top layer of pieces, so that the initial rate of loss of weight from a heavily loaded tray is little, if any, greater than from a lightly loaded tray.   So long as the tray surface is at least completely covered with pieces, the initial drying rate determined by weighing the whole trayload must therefore be approximately inversely proportional to the initial loading per square foot of tray.

TEMPERATURE, HUMIDITY, AND VELOCITY OF AIR OVER THE MATERIAL BEING DRIED

Wet-bulb Depression

The most important single factor correlated with drying rate is the wet-bulb depression of the air flowing past the wet body—that is, $t - t_w$, the difference between dry-bulb and wet-bulb air temperatures. If this difference is zero the air is saturated and no drying takes place (Carrier 1921).

Fig. 32, adapted from Ede and Hales (1948) and Ede (1958), shows gross drying rate of single potato strips, $5/16$ x $5/16$ x $2^1/2$ in., in air at 70°C. (158°F.), flowing at 10 ft. per sec., and with wet-bulb depressions ranging from less than 10°C. to almost 40°C.   The three curves show that during the early phases of drying ($W = 3.0$ lbs. water per pound dry solids) the drying rate is very nearly proportional to the wet-bulb depression; at an intermediate phase ($W = 1.4$) increasing wet-bulb depression from 20° to 30°C. increases the rate only a little, and increasing the depression further would have even less effect; in the fairly dry strips ($W = 0.6$) increasing the depression to more than about 20°C. has little or no effect on rate.   In all cases, of course, the rate drops off sharply when the wet-bulb depression falls further and approaches zero.

These relationships reflect the drastic change in the permeability of potato tissue to water as the moisture content is reduced (see Figs. 11, 12, and 14, pp. 48, 50 and 57). In the early stages of drying internal transfer of water takes place readily and drying rate is controlled almost exclusively by the surface resistances to evaporation, while in later stages the rate is mainly controlled by the internal resistances to moisture flow, so that an increase in the external drying potential (by increasing the wet-bulb depression) has little effect.

Ede and Hales (1948) reported that the drying rates of carrot strips and shredded cabbage are, like the drying rate of potato strips, approximately proportional to wet-bulb depression at the higher levels of moisture content. Guillou (1942) and Perry (1944), on the other hand, showed that the drying rate of whole prunes is substantially independent of wet-bulb depression so long as the relative humidity of the air is less than about 40 per cent; in this case the main resistance to be overcome is evidently always the internal resistance to moisture movement.

Wet-bulb depression, it will be observed, is a very simple measure of the "drying potential" of a stream of air. In an earlier paragraph we applied the same term to the distance along an adiabatic cooling line on a psychrometric chart from the point representing the air condition to the saturation curve. For practical purposes the two meanings are equally useful and acceptable.

The proportionality of drying rate to wet-bulb depression, and to vapor pressure difference during the constant-rate phase of drying (Carrier 1921), leads to the following widely used expression:

$$\left(\frac{dW}{d\theta}\right)_e = aG^{0.8}(t_a - t_w) \tag{51}$$

equivalent to Equations (40) and (41) quoted earlier (p. 60) which also relate this rate to humidity difference.

Air Temperature (Dry-bulb)

The effect of changing the air temperature at constant wet-bulb depression is illustrated by the curves in Fig. 33, computed for the drying of potato half-dice on metal-mesh trays at temperatures of 140°, 150°, 160°, and 170°F., and a wet-bulb depression of 50°F. in every case. The trays were loaded at 1.5 lbs. per sq. ft., air velocity was 800 ft. per min.

The initial rate of drying, down to a moisture content of about 1.0, is substantially identical in all four curves, but in the low-moisture range the drying rate is substantially greater at the higher temperatures. Fig. 34, adapted from Ede and Hales (1948), shows the course of final drying of potato strips below a moisture content of 0.10 at temperatures of 60°, 70°, and 80°C.; neither wet-bulb depression

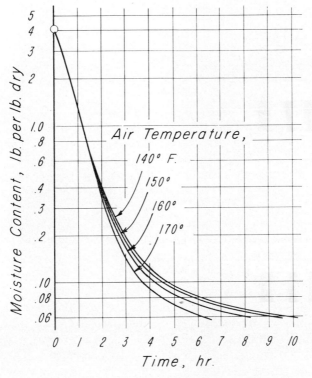

Air Temperature,
140° F.
150°
160°
170°

From Van Arsdel 1951

FIG. 33. EFFECT OF AIR TEMPERATURE ON COURSE OF
DRYING POTATO HALF-DICE AT CONSTANT
WET-BULB DEPRESSION

nor air velocity has any further appreciable effect on the drying time, but the air temperature does. In this low-moisture range the drying is so slow that the cooling effect of evaporation is inappreciable and the pieces of material assume very nearly the dry-bulb temperature of the air. The internal redistribution of moisture, which is the rate-determining factor in this phase, is accelerated by this rise of the material temperature.

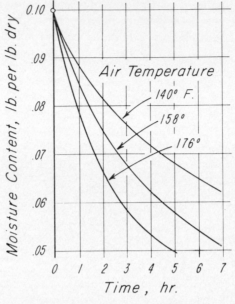

From Ede and Hales 1948

FIG. 34. EFFECT OF AIR TEMPERATURE ON COURSE OF
DRYING POTATO STRIPS IN THE LOW-MOISTURE RANGE

Air Velocity

Fig. 35 illustrates the course of drying as computed for four conditions in which the air velocity across the tray of potato half-dice is the
only variable. Tray loading is 1.5 lbs. per sq. ft., air temperature is
160°F., and wet-bulb depression is 60°F. Air velocities are 400, 600,
800, and 1,000 ft. per min. across the tray surface. The curves for
velocities of 800 and 1,000 ft. per min. are virtually identical, and
only the curve for the lowest velocity is significantly different; the
differences are all at the high-moisture end of the curves, and below a
moisture content of about 0.50 the drying rate appears to be substantially independent of air velocity. Other comparisons made in
the Western Regional Research Laboratory showed, however, that a
change in air velocity exerts a more pronounced effect if the trays
are more heavily loaded than 1.5 lbs. per sq. ft. Apparently an increase in air velocity, and the accompanying increase in the turbulence
of the air stream passing between trays, produces a greater proportion
of through-circulation in the heavier layers.

According to Ede and Hales (1948) the initial rate of drying of
small trays of potato strips is proportional to about the 0.7 or 0.8

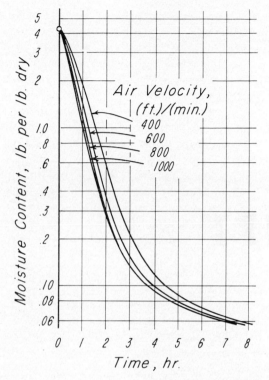

From Van Arsdel 1951

FIG. 35.   EFFECT OF AIR VELOCITY ON COURSE OF DRYING
POTATO HALF-DICE

power of the air velocity, see Equation 51, (p. 110).   This corresponds
with the velocity exponent for the rate of evaporation from a free
water surface.

Barometric Pressure

The experiments upon which published drying rates are based were
all conducted in locations not far above sea level, and hence at a barometric pressure not far different from the "normal," 1.00 standard
atmosphere, 29.92 in. of mercury.   The effect of a substantially lower
pressure, such as will prevail in a mountainous area, can, however,
be predicted with some assurance from general physical principles.
It is not a very marked effect in any air-convection type of dehydrator.

Regardless of the barometric pressure, the temperature of moist
material in the dehydrator will at first quite closely approximate the
wet-bulb temperature of the air and will gradually rise closer and

closer to the dry-bulb temperature of the air. During the early stages the rate of drying will be approximately proportional to the difference between the vapor pressure of water at the wet-bulb temperature and the partial pressure of water vapor in the air (Equation (40), p. 60). This difference will be less if the barometric pressure is low, as will be evident from the following example:

We are drying a material in air at a temperature of 160°F. and wet-bulb temperature of 100°F., but under a barometric pressure of only 23.94 in. (0.80 standard atmosphere, corresponding to an altitude of about 5,900 ft, above sea level) instead of 29.92 in. The material temperature will quickly come close to the wet-bulb temperature of the air, 100°F. The initial rate of evaporation will be proportional to $p_{sw} - p_w$, where p_{sw} is the vapor pressure of water at the wet-bulb temperature and p_w is the partial pressure of water vapor in the air. The Ferrel psychrometric formula, Equation (14), can be rearranged as follows:

$$p_{sw} - p_w = \frac{P}{2,730} (t_a - t_w) \left(1 + \frac{t_w - 32}{1,571}\right) \tag{52}$$

Thus for a given value of air temperature, t_a, and wet-bulb temperature, t_w, the initial driving force for evaporation will be directly proportional to the barometric pressure, P. In the example, the initial rate of evaporation should be only 80 per cent as great under the barometric pressure of 23.94 in. as at the standard pressure of 29.92 in. Assuming that the initial rate is proportional to wet-bulb depression, the latter would have to be increased from 60° to 75°F. in order to maintain the same rate as at normal barometer—for example, a wet-bulb temperature of 85° instead of 100°F.

Far more important, however, in determining the effect on total drying time is the influence the barometric pressure may have on drying rates in the low-moisture range. The main rate-determining factor there, namely the internal resistance to translocation of moisture, should be nearly unaffected by barometric pressure; the diffusivity of water in the partly dry material is controlled by the moisture content and temperature of the piece, and the latter will be substantially the same as the dry-bulb temperature of the air.

Summing up, the effect of a lower barometric pressure is to require a somewhat greater wet-bulb depression to produce the same drying rate, but the difference will be appreciable only in the early phases of the drying. This result may be set against the fallacious belief of some dehydrator designers and operators that more rapid drying can be realized if the air circulation fan and dampers are placed so that the drying compartment will be under "suction"—that is, below the outside atmospheric pressure rather than above it. The arrangement may have its advantages for other reasons, but not for that one. In the first place, the "suction" produced by the types of circulating fan used in dehydrators is negligible in comparison with the atmospheric pressure; the pressure in the dehydrator would be reduced at most only a few tenths of an inch of mercury. The effect on drying rate, however slight, is in the opposite direction—that is, the rate is reduced—if the dehydrator temperatures are maintained unchanged.

CONDUCTIVE AND RADIATIVE SOURCES OF ADDITIONAL HEAT SUPPLY TO MATERIAL BEING DRIED

The drying experiments conducted at the Western Regional Research Laboratory and those described by Ede and Hales (1948) show that even minor differences in tray design and construction and drier arrangement will produce substantial differences in drying rate. No complete theoretical analysis of the effective factors is available. Results of operation in full-size driers have, however, been in reasonably good accord with design predictions based on small-scale experiments, especially if certain rather obvious factors are taken into account. Among these factors are the conductive and radiative heat sources over and above the main heat supply carried as sensible heat in the main air stream; the magnitude and arrangement of these supplementary heat sources will affect particularly the equilibrium temperature of wet material on the trays.

In the experiments at the Western Regional Research Laboratory, drying of vegetable pieces was found to be as much as 20 per cent faster during the early drying stages on trays whose bottoms were made by rolling "expanded metal" into a fairly heavy diamond-mesh sheet than on trays with bottoms of thin wood slats spaced about $1/_8$ in. apart. Some of the increased rate on the metal mesh bottoms may have been a consequence of the higher proportion of opening, but the greater effect was probably a rise in temperature of the wet material to several degrees above the wet-bulb temperature of the air, because of the high heat conductivity of the metal mesh. The metal itself would assume a temperature somewhere between the dry-bulb temperature of the air, to which it would be exposed on one side, and the temperature of the wet material in contact with its other side.

The wet-bulb temperature itself is the resultant of a heat balance between evaporative cooling and convective and radiative transfer of heat from the hotter surroundings. In the standard case all of these surroundings are at the dry-bulb temperature. This will also be approximately true for all of the closely stacked trays in a dehydrator; the wet material on a tray will "see" only the bottom surface of the tray above. On the other hand, if a body at higher temperature, such as an infrared radiator, is introduced into the drier the heat balance will be shifted and the material on the tray will assume a temperature higher than the wet-bulb temperature of the air (see p. 41). In vacuum drying, heat transfer by convection being greatly reduced, infrared radiation is often used to supplement what heat can be conducted to the wet material from a heated supporting shelf or conveyor belt. When the drying rate decreases as the material approaches dryness, the energy input to the radiators must be reduced or the temperature of the material will exceed the allowable maximum.

BIBLIOGRAPHY

BRITISH MINISTRY OF FOOD.   1946.   Vegetable Dehydration.   H. M. Stationery Office, London.

BROWN, A. H., and KILPATRICK, P. W.   1943.   Drying characteristics of vegetables—riced potatoes.   Trans. Am. Soc. Mech. Eng. 65, 837–842.

CARRIER, W. H.   1921.   The theory of atmospheric evaporation, with special reference to compartment dryers.   Ind. Eng. Chem. 13, 432–438.

CULPEPPER, C. W., and MOON, H. H.   1937.   Factors affecting the rate of drying of Kieffer pears.   U. S. Dept. Agr. Tech. Bull. 592.

EDE, A. J.   1958.   Some physical data concerning the drying of potato strips. In Fundamental Aspects of the Dehydration of Foodstuffs.   Soc. Chem. Ind. 136–142.

EDE, A. J., and HALES, K. C.   1948.   The physics of drying in heated air, with special reference to fruit and vegetables.   Dept. Sci. Ind. Research, Food Investigations Spec. Rept. 53.

EDE, A. J., and PARTRIDGE, S. M.   1943.   Dried meat.   IV.   The effect of some physical factors on the rate of drying of minced meat in heated air.   J. Soc. Chem. Ind. 62, 194–200.

EIDT, C. C.   1938.   Principles and methods involved in dehydration of apples. Canada Dept. Agr. Tech. Bull. 18.

GUILLOU, R.   1942.   Development of a fruit dehydrator design.   Agr. Eng. 23, 313–316.

KILPATRICK, P. W., LOWE, E., and VAN ARSDEL, W. B.   1955.   Tunnel dehydrators for fruits and vegetables.   In Advances in Food Research 6, 314–369.

LEWIS, W. K.   1921.   The rate of drying of solid materials.   Ind. Eng. Chem. 13, 427–432.

PERRY, R. L.   1944.   Heat and vapor transfer in the dehydration of prunes. Trans. Am. Soc. Mech. Eng. 66, 447–456.

PERRY, R. L., MRAK, E. M., PHAFF, H. J., MARSH, G. L., and FISHER, C. D. 1946.   Fruit dehydration.   I.   Principles and equipment.   Calif. Agr. Expt. Sta. Bull. 698.

UNITED STATES DEPARTMENT OF AGRICULTURE.   1944.   Vegetable and Fruit Dehydration—a Manual for Plant Operators.   Misc. Pub. 540.

VAN ARSDEL, W. B.   1942.   Tunnel dehydrators and their use in vegetable dehydration.   I.   Factors governing the choice of a dehydrator and types of tunnels.   Food Inds. *14*, No. 10, 43–46, 106;   II.   Physical laws of dehydrator operation.   *Ibid. 14*, No. 11, 47–50, 103;   III.   Operating characteristics of tunnels.   *Ibid. 14*, No. 12, 47–50, 108–109.

VAN ARSDEL, W. B.   1943 A.   Tray and tunnel drying methods and equipment. Proc. Inst. Food Technologists 1943, 45–51.

VAN ARSDEL, W. B.   1943 B.   Some engineering problems of the new vegetable dehydration industry.   Heating, Piping, Air Conditioning, ASHVE Sec. *15*, No. 3, 157–160.

VAN ARSDEL, W. B.   1947.   Approximate diffusion calculations for the falling-rate phase of drying.   Chem. Eng. Progr. *43*, 13–24.   Also issued as U. S. Dept. Agr. Bur. Circ. AIC-152.

VAN ARSDEL, W. B.   1951.   Principles of the drying process, with special reference to vegetable dehydration.   U. S. Dept. Agr. Bur. Circ. AIC-300.

CHAPTER 7

Applying Data on Drying Rate Factors to
Estimation of Drying Time

INTRODUCTION

. In the preceding section we have discussed the effects of various external conditions upon the course of drying, in each case assuming that all variables except the one under discussion are held constant. In many important kinds of dehydrator, however, the principle of the operation imposes an inherent and determinate kind of variation on the drying conditions. A quantitative description of the operation then requires determination of the course of drying, and especially the total drying time, under a particular set of these variable conditions. For a specific example, in a quasi-continuous (or "progressive") tunnel-and-truck dehydrator a single piece of the product experiences a marked change in the temperature and humidity of the air flowing over it during the residence time of the piece of material. The air velocity will also change somewhat as a consequence of these temperature and humidity changes and the gradual volume-shrinkage of the product. Both the drying time (and hence the daily output capacity of the dehydrator) and the quality of the product are affected by the manner in which these changes occur.

CHANGES IN DRYING CONDITIONS WITHIN A DEHYDRATOR

Approximation to Adiabatic Conditions in Tunnels

The kind of food dehydrator called a "tunnel" (see Van Arsdel 1951 B; and Kilpatrick *et al.* 1955) is operated as a quasi-continuous steady-state system in which the wet material is introduced at one end of the drier, is moved progressively in a number of steps through the long enclosure, or tunnel, in which the hot air stream is flowing, and is removed at the other end of the drier. For purposes of analysis and preliminary design we can usefully regard an ideal tunnel operation as truly continuous and truly steady-state.

A further great simplification is accomplished by regarding the drying section of the tunnel as adiabatic in operation. This can be no better than an approximation. Adiabatic operation of a tunnel would be a condition in which the trucks, trays, and other equipment, and the dry substance of the material, all have negligible heat capacity.

that heat losses through the walls of the tunnel are negligible, and
that the temperature of the wet product is, and remains at, the thermodynamic wet-bulb temperature of the air flowing in the tunnel; all of
the heat absorbed through the evaporation of water would then be
accounted for by the decrease in dry-bulb air temperature. Brown
(1943 A) and Lazar (1944) examined this approximation critically and
concluded that for the range of conditions encountered in tunnel
dehydrators for vegetables the errors resulting from its use are smaller
than the other inherent uncertainties of such systems. This is mainly
a consequence of the high initial moisture content of these materials
and the resulting overwhelming importance of the heat of evaporation
in comparison with the sensible heat lost in the outgoing trays, trucks,
and dry product. The wet-bulb temperature of air in practical tunnels will usually fall less than 1°F. between the "hot end" and the
"cool end" of the tunnel. The British Ministry of Food, in its
bulletin "Vegetable Dehydration" (1946) described the performance
of two-stage tunnels in potato dehydration; the fall in wet-bulb temperature through the tunnel was somewhat less than 0.5°F.

Approximate Proportionality Between Air Temperature Change and Change of Moisture Content

Besides the approximate constancy of wet-bulb temperature,
adiabatic conditions imply that the change in temperature of the air
between any two points along the tunnel is approximately proportional
to the change in mean moisture content of the material between the
same two points. This follows from a simple mass balance on the
water transferred from material to air between the two points and
the fact, apparent upon inspection of the psychrometric chart, that an
adiabatic cooling line—that is, a line of constant (thermodynamic)
wet-bulb temperature—is very nearly straight. We can write the
following expression for the resulting relation:

$$\Delta t = -1,000 \, z \, \Delta H \tag{53}$$

where

Δt = change in air temperature between two points on an adiabatic
   cooling line (°F.)
ΔH = change in absolute humidity between the same two points (lb.)/(lb.
   dry air)
z = nearly constant slope of the lines, and the multiplier 1,000 is used
   to give z a convenient magnitude

Thus z is the decrease in air temperature for an increase of 0.001 in
absolute humidity. The negative sign signifies that temperature
decreases as humidity increases.

The slope of adiabatic cooling lines changes slightly from point to point on the psychrometric chart. Values of z at four widely separated points are as follows:

Wet-bulb temperature 90°F.
  Air temperature 120°, $z = 4.28°$F.
              180°, $z = 4.35°$F.
Wet-bulb temperature 120°F.
  Air temperature 140°, $z = 3.81°$F.
              200°, $z = 3.96°$F.

Losses of sensible heat in practical equipment always result in a somewhat greater fall in air temperature than this for a rise of 0.001 in absolute humidity. Many approximate drier calculations are, in fact, made on the assumption that $z = 5°$F.

As stated above, a mass balance on the water in the moist material and in the air at any two points along the continuous tunnel equates the amount of water vapor added to the air between those two points in a given length of time such as 1 hr. with the fall in water content of the material passing through that section of the tunnel in the same length of time:

$AG(H_2 - H_1)$ = water vapor added to the air flowing in 1 hr. between points 1 and 2

where

A	= cross-section area of the tunnel (sq. ft.)
G	= mass velocity of the air (lb. dry air)/(hr.)(sq. ft. cross-section)
H_2 and H_1	= absolute humidities of the air at the two points (lb. water vapor)/(lb. dry air)

$\dfrac{L_0 Sl(W_1 - W_2)}{\theta_R(W_0 + 1)}$ = weight of water evaporated per hour in section of tunnel between points 1 and 2

where

L_0	= initial load of wet material per square foot of tray surface (lb.)/(sq. ft.)
S	= area of tray surface per foot of tunnel length (sq. ft.)/(ft.)
l	= total length of the tunnel (ft.)
W_1 and W_2	= mean moisture contents of material in the tunnel at points 1 and 2 (lb.)/(lb. dry solids)
θ_R	= total residence time of material in the tunnel (hr.)
W_0	= initial moisture content of the material as it is loaded into the tunnel (lb.)/(lb. dry solids)

Equating the two expressions and rearranging, we have,

$$H_2 - H_1 = \pm \frac{L_0 Sl}{AG\theta_R(W_0 + 1)} (W_1 - W_2) \tag{54}$$

and if we replace $H_2 - H_1$ by its value as given by Equation (53) we obtain,

$$t_2 - t_1 = \pm \frac{1{,}000 z L_0 S l}{A G \theta_R (W_0 + 1)} (W_1 - W_2) \tag{55}$$

This we might call the "tunnel equation." The plus sign applies before the second member if the tunnel is in counterflow operation (that is, loading at the "cool end" of the tunnel, discharging at the "hot end"), while the minus sign applies if the tunnel is in parallel or concurrent flow operation ("hot end" loading). If we are satisfied to use the approximate value $z = 5$ for the relation between temperature fall and humidity rise the equation becomes:

$$t_2 - t_1 = \pm \frac{5{,}000 L_0 S l}{A G \theta_R (W_0 + 1)} (W_1 - W_2) \tag{56}$$

The coefficient of $W_1 - W_2$ in the right-hand member is constant under this assumption, and we can collect all the terms into a single constant, the "tunnel constant,"

$$t_2 - t_1 = \pm b(W_1 - W_2) \tag{57}$$

where $$b = \frac{5{,}000 L_0 S l}{A G \theta_R (W_0 + 1)}$$

Equations (53) through (57) can easily be transformed so as to express the approximate proportionality between rise in air humidity and fall in air temperature in terms of the rate of supply of wet material to the tunnel or the rate of output of dry material from it, instead of the total residence time of material in the tunnel, θ_R. Also by slight modification of some of the terms in these equations they can be made to apply directly to continuous conveyor dehydrators.

ESTIMATION OF DRYING TIME IN A PARTICULAR DRIER

All this discussion of factors that influence drying rate is necessitated by the fact that we always need to know the *time* that will be required to reduce the moisture content of a specified body of material from some initial value to a specified lower value. Every element of the design and operation of the drier hangs on this drying time, however it may have been determined. In general, three procedures might be considered. The first of these, prediction directly on the basis of general physical principles, is beyond our power at present, for reasons that have been discussed in the paragraphs above, dealing with the mechanism of moisture movement within a moist hygroscopic body. The other two general procedures are analogue experimentation and integration of instantaneous drying rates.

Drying Time by Analogue Experimentation

Analogue experimentation simply consists in setting up small-scale controllable drying equipment in which all the circumstances of a practical drying operation are duplicated, insofar as possible, in everything but scale; drying time is then determined directly from the results of that operation. In other words, this is a pilot-scale simulation of practical conditions. The method could conceivably be applied to investigations of any type of drying whatever, and in fact it is the only satisfactory way to test systems which, although simple enough to operate, are hopelessly complicated in theory. This is the case, for example, with continuous conveyor-type through-flow dehydrators and belt-trough driers. On the other hand, small-scale simulation of spray drying is not fully satisfactory because the operation can only be duplicated in a full-scale drying chamber.

Analogue simulation of tunnel dehydration, particularly of vegetables, has been studied more extensively than most other design procedures. A well designed experimental "cabinet" drier (*i.e.*, a drier in which a suitable sample of the wet material is disposed as it would be in the full-scale drier, but is dried as a stationary batch under controlled conditions of air temperature, humidity, and velocity) is required for this purpose. Sketches of a pilot-scale cabinet drier which has given satisfactory service have been published by the Western Regional Research Laboratory, Agricultural Research Service, U.S. Department of Agriculture, Albany, California (Drawings C-112 and C-113, 1943). The drier is designed to take trays 3 ft. sq. and is constructed mainly of plywood, with mineral wool insulation. It is steam heated by finned coils capable of transferring 1,100,000 B.t.u. per hr. to air at 60°F. The centrifugal circulating fan delivers 9,000 cu. ft. of air per min. at a static pressure of $1^1/_2$ in. of water.

Broughton and Mickley (1953) describe an especially thorough study of the analogue procedure, illustrated by the experimental drying of soap and wet insulating board. The drier is specially equipped with thermocouples embedded in the stock being dried, so that material temperature, as well as air temperature, can be monitored continuously, along with the net weight of material on the tray. In advance of the experiment general heat- and mass-balance equations are set up, incorporating the specified conditions of air temperature, humidity, and mass velocity so as to relate the change of moisture content of the sample at any time to the corresponding change of air temperature in the hypothetical tunnel drier. Equation (55), it will be remembered, is a somewhat simplified form of a similar balance.

Now a short time after the beginning of the experiment the weight and temperature of the sample are measured. Air temperature is immediately changed by the amount prescribed by the balance equation. Drying is continued in this way, temperature of the air being changed in increments as required by the change in weight of the sample. Then the drying time for that material under the combination of conditions prescribed is given directly by the time required in the experimental drier for the sample to reach the specified final moisture content (or sample weight).

A somewhat simpler procedure, involving no attempt to include control of stock temperature in the analogue set-up, and probably suffering somewhat in faithfulness of reproduction of full-scale conditions on that account, has been described by Van Arsdel (1951 A). The procedure can be described most clearly by means of an example. Suppose that carrot dice are to be dehydrated in a counterflow truck-and-tray tunnel (assumed continuous in operation) which will hold ten truckloads, each with a tray area of 540 sq. ft. The prepared carrot dice, with an initial moisture content of $W_0 = 8.40$, are to be spread on metal-mesh trays at a loading of 2 lbs. per sq. ft. The circulating fan is to supply 40,000 cu. ft. per min. of air at 160°F. and a wet-bulb temperature of 95°F. to the hot end of this tunnel. The product is to be dried to a final moisture content of five per cent, moist basis ($W_f = 0.053$). We wish to carry out the drying experiments that will be needed to determine drying time under these conditions and hence the output capacity and other performance characteristics of the tunnel.

First we need to know what air velocity to use in the drying tests; a fairly rough approximation will suffice. The temperature at the cool, or loading, end of the tunnel may be expected to be perhaps 110°F.; air flow at that temperature should be 37,000 cu. ft. per min. (application of Charles' law, p. 13). Now if the free cross-section area around the trucks and between loaded trays is, say, 33 sq. ft., the mean air velocity over the trays in the cool end of the tunnel should be 1,120 ft. per min.

Next, we find from the psychrometric chart that the absolute humidity of air at 160° and wet-bulb temperature 95° is 0.0210 and its humid volume is 16.2 cu. ft. per lb. of dry air. Then the mass air flow through the tunnel is 2,465 lbs. of dry air per min.

Our immediate object is to lay out a schedule of change for the air temperature in the test run that will simulate the temperature change in the tunnel. However, we do not yet know what retention time in the tunnel will suffice to bring mean moisture content of the product

down to five per cent.   We can find out by making a minimum of two,
and preferably three, test drying experiments which will bracket the
true unknown figure.   This can be accomplished as follows:

We know from the form of Equation (55) or (57) that if the air
temperature at points along the tunnel is plotted on coordinate paper
against the mean moisture content of the product at the same points a
straight line will result, within the accuracy of the simplifying assumptions made in the preceding section.   We shall therefore set up a
diagram like Fig. 36, in which air temperature is the ordinate, mean

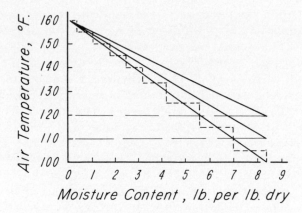

From Van Arsdel 1951 A

FIG. 36.   DIAGRAM USED FOR SCHEDULING
EXPERIMENTAL DRYING RUN

moisture content the abscissa.   We know the coordinates at one end
of the line—temperature 160°F., moisture content 0.053—and the
moisture content, 8.40, but not the temperature at the other end.   We
assume three different temperatures, say 100°, 110°, and 120°F., in
the expected range of this unknown temperature, and draw the three
corresponding straight lines.   Each of these lines maps a schedule for
carrying out one of the three test runs;   the temperature in the experimental cabinet will start at, say, 100°, and will be raised in small
increments in accordance with the mean moisture content of the
material on the tray, as estimated from frequent weighings of the tray.
The wet-bulb temperature of the air in the test drier will be maintained
unchanged at 95°F. during the entire experiment (for a closer approximation, wet-bulb temperature can also be changed from time to
time to correspond to known heat losses rather than adiabatic operation).   Practically it is unnecessary to make the weighings and ad-

justments of temperature continuously; the desired straight-line relationship can be closely approximated in a series of small steps, as shown in one of the lines in Fig. 36.

The three test runs will give us three different values of the time required to dry the product to a moisture content of five per cent. The lower the wet-end temperature we have chosen, the longer this time will be. Now the three drying times will be plotted, as in Fig. 37, against the wet-end air temperature. On the same diagram we

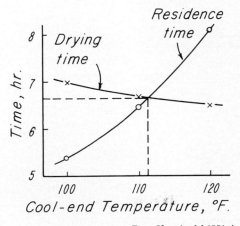

From Van Arsdel 1951 A

FIG. 37. ESTIMATION OF DRYING TIME FOR SPECIFIED
TUNNEL CONDITIONS

shall plot another curve which we take from the tunnel equation, Equation (55), to show the relation of residence time to wet-end air temperature in this tunnel:

$$t' - t'' = \frac{1{,}000\, z\, L_0 Sl}{AG\theta_R(W_0 + 1)}\, (W_0 - W_f) \tag{58}$$

If we insert the numerical values of our example this reduces to:

$$160 - t'' = \frac{1{,}000 \times 5 \times 2 \times 5{,}400}{2{,}465 \times 60 \times 9.40\theta_R}\, (8.40 - 0.053)$$

$$= \frac{323}{\theta_R}$$

For a wet-end air temperature of 100° this gives a residence time of 5.38 hr.; for 110°, 6.46 hr.; and for 120°, 8.07 hr. These are the points which determine the residence-time curve on Fig. 37.

Now the point at which the drying-time and residence-time curves intersect gives us the values we have been seeking, namely, a cool-end temperature of 112°F. and a time of 6.65 hr. Retention of the material in the tunnel for that length of time (that is, inserting a freshly loaded truck about every 40 min. and withdrawing a dry one at the same time) will, we are predicting, just dry it to a mean moisture content of five per cent. The 24-hr. output of dry product should be

$$\frac{5,400 \times 2 \times 1.053 \times 24}{9.40 \times 6.65} = 4,375 \text{ lbs.}$$

The same kind of procedure can be used to predict the behavior of a two-stage tunnel, such as the widely used combination of a parallel flow first stage and a counterflow finishing stage. A more elaborate series of test runs must be made, however, because the moisture content of the product at the point of change-over from first to second stage will not be known in advance. In practice, because of the inevitable variability of experimental raw materials and conditions in predrying steps, it may be necessary to replicate experimental runs and apply the *mean* results to the graphical determination of drying time. In addition, of course, results should be discounted enough to allow for the expected imperfections of design and operation of practical dehydrators. Only experience can give any guidance in this. The usual causes of poorer performance than expected are uneven distribution of hot air flowing through the tunnel, careless loading and careless stacking of trays, and major air leaks at the high-pressure end of the tunnel.

The experimental procedure used to secure an analogue prediction of drying time in a continuous conveyor-type through-flow dehydrator must, of course, be quite different from the method just described. A through-flow experimental drier will be used. The perforated support will be similar to the perforated conveyor. The volume of air flow per square foot of supporting surface will be made equal to that expected in the full-scale drier; the direction of air flow must be reversible, and the temperature and humidity of the air be controllable by the operator. Temperature and humidity conditions must be chosen in advance for each of three or four segments of a single test, corresponding to the three or four separately controllable sections of the conveyor dehydrator. These drying conditions will be kept constant during each segment. The time of exposure in each segment will be made equal to the length of time the product will remain in that section of the continuous conveyor for some one chosen value of the rate of travel of the conveyor. If, as is sometimes done, the product is to be dumped from one conveyor onto a slower moving one, a similar mixing and respreading will be done in the experimental unit. Ordinarily three such runs will be required, corresponding to three different rates of conveyor travel. When the moisture contents of the products of the experimental runs have been determined the proper conveyor speed (and therefore drying time and evaporative capacity) can be estimated by a graphical interpolation process. Obviously a considerable number of test runs must be made if various combinations of temperature and humidity in the different sections of the drier are to be tried; for example, to find the combination which gives the highest production of acceptable dry product.

Drying Time From Drying Rates Determined Under Constant Conditions

The "Point-Condition" Method.—The classical method of estimating drying time, as described by Lewis (1921) and Walker *et al.* (1937), assumes that drying rates determined by means of a series of experiments at a number of different constant drying conditions can simply be integrated over the specified sequence of changing conditions.

$$\theta = \frac{1}{A_0} \int_{W_1}^{W_2} \frac{-dW}{(dW/Ad\theta)} \tag{59}$$

This has been known as the "point-condition" method of solution. It has been shown to give satisfactory agreement with experience in the drying of many non-hygroscopic materials. Broughton and Mickley (1953) comment, however, that the conditions for its applicability are so stringent that it has not been very widely useful.

Integration of Drying Rate Data.—Direct integration of drying rates, as in Equation (59), is theoretically allowable only if the rate of drying of a moist body is strictly determined by the value of its mean moisture content at any instant, and not at all by the previous drying history. This can never be exactly true in any actual case; the drying rate of a moist body at any instant is determined by the surrounding air conditions and the temperature and moisture content at the *surface* of the body, not the mean. In turn, the surface moisture content and temperature reflect the internal gradients which have become established in the course of all that has gone before. Extensive studies of the drying rates of several vegetables have shown that this effect of previous drying history is substantial and must be taken into account. It is automatically eliminated as a factor, of course, in the analogue procedures described above.

Development of the "point-condition" method for taking account of the change in drying conditions encountered by a piece of wet material in its progress through a tunnel is simple and straightforward if the drying rate is a linear or other simple function of mean moisture content and air temperature and humidity.   Badger and McCabe (1936) and Walker *et al.* (1937) gave the integrated forms of Equation (59) for adiabatic counterflow and parallel-flow driers, based on the assumptions, first, that in the initial constant-rate phase the rate is proportional to $H_s - H$ (the difference between the air humidity and saturation humidity at the same wet-bulb temperature), and second, that in the entire falling-rate phase the resistance to surface evaporation is the controlling factor and the rate is proportional to the remaining "free" moisture content, $W - W_e$. However, the actual drying behavior of important food materials is so far from conformance with these or any other very simple relationships that the analytical integration of Equation (59) has little practical interest.

Nomographic Estimation of Drying Time.—If a material whose drying characteristics are not very completely known is to be dried, use of one of the analogue experimental procedures described above is the only satisfactory recourse, laborious though it may be.   However, there is a large and important class of drying problems in which the specific behavior of a particular raw material is relatively unimportant; this includes such questions as determining the preferable arrangement of a dehydrator (counterflow, parallel-flow, or multiple-stage), the optimum proportion of air recirculation in a tunnel, the relation between tray loading and tunnel drying capacity, and the optimum proportion between lengths of primary and secondary stages of a two-stage tunnel.   Solution of such problems as these is best attacked through application of generalized drying rate relations which can typify the drying behavior of broad classes of materials.

Guillou (1942) showed that the drying rate of prunes in a tunnel dehydrator, down to the usual "dried fruit" moisture level of about 17 per cent, is proportional at all times to the "free" moisture content; the empirically determined constant contains the factors of air temperature, humidity, and velocity, and the size of the fruit. He, and later Perry (1944) and Perry *et al.* (1946) applied the generalized relation to the design of a dehydrator in which an optimum balance is found between heat costs and combined power, labor, and capital costs.

A group of investigators at the Western Regional Research Laboratory (Brown and Kilpatrick 1943; Van Arsdel 1942, 1943 B, 1951 A; Brown 1943 B, 1951 A, 1944, 1951 B; Brown and Van Arsdel 1944, 1951; Brown and Lazar 1944, 1951; Lazar *et al.* 1944, 1951; Lazar

and Brown 1945, 1947, 1951; and Van Arsdel *et al.*, 1947, 1951), analyzed various ways of correlating and reporting their extensive studies
of the drying rates of white potato in riced, strip, and half-dice forms,
carrot pieces, shredded cabbage, onion slices, sweet corn, and sweet
potato strips. Empirical equations proved to be impractical. The
results were eventually published by the U. S. Department of Agriculture as a series of nomographic charts under the designation,
"Drying Rate Nomographs—AIC-31." They were numbered I
through VIII.

In each case at least two separate charts were drawn for each material—one giving the time required to dry from the initial moisture
content, W_0, down to an intermediate value ranging from $W = 0.10$
to 0.25, and the other giving the additional time required to bring the
moisture content from that intermediate level to a final level ranging
from 0.02 for cabbage to 0.06 for corn and sweet potatoes. The charts
are thus designed to read in drying times directly, instead of proceed-
ing by way of integration of drying rates; in fact, the authors counsel
caution in the use of the charts to compute drying rates. For example, the nomographic solution exhibits a perceptible discontinuity
of drying *rate* at the point marking passage from the high-moisture
chart to the low-moisture chart, but the slight discontinuity in the
slope of the drying curve is negligible in the estimation of total drying
time.

Fig. 38 illustrates the type of chart used in these nomographs. The
one shown here on a reduced scale gives an estimate of the drying
time of potato half-dice from an initial moisture content of $W_0 =$
3.4 to a moisture content of 0.20 at the end of the high-moisture
segment of the estimate. The other conditions are a tray-loading of
1.5 lbs./sq. ft. (metal-grid trays), an air velocity of 800 ft. per min.,
temperatures in the range of 110° to 200°F., and wet-bulb temperature
depressions in the range of 20° to 80°F. Alignment of a point in the
temperature network on the right of the chart with any point on the
left-hand scale of moisture contents gives a time, in hours, at the inter-
section with the center scale. A second alignment chart then provides
the value of a multiplying factor, which converts the time required
under the conditions specified above to the time required at some
other air velocity in the range of 400 to 1,200 ft. per min., and some
other tray loading in the range of 0.5 to 2.5 lbs./sq. ft. A third chart
supplies a drying time from $W = 0.20$ to the final moisture content,
W_f, for temperatures from 120° to 170°F. and wet-bulb temperatures
from 80° to 110°F. A final nomograph supplies a value for the length
of time required to dry to the "reference value" of W_0, namely 3.4,

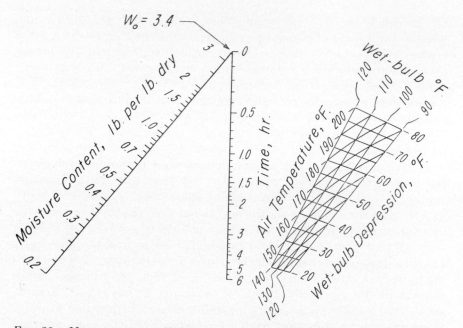

FIG. 38.   NOMOGRAPH FOR ESTIMATING DRYING TIME OF POTATO HALF-DICE—
HIGH-MOISTURE SEGMENT

from any higher initial value that may have been found in a different
raw material.

A partial test of the validity of the procedure was made by P. W.
Kilpatrick, of the Western Regional Research Laboratory, by con-
ducting a long series of experimental runs with shredded cabbage as
the raw material, simulating a wide range of counterflow tunnel operating conditions.   Results summarized in an unpublished report dated
January 21, 1946, indicated that nomographic predictions of drying
time are adequately conservative.   For example, when the tray-
loading was 1.5 lbs. per sq. ft. the experimental drying time down to a
final moisture content of 0.05 under counterflow temperature conditions was 7.7 ± 0.2 hr., whereas the nomographic solution gave a
time of 7.9 hr.

The nomographic charts of the AIC-31 series, being based upon
tray drying experiments, are much more helpful in the design and
operation of practical dehydrators than in throwing light on the
theory of drying.   They lend themselves readily to investigation of
the effects of any of the operating conditions upon the performance
of a tunnel dehydrator.   The typical procedure is closely similar to
that described above for analogue simulation of tunnel drying.   A

set of tunnel operating conditions (tunnel arrangement, total tray surface, unit tray-loading, total air flow, hot-end air temperature, and wet-bulb temperature) and initial material moisture content are combined with three values of cool-end air temperature to give three straight lines relating air temperature to mean moisture content, as in Fig. 36 (p. 124). Each of these lines is replaced by a series of small steps (for example, 5° change in air temperature), as suggested in the Figure. The nomograph is then applied to obtain the successive small segments of drying time, which are summed to give three values of total drying time. The latter are plotted against cool-end air temperature, as in Fig. 37. A plot of residence time versus cool-end temperature on the same chart then intersects with the drying-time curve at a point which gives the required solution to the problem.

BIBLIOGRAPHY

BADGER, W. L., and McCABE, W. L.   1936.   Elements of Chemical Engineering. Second Ed.   McGraw-Hill Book Co., New York.

BRITISH MINISTRY OF FOOD.   1946.   Vegetable Dehydration.   H. M. Stationery Office, London.

BROUGHTON, D. B., and MICKLEY, H. S.   1953.   Design of full-scale continuous tunnel driers.   Chem. Eng. Progr. 49, 319–324.

BROWN, A. H.   1943 A.   Heat balance in tunnels.   Unpublished report to Western Regional Research Laboratory, U. S. Dept. Agr., May 20.

BROWN, A. H.   1943 B, 1951 A.   Drying rate nomographs.   II.   Blanched sweet corn.   U. S. Dept. Agr. Bur. Circ. AIC-31-II.

BROWN, A. H.   1944, 1951 B.   Drying rate nomographs.   IV.   Shredded cabbage.   U. S. Dept. Agr. Bur. Circ. AIC-31-IV.

BROWN, A. H., and KILPATRICK, P. W.   1943.   Drying characteristics of vegetables—riced potatoes.   Trans. Am. Soc. Mech. Eng. 65, 837–842.

BROWN, A. H., and LAZAR, M. E.   1944, 1951.   Drying rate nomographs.   V. Onion slices.   U. S. Dept. Agr. Bur. Circ. AIC-31-V.

BROWN, A. H., and VAN ARSDEL, W. B.   1944, 1951.   Drying rate nomographs. III.   White potato strips—vertical air flow.   U. S. Dept. Agr. Bur. Circ. AIC-31-III.

GUILLOU, R.   1942.   Development of a fruit dehydrator design.   Agr. Eng. 23, 313–316.

KILPATRICK, P. W., LOWE, E., and VAN ARSDEL, W. B.   1955.   Tunnel dehydrators for fruits and vegetables.   Advances in Food Research 6, 314–369.

LAZAR, M. E.   1944.   Deviations from adiabaticity in tunnel dehydrators. U. S. Dept. Agr. Western Regional Research Laboratory.   Unpublished report.

LAZAR, M. E., and BROWN, A. H.   1945.   Drying rate nomographs.   VII. White potato half cubes.   U. S. Dept. Agr. Bur. Circ. AIC-31-VII.

LAZAR, M. E., and BROWN, A. H.   1947, 1951.   Drying rate nomographs.   VIII. Carrot pieces.   U. S. Dept. Agr. Bur. Circ. AIC-31-VIII.

LAZAR, M. E., KILPATRICK, P. W., and BROWN, A. H.   1944, 1951.   Drying rate nomographs.   VI.   Sweet potato strips.   U. S. Dept. Agr. Bur. Circ. AIC-31-VI.

LEWIS, W. K.   1921.   The rate of drying of solid materials.   Ind. Eng. Chem. 13, 427–432.

PERRY, R. L. 1944. Heat and vapor transfer in the dehydration of prunes. Trans. Am. Soc. Mech. Eng. *66*, 447–456.

PERRY, R. L., MRAK, E. M., PHAFF, H. J., MARSH, G. L., and FISHER, C. D. 1946. Fruit dehydration. I. Principles and equipment. Calif. Agr. Expt. Sta. Bull. *698*.

VAN ARSDEL, W. B. 1942. Tunnel dehydrators and their use in vegetable dehydration. I. Factors governing the choice of a dehydrator and types of tunnels. Food Inds. *14*, No. 10, 43–46, 106; II. Physical laws of dehydrator operation. *Ibid. 14*, No. 11, 47–50, 103; III. Operating characteristics of tunnels. *Ibid. 14*, No. 12, 47–50, 108–109.

VAN ARSDEL, W. B. 1943 A. Tray and tunnel drying methods and equipment. Proc. Inst. Food Technologists 1943, 45–51.

VAN ARSDEL, W. B. 1943 B. Some engineering problems of the new vegetable dehydration industry. Heating, Piping, Air Conditioning, ASHVE Sec. *15*, No. 3, 157–160.

VAN ARSDEL, W. B. 1951 A. Principles of the drying process, with special reference to vegetable dehydration. U. S. Dept. Agr. Bur. Circ. AIC-300.

VAN ARSDEL, W. B. 1951 B. Tunnel-and-truck dehydrators, as used in vegetable dehydration. U. S. Dept. Agr. Bur. Circ. AIC-308.

VAN ARSDEL, W. B., BROWN, A. H., and LAZAR, M. E. 1947, 1951. Drying rate nomographs. I. Riced white potatoes. U. S. Dept. Agr. Bur. Circ. AIC-31-I.

WALKER, W. H., LEWIS, W. K., McADAMS, W. H., and GILLILAND, E. R. 1937. Principles of Chemical Engineering. Third Ed. McGraw-Hill Book Co., New York.

CHAPTER 8

Theoretical Tunnel Drying Characteristics

Although the basic idea of the tunnel drier goes back at least to Yule (1845), its development in substantially the present form dates from the period 1919–1923. It was especially adapted to the drying of prunes, as a simple, rugged, low-cost unit, most of which could be constructed by local labor in the middle of a fruit-growing area. The names Cruess (1919), Cruess and Christie (1921 A, B), Ridley (1921), and Wiegand (1923) were prominent in this development, which has been described in some detail by Kilpatrick *et al.* (1955).

Counterflow and Parallel-Flow Tunnels

Most of the prune drying tunnels were arranged for counterflow operation (Fig. 39). The hot dry air is blown into the "dry end" of the tunnel (*i.e.*, the end where dry product is removed), and moves through it in a direction opposite to the direction of movement of the fruit. The moisture-laden air at the far end of the tunnel may be partly exhausted and partly recirculated back to the air intake. Parallel-flow (or concurrent) operation involves only a reversal of the direction of movement of the trucks of material through the tunnel.

The main characteristics of drying conditions in these two tunnel arrangements are illustrated in Fig. 40. Here the nomographic charts for potato half-dice (AIC-31-VII) have been used to determine curves representing the changes in material moisture content and air temperature in two tunnels of the same length, one being operated counterflow, the other parallel-flow, and air temperatures being chosen so as to make the two drying times equal. This combination turns out to be a hot-end air temperature of 150°F. in the counterflow tunnel, 185°F. in the parallel-flow tunnel, with a wet-bulb temperature of 85°F. in the former, 90°F. in the latter. Total tray surface in each tunnel is taken to be 6,480 sq. ft., unit loading of prepared material 1.50 lbs./sq. ft., and air velocity between trays 1,000 ft./min. The drying time is slightly over 7 hr. It will be observed that although air temperature starts out very much higher in the parallel-flow tunnel, it ends by being somewhat lower than temperature in the counterflow tunnel in about two-thirds of the entire tunnel length. The initial drying rate of material in the parallel-flow tunnel is very high, but the final drying

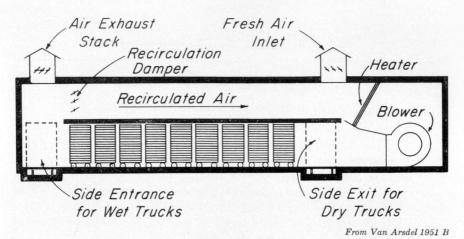

From Van Arsdel 1951 B

FIG. 39.   DIAGRAM OF SIDE-ENTRANCE COUNTERFLOW TUNNEL (ELEVATION)

rate is very low.   These differences in drying rate at various stages of the operation will undoubtedly cause noticeable differences in the quality of the product.   Material dried by the parallel-flow operation will be more bulky because shrinkage stresses will open up internal cracks and voids, and it may exhibit less "heat damage" than the counterflow dried product because of the slightly lower temperature during the last two-thirds of the time.

A set of conditions postulated by Van Arsdel (1951 B) illustrates strikingly how the behavior of a tunnel is affected if its evaporative capability is overloaded.   A counterflow tunnel similar to the one referred to in the above example is operated with trays loaded at 3.0 lbs./sq. ft. (instead of 1.5), air velocity is 500 ft./min. (instead of 1,000), and wet-bulb temperature level is held at 100°F. (instead of 85°).   Drying time increases from about 7 to 22 hr., and the air at the cool end has a relative humidity of about 96 per cent; indeed if a truckload of wet material enters the tunnel at a temperature of 80°F., about 35 lbs. of water will condense on it from the nearly saturated exhaust air (i.e., the truckload "sweats") before the wet material finally warms up to 100°F. and begins to dry.   The material remains for many hours at a temperature favorable to very rapid bacterial growth, with accompanying souring and development of off-flavor.

Two-Stage and Multiple-Stage Tunnels

Two-stage tunnels now generally comprise a parallel-flow first stage and counterflow second stage, the arrangement first suggested by Eidt (1938) for the dehydration of apple slices.   Fig. 41 is a diagram-

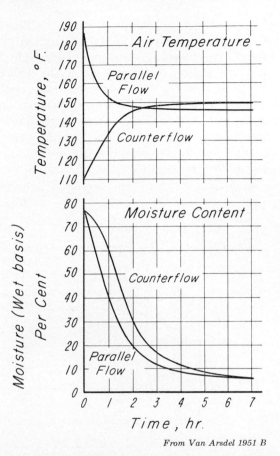

From Van Arsdel 1951 B

FIG. 40.   COMPARISON OF COUNTERFLOW AND PARALLEL-
FLOW TUNNEL DRYING OF POTATO HALF-DICE

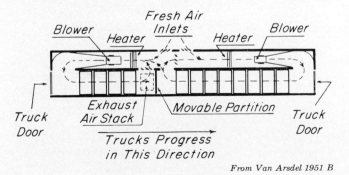

From Van Arsdel 1951 B

FIG. 41.   DIAGRAM OF TWO-STAGE SINGLE-TUNNEL
DEHYDRATOR—PLAN VIEW

matic plan view of one form of two-stage tunnel. Trucks move one step at a time first through the primary section at the left, then straight on through the finishing section at the right; a movable partition between the stages is opened when the trucks are to be moved. Fig. 42 illustrates the course of moisture content and air temperature in such a dehydrator. This example was computed from the nomographs for potato half-dice, assuming total tray surface of 4,160 sq. ft., tray-loading of 1.50 lbs./sq. ft., air velocity between trays 1,000 ft./min., initial air temperature in the primary stage 220°F., with wet-bulb temperature 100°F., and hot-end air temperature in the secondary stage 147°F., wet-bulb temperature 80°F.

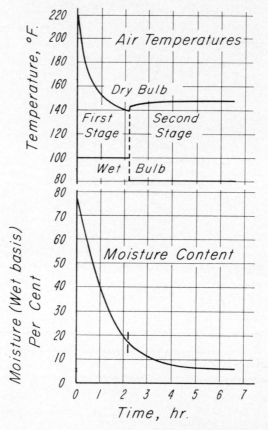

FIG. 42. MOISTURE CONTENT OF MATERIAL AND TEMPERATURE OF AIR IN TWO-STAGE TUNNEL DRYING OF POTATO HALF-DICE

The primary stage is assumed to be just half as long as the secondary. Calculation showed that this combination should produce about seven per cent more product dried to six per cent moisture than two counter-flow tunnels carrying the same total tray surface.   The drying time would be correspondingly shorter and somewhat less heat damage might be expected.

Gooding and Tucker (1958) made extensive studies of multistage dehydration at the Aberdeen Experimental Factory of the British Ministry of Agriculture, Fisheries, and Food.   Their conclusion was that the usual two-stage tunnel, more or less similar to the form just discussed, is somewhat wanting in flexibility because of the necessary dependence of conditions in either stage upon the rate of drying in the other stage.   They favor a three- or four-stage system, employing a general countercurrent flow of air, but also introducing reheating of the air between stages and finishing the drying by through-flow of warm dry air in deep bins.   Reheating results in a very considerable rise in the wet-bulb temperature level, as may be seen from the following conditions finally adopted in the Aberdeen Factory for drying $1/8 \times 5/16$ in. strips of potato or carrot:

Stage	Time (min.)	Temperature (°F.)	
		Dry-Bulb	Wet-Bulb
1	30	230	125
2	30	175	120
3	120	155	115–105
4	180	145	90–80

HEAT, POWER, AND LABOR COSTS

In any convection drier, of which the tunnel drier is an example, circulating air is artificially heated and then circulated into contact with the wet material in order to convey to it the heat energy required to evaporate the water—at least 1,000 B.t.u. for every pound of water to be evaporated.   The air is primarily a carrier of heat; it must be moved out of the way, once it has discharged its heat burden, to make room for some more carrier fully charged with available heat energy.

Full-scale dehydrators of various types require a supply of heat ranging from as little as about 1,200 B.t.u. per lb. of water evaporated to as much as 5,000 or 6,000 B.t.u. per lb., depending upon the factors that determined the basic design and numerous conditions of operation.   Careful economic analysis of the job to be performed and all of the operating costs connected with it may result sometimes in choice of a design and mode of operation that necessarily involve high usage of heat per unit of evaporation, because other economic factors outweigh heat cost. This appears to be the case at present in some important vegetable dehydration operations. Historically, design and operation of the early fruit-drying tunnels was strongly influenced in the other direction, that is, toward good heat economy. The familiar counterflow prune-drying tunnel was designed on that basis.

The air leaving the cool end of a dehydration tunnel will usually have a temperature of at least 110°F., which is higher than the usual outdoor temperature; air leaving the second stage of a two-stage tunnel may be only a few degrees cooler than at the incoming end. A substantial saving of heat can therefore be made by reheating this air and returning a part of it to the system, instead of exhausting it all after one pass through the tunnel. In addition, control of this "recirculation" provides a simple way to control the humidity level and wet-bulb temperature in the tunnel. (See the section on computation of recirculation, pp. 29–31.)

Heat usage in a simple tunnel can be estimated as follows (Van Arsdel 1951 A):

Of the total air flow entering the hot end of the tunnel the proportion r_d is recirculated air, the proportion $1 - r_d$ is fresh air, drawn in from the surroundings at a temperature of t_0. The fresh air must be heated from t_0 to t', the hot-end temperature, while the recirculated air must be heated only from t'' to t'. If we neglect the slight difference in humid heats of the two sources of air and take the mean as 0.25, the heat required per pound of air circulating is $0.25 \ [r_d(t' - t'') + (1 - r_d)(t' - t_0)]$ (B.t.u.)/(lb. dry air). Now the evaporation into this pound of air in its passage through the tunnel is $H'' - H'$ lbs. per lb. of dry air, and this is coupled with a change in air temperature (Equation (53)) of $- 1,000 \ z \ (H'' - H')$ (°F.). The result is as follows:

$$F = 250\, z \left[r_d + (1 - r_d) \frac{t' - t_0}{t' - t''} \right] \tag{60}$$

where F = heat usage (B.t.u.)/(lb. water evaporated).

Lazar (1944), in investigating the amount of departure of practical tunnels from theoretical adiabatic evaporation, found that if heat losses due to air leakage and conduction through the walls were set aside, about 95 per cent of the heat supplied in a typical case would go into heat of evaporation of the water. The absorption of sensible heat by trucks, trays, and material during the warm-up period would take about four per cent in this ideal case and exhausting the air at a higher temperature than the wet-bulb temperature would take the remaining one per cent.   Temperature would fall about 2.5°F. farther than in an adiabatic drier, and wet-bulb temperature would fall about 0.5°F. instead of remaining constant.

We have already stated that many approximate drier calculations are made on the assumption that z, the fall in air temperature corresponding to a rise of 0.001 in humidity, is 5°F., whereas the adiabatic ratio is approximately 4°F.   This, it will be seen, corresponds to only about 80 per cent of the heat input going into heat of evaporation. This figure is sometimes called the thermal efficiency, with symbol η.   The quantity F, heat usage per pound of evaporation, is generally more useful.

Optimum Recirculation of Air

Ramage and Rasmussen (1943) pointed out that an increase in proportion of recirculation in a tunnel drier will ordinarily diminish the rate of drying somewhat (because the drying potential, or wet-bulb depression, will have been decreased), so that the saving in cost of heat must be balanced against probable increases in the cost of power, labor, and capital per pound of product made.   Kilpatrick et al. (1955) computed two illustrative examples, using the AIC-31 nomographs, and the results of one are reproduced in Fig. 43.   Here a counterflow tunnel long enough to hold a maximum of eleven 3-ft. trucks (400 sq. ft. of useful tray surface on each truck) is to be used to dehydrate potato half-dice to 6.55 per cent moisture.   Trays will be loaded with 2.50 lbs. of blanched potato pieces per square foot.   The

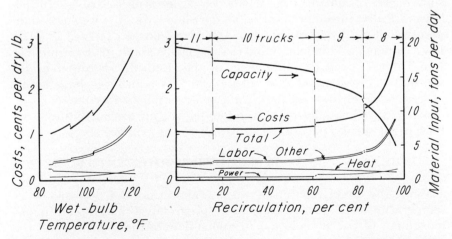

From Kilpatrick et al. 1955

FIG. 43.   EFFECT OF AIR RECIRCULATION ON DRYING COSTS

centrifugal fan supplying the air through a "twin-tunnel" pair is of the limit-load type, double width, with a standard air rating of 54,000 cu. ft. per min. against 1.5 in. (water) static pressure; when operated at 423 r.p.m. it absorbs approximately 17 h.p. The hot-end temperature will be 150°F. The power absorbed by the fan at operating temperature is approximately 15 h.p. The outside fresh-air temperature is 60°F., absolute humidity 0.010 lb. water per lb. dry air. The tunnel will be operated with a minimum of 15°F. wet-bulb depression at the cool end; if an increase in recirculation would result in a lower wet-bulb depression than that, the load on the tunnel will be reduced by decreasing the number of trucks in it. The cost of heat is taken as 35 cents per million B.t.u. transferred to the air stream, the cost of power two cents per kilowatt-hour, operating labor cost for each side of the double tunnel $1.45 per hr., regardless of output within the range considered in the example, and all other costs (plant overhead and fixed charges) $1.35 per hr. From Fig. 43 it is evident that although the cost of heat per dry pound drops continuously as proportion of recirculation is increased, minimum total cost would be realized by employing little or no recirculation.

This theoretical conclusion appears to have been accepted by the designers of some important commercial vegetable dehydration tunnels built within the past few years; heated air flows straight through these tunnels and discharges to atmosphere without any provision for recirculation. A radical simplification of single-stage tunnel construction is thus made possible. It must be noted, however, that some degree of control of the drying conditions is necessarily sacrificed. Theoretically, in such a location as Portland, Me., the wet-bulb temperature of outdoor air heated to 160°F. would be expected to go as low as about 77°F. in winter and rise as high as about 92°F. in summer (see Table 7, page 19); the effect of the resulting 15° difference in wet-bulb depression would be substantial. In a multiple-stage tunnel at least some of the gain that could be accomplished by recirculation can be realized equally well by employing the air discharged from the finishing stage as a part of the air supply to the primary stage.

THE "SAW-TOOTH" EFFECT OF INTERMITTENT TRUCK MOVEMENT

While the direct relation between evaporation and decrease in air temperature holds just as truly in a "progressive" and discontinuous movement of trucks as in a continuous flow of material through the dehydrator, such as was assumed for purposes of simplification in most of the foregoing analysis of tunnel drying, details of change in temperature and moisture content are much more complicated; the system is not actually in a steady state at any time. The effects upon equipment capacity and product characteristics are relatively small in dehydrators of usual types and sizes, but should not be overlooked.

Consider the course of events in a short parallel-flow tunnel, built to hold six trucks. During operation this string of trucks remains stationary for successive intervals of one-sixth of the total drying time. When a fresh truckload of material is placed in the tunnel the hot air at first spends much of its available energy in heating up the truck, trays, and wet material and the temperature of air passing on down the tunnel drops sharply. The heating-up period passes quickly, but is succeeded by extremely rapid evaporation from the new truckload; air temperatures throughout the tunnel remain relatively low. However, the period of rapid evaporation hardly lasts for as much as one-sixth of the total drying time, and air temperatures down through the tunnel rise appreciably before the time comes to insert another freshly loaded truck. The result, as it might be reflected in a record of air temperature at the exhaust end of the tunnel, is a kind of "sawtooth" variation, as illustrated in Fig. 44.

We are of course primarily concerned with the environmental history of any portion of the food material during its stay in the tunnel. Fig. 45 shows what the conditions would be for two pieces of product passing through a six-truck parallel-flow tunnel, one of the pieces being located near the "leading" edge of a tray (nearest to the hot-air inlet), and the other near the "trailing" edge. A large part of the total evaporation takes place in the first truck position, and the

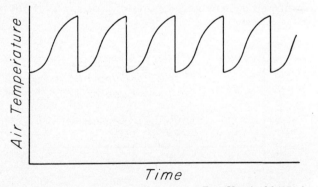

From Van Arsdel 1951 A

FIG. 44.   FLUCTUATION OF COOL-END AIR TEMPERATURE
IN PARALLEL-FLOW TUNNEL

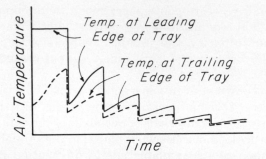

From Van Arsdel 1951 A

FIG. 45. TEMPERATURE OF AIR PASSING OVER A GIVEN
PIECE OF MATERIAL DURING ITS PASSAGE THROUGH A
PARALLEL-FLOW TUNNEL

material near the leading edges of the trays is always exposed to
more severe drying conditions than material near the trailing edge.

Fig. 46 is a comparable diagram showing the environmental temperatures that might be experienced by material dried in a six-truck
counterflow tunnel. The saw-tooth effect is much less pronounced
and there is less difference between the temperature experiences of
front and back positions on the trays.

MATERIAL TEMPERATURE

Generally we strive to operate a food dehydrator so as to minimize
the various kinds of quality loss or damage that have been described
in earlier paragraphs, and yet maximize the output of dry product
per dollar of total expense. The most serious quality impairment
usually encountered is browning, or "heat damage." This, as we have

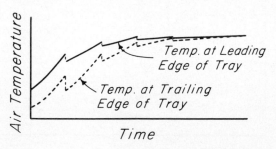

From Van Arsdel 1951 A

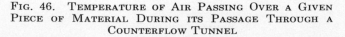

FIG. 46. TEMPERATURE OF AIR PASSING OVER A GIVEN
PIECE OF MATERIAL DURING ITS PASSAGE THROUGH A
COUNTERFLOW TUNNEL

pointed out, is the result of complex chemical reactions in the material and takes place at a rate which is strongly increased by a rise in temperature and is greatest at intermediate and low moisture contents. The course of the latter as a function of time has already been discussed in detail; the simultaneous course of material temperatures can be approximately calculated for the conditions of tunnel dehydration by a method described by Kilpatrick *et al.* (1955). Drying rate as a function of distance the material has traveled in the tunnel, as estimated from drying time nomographs, is combined with a heat balance. A convective heat transfer coefficient is evaluated for the conditions near the "wet end" of the tunnel, where the material temperature is equal, at least momentarily, to the wet-bulb temperature of the air, and a term is introduced to express the change in area due to shrinkage of the material.

Fig. 47 shows the computed course of material temperature in a lightly loaded counterflow tunnel drying potato half-dice. Loading is 1.5 lbs./sq. ft. in a tunnel containing 12 trucks, each of 540 sq. ft. surface. Air velocity between trays at the wet end is 1,000 ft./min., wet-bulb temperature of the air 85°, and hot-end temperature 150°F. Drying time to a moisture content of six per cent (moist basis) is 7.03 hr.

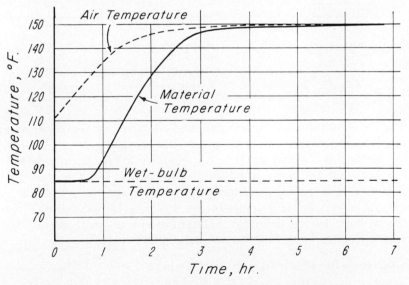

From Van Arsdel 1951 B and Kilpatrick et al. 1955

FIG. 47.   AIR TEMPERATURE AND MATERIAL TEMPERATURE IN COUNTERFLOW TUNNEL DRYING OF POTATO HALF-DICE

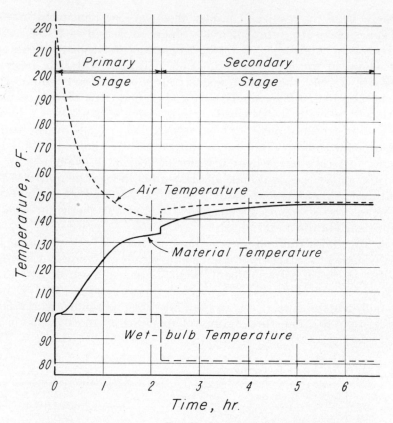

FIG. 48. AIR TEMPERATURE AND MATERIAL TEMPERATURE
IN TWO-STAGE TUNNEL DRYING POTATO HALF-DICE

From Van Arsdel 1951 B and Kilpatrick et al. 1955

Fig. 48 shows the similarly computed course of air temperature and material temperature in a two-stage tunnel drying potato half-dice. Tray-loading is 1.5 lbs./sq. ft. Air velocity in the parallel-flow first stage is 1,000 ft./min., wet-bulb temperature 100°, hot-end temperature 220°. In the counterflow second stage the wet-bulb temperature is 81°, hot-end temperature 147°. The secondary stage is twice as long as the primary. Retention times are 2.20 hr. in the primary, 4.40 hr. in the secondary, total 6.60 hr.

Conditions for Minimum Heat Damage

It is evident that there is always a race between the two processes, drying and browning, and we want to arrange conditions so that the former will win. Both processes proceed faster the higher the temperature, but they have different temperature coefficients, so it should be possible to devise an optimum temperature schedule, calling for maintenance of a relatively low material temperature during the period while mean moisture content is in the most sensitive range, W about 0.15 to 0.30, and then allowing the material temperature to rise moderately during the remainder of the finishing phase. Hendel (1956) was able to demonstrate that potato dice can be dried to a low moisture content without browning by proper control of the temperature and humidity of the drying air, but in general found that temperature cannot safely be raised during the finishing phase, as had been hoped. In the commercial practice of bin finishing of certain dehydrated vegetables, the maximum air temperature is usually at least 5° to 10° lower than the temperature found suitable for the second stage of a two-stage tunnel which discharges product at a moisture content of, say, 0.15 to 0.20.

BIBLIOGRAPHY

CRUESS, W. V. 1919. Evaporators for prune drying. Calif. Agr. Expt. Sta. Circ. *213*.

CRUESS, W. V., and CHRISTIE, A. W. 1921 A. Dehydration of fruits—a progress report. Calif. Agr. Expt. Sta. Bull. *330*.

CRUESS, W. V., and CHRISTIE, A. W. 1921 B. Some factors of dehydrator efficiency. Calif. Agr. Expt. Sta. Bull. *337*.

EIDT, C. C. 1938. Principles and methods involved in dehydration of apples. Canada Dept. Agr. Tech. Bull. *18*.

GOODING, E. G. B., and TUCKER, C. G. 1958. Dehydration of vegetables in multi-stage cross-flow systems. *In* Fundamental Aspects of the Dehydration of Foodstuffs. Soc. Chem. Ind. 225–238.

HENDEL, C. E. 1956. Browning rates and equilibrium vapor pressures of white potatoes in later stages of dehydration. Diss. Univ. Calif., Berkeley.

KILPATRICK, P. W., LOWE, E., and VAN ARSDEL, W. B. 1955. Tunnel dehydrators for fruits and vegetables. Advances in Food Research 6, 314–369.

LAZAR, M. E. 1944. Deviations from adiabaticity in tunnel dehydrators. U. S. Dept. Agr., Western Regional Research Laboratory. Unpublished report.

RAMAGE, W. D., and RASMUSSEN, C. L. 1943. This is what it costs to dehydrate vegetables. Food Inds. *15*, No. 7, 64–71, 137–138; No. 8, 66–67, 118–119; No. 9, 75–77, 126.

RIDLEY, G. B. 1921. Tunnel driers. Ind. Eng. Chem. *13*, 453–460.

VAN ARSDEL, W. B. 1951 A. Principles of the drying process, with special reference to vegetable dehydration. U. S. Dept. Agr. Bur. Circ. AIC-300.

VAN ARSDEL, W. B. 1951 B. Tunnel-and-truck dehydrators, as used in vegetable dehydration. U. S. Dept. Agr. Bur. Circ. AIC-308.

WIEGAND, E. H. 1923. Recirculation driers. Oregon Agr. Expt. Sta. Circ. *40*.

YULE, W. T. 1845. English patent, Jan. 28, for method of drying. Abstracted in J. Franklin Inst., Ser. III, *11*, 179–180 (1846).

CHAPTER 9

Some Theoretical Characteristics of
Other Types of Drying

CONTINUOUS THROUGH-FLOW CONVEYOR DRYING

Much of the recent modernization of vegetable dehydration plants has been stimulated by the development of continuous and substantially automatic driers. The truck-and-tray tunnel, although quasi-continuous, remains basically a series of batch driers; some mechanized forms have been tried, but their complexity has worked against them. As we have seen, however, some approximate relationships enable us to draw a great many useful conclusions about tunnel design and operation, while on the other hand the theory of the modern automatic through-flow drier, an inherently simple machine, remains forbiddingly complex. So far as we know, a satisfactory theory for the drying of hygroscopic materials in this kind of drier has never been developed. Some characteristics of conveyor driers used for commercial vegetable dehydration are described in the Management Handbook (U. S. Dept. of Agriculture 1959).

The analogue procedure commonly used as a basis for design calculations has been briefly described on pp. 126–127, above. Brown and Van Arsdel (1944, 1951) have published a nomograph for estimation of drying time of potato strips $5/_{32}$-in. square, by through-flow of air. Data are given for bed thicknesses ranging up to a unit loading of 4 lbs./sq. ft. and air flows from 100 to 250 cu. ft. per min. per sq. ft. A heavier layer of material is analyzed as though it were two or more superposed layers, independent of one another. This design procedure has not been tested experimentally.

For descriptions of commercial driers of this and related types see especially Marshall and Friedman pp. 823–828 (1950) and Kröll pp. 262–266 (1959). See also Volume II of this work.

BIN-DRYING, BATCH AND CONTINUOUS

Through-flow drying of a deep bed of granular, non-sticky material is now very widely used as a finishing step in the dehydration of piece-form vegetables, just as it has been used for a long time to reduce the moisture content of wet grain to a safe storage condition. (See especially the publications by Babbitt 1940; Hukill 1947; Simmonds et al. 1953; Becker and Sallans 1955; Hukill and Shedd 1955; and

O'Callaghan 1956.) In some respects the theory of the deep-bed finishing drier is simpler than the general theory of through-flow drying. In particular, all of the drying takes place in the lower end of the falling-rate domain, so that air velocity has no effect; no substantial further volume shrinkage occurs; finally, only a slight difference exists at any point in the bed between the temperatures of the material and of the air passing through it. At the same time, mathematical formulation of the behavior of this kind of drier is difficult because the interrelations between moisture content, temperature, and instantaneous drying rate at any point at any moment are non-linear, and temperature cannot be assumed constant. Van Arsdel (1955) derived the partial differential equations relating instantaneous moisture content of a material at a point in a deep bed to the temperature and humidity of drying air at the same point and to the drying rate and thermal properties of the material. He also described a procedure for numerical solution of these equations. Only fragmentary quantitative data of the kind necessary for a test of the procedure are available, but a partial test showed good qualitative agreement with known behavior of potato half-dice being dried from an initial moisture content of 0.12 by 130°F. air in a bed 3 ft. deep. Examples of application of the method both to a batch operation and to continuous drying in a stack-type drier were given. Application of bin driers in certain vegetable dehydration plants is described in the Management Handbook (U.S. Dept. of Agriculture 1959). See also Volume II of this work.

PNEUMATIC, OR AIR-SUSPENSION, DRYING

The well known method of drying finely divided solids while they are being conveyed in a hot air stream, often applied to the drying of wet minerals after passage through a hammermill or other disintegrator, has been used by a number of workers for the first-stage or rough drying of granulated cooked potatoes in the manufacture of potato granules. The method has also been applied on a large scale to reduction of the moisture content of spray dried egg powder from around three to four per cent to a maximum of 0.5–1.0 per cent in order to increase its stability in subsequent storage (Conrad et al. 1948). For descriptions of commercial driers of this type see especially Marshall and Friedman, pp. 834–838 (1950), and Kröll pp. 282–298 (1959).

The partial drying desired for potato granules takes place in a few seconds in the finely granulated wet potato, whose initial moisture content generally has been reduced to around 35 to 40 per cent by admixture of the fresh mash with recycled dry product ("add-back"). Most of the material is finer than 60-mesh, but a small proportion may be 20-mesh or coarser.   The moist granulated material is usually sucked into the conveying pipeline at a low-pressure throat ("Venturi").   Air velocity in the pipeline is sufficient to keep the coarser particles suspended—i.e., greater than the free-fall velocity of these particles—but not much greater, so as to avoid unnecessary abrasion damage to the delicate potato cells.   The length of the pipe is made great enough to give the necessary retention time at that air velocity. Ordinarily the conveying pipe will be disposed vertically, rather than horizontally, so that the product will not tend to settle out and drift along the bottom of the pipe.

The conveying section is generally terminated by a diverging section which helps to separate the light, completely dry particles from the heavier, still somewhat moist ones, and give the latter a longer residence time in the hot air.   The conveying riser ends with a cyclone collector where the granular solid is separated from the outgoing air stream.

Neel et al. (1954) obtained satisfactory single-stage drying of add-back mix from about 38 per cent moisture down to 11 per cent moisture when the inlet air temperature was from 280° to 380°F., air velocity 1,500 to 2,030 ft. per min., and the fall in air temperature ranged from 100° to 200°F.   Retention time in the drying section was of the order of only 2 to 3 sec.

Cooley et al. (1954) reported results from a pneumatic drier for potato granules, operated at a somewhat lower initial air temperature (250°F.) and higher air velocity (2600 ft. per min.).   By determining temperatures at various points along the vertical duct he was able to compute the moisture content of the granules as a function of distance traveled through the duct.   Fig. 49 shows that drying rate decreased very rapidly at first, but below a moisture content of about 0.25 the further decrease in moisture content was substantially linear with time of contact.

The information available is not sufficient to permit correlations with unit heat-transfer or mass-transfer rates, and equipment design remains limited by empirical knowledge of reasonably satisfactory existing installations.   The experience element is especially important in dealing with this particular product; even rather slight changes in design or operation are said to be reflected in substantial differences in the packing density of the dry granules (important from the standpoint of space-saving for military use) and the palatability of the reconstituted mashed potatoes.

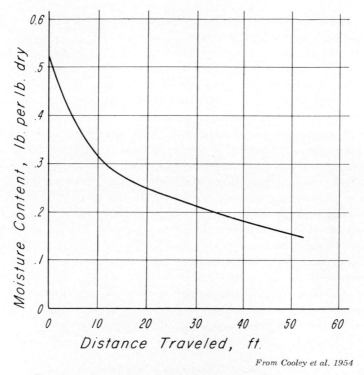

From Cooley et al. 1954

FIG. 49. COURSE OF MOISTURE CONTENT IN POTATO
GRANULES DURING TRAVEL IN VERTICAL
AIR-SUSPENSION DRIER

FLUIDIZED-BED DRYING

Neel *et al.* (1954) described application of the "fluidization" phenomenon to the finishing stage of potato granule manufacture. The phenomenon, used industrially on a very large scale for securing intimate contact between a powdered or granular solid and a gas, for example, in the catalytic cracking of petroleum vapors, is observed when gas pressure is applied beneath a finely porous diaphragm supporting a horizontal bed of fine granular material. At low gas pressure the gas flows between and around the solid particles without disturbing them, but if the pressure is gradually increased so that gas flow through the bed increases, a point is reached where the gas pressure almost lifts the entire bed. Any slight disturbance then causes a bubble of gas to break up through the bed, just as though the latter were liquid. The bed then continues in a condition of vigorous turbulence and "boiling"—and indeed, the bed acts like a fluid, seeking its own level like a fluid would. If the gas is hot and the solid particles in the granular bed are somewhat moist, excellent conditions for heat transfer and drying are created.

In application to potato granules (Olson and Harrington 1955), the moisture content of partially dried granules was readily reduced from 11 or 12 per cent moisture to three to five per cent in from 15 min. to $^1/_2$ hr. residence as a fluidized bed, using air at a temperature of from 300° to 400°F. below the porous diaphragm. In these experiments the bed was arranged for continuous flow, moist granules being continuously supplied at one end of the bed and dry granules continuously collected at the other end, which was arranged as a weir to meter the discharge, just as though the material were a liquid. Air supply to the bed was at a rate of 10 cu. ft. per min. per sq. ft. of bed area. Temperature measurements at the center of the porous plate showed a large temperature gradient through the plate, meaning that much of the heat used for drying is transferred through the plate by conduction, and that the hot air is cooled considerably before it comes into contact with the potato granules in the bed. Under these conditions the amount of heat added to inlet air per pound of water evaporated was only about 2,000 to 2,500 B.t.u.

For descriptions of commercial fluidized-bed installations see especially Kröll, pp. 275–281 (1959).

BELT-TROUGH DRYING

See Lowe *et al.* (1955) and the Management Handbook (U. S. Dept. Agriculture 1959) for a description of this very recent type of continuous through-flow drier, which has not yet been analyzed theoretically. Unusually high drying rates have been observed, probably because very high air temperature (as high as 300°F.) has been used without producing appreciable heat damage in vegetable pieces, and also because any individual piece of vegetable is exposed only momentarily to this very hot dry air and then spends a considerably longer time surrounded by air at a much lower temperature. During the latter phase the moisture inside individual pieces has some opportunity to "equalize"—that is, diffuse from wet centers into the very dry surface layers of the pieces. Thus when the piece travels again into the zone of intense drying, relatively rapid evaporation can take place once more.

DRUM DRYING

Drum drying has found application for production of a number of dry food products such as dry skim milk and dry whey, tomato juice flakes, comminuted chicken and other meat, potato flour, and especially since the development by Cording *et al.* (1954) at the Eastern Regional Research Laboratory, mashed potato flakes. In all of these uses the single-drum drier has been found superior to the double drum which is more widely used for drying industrial materials. Spadaro and Patton, however, of the Southern Utilization Research and Development Division (1961), have recently produced sweet potato flakes successfully by drying the precooked and puréed material on a double-drum drier (see also Deobald *et al.* 1962).

Little has been published on the principles of this operation. Marshall and Friedman, in the Chemical Engineers Handbook, pp. 863–866 (1950) give a few data on the over-all heat transfer coefficient from high pressure steam to moist material on a double-drum drier, but nothing on the single-drum drier. Cording *et al.* (1957) studied the relation between solids content of a potato mash, drum speed, steam pressure, product moisture content, rate of product output, and bulk density of dry sheet leaving the drum, but did not derive a heat transfer coefficient. A mash containing 80 per cent moisture can be reduced to five per cent moisture in about 20 sec. The air surrounding the drum, containing much water vapor, is usually moved into an exhaust stack by natural ventilation, but sometimes is exhausted mechanically so that the humidity at this point can be controlled at a desired level.

SPRAY DRYING

This method of drying, appropriately for its high industrial importance, appears to have received more intensive (and perhaps more sophisticated) study by physicists and engineers than any other. Its inherent theoretical complexity, which makes it a forbidding subject for experimental attack, contrasts strongly with its basic simplicity; one just sprays the liquid material into a stream of hot air and collects the resulting dust. Concentrated non-fat milk is spray dried; so are egg products and concentrated coffee and tea extracts. Many other food products, ranging from mashed potato to ground and homogenized chicken meat, have also been spray dried. The types of equipment used are described in considerable detail by Marshall and Friedman, pp. 838–848 (1950) and Kröll, pp. 303–324 (1959).

The principles of spray drying, with special emphasis on the principles of the formation of very fine sprays, have recently been treated in a monograph by Marshall (1954). Other important publications are those of Philip (1935), Fogler and Kleinschmidt (1938), Lapple and Shepherd (1940), Johnstone *et al.* (1941), Diemair (1941), Seltzer and Settelmeyer (1949), Marshall and Seltzer (1950), Duffie and

Marshall (1953), Lazar *et al*. (1956), Dlouhy and Gauvin (1960), and Charlesworth and Marshall (1960).

Complex and difficult physical problems, still only partially solved, arise in analysis of all three of the steps that make up a spray-drying operation—forming the spray, contacting the spray droplets with hot air in the drying chamber, and separating the resulting dry powder from the cooler and more humid exhaust air. Only the second of these is a drying problem pure and simple, but the three steps cannot usefully be considered apart from one another. The atomization step is so crucial that Marshall felt justified in devoting more than half of his monograph to that topic alone.

Three types of spray-forming device are most important—centrifugal or swirl-type, spinning disk, and pneumatic or two-fluid atomizer. Theoretical and experimental investigations have combined to give a fair quantitative picture of the statistical distribution of droplet sizes in sprays produced in each of these ways, and of the operating characteristics and power consumption of the atomizers. Such variables as density, viscosity, and surface tension of the liquid, and the relative velocity of the liquid and the surrounding air at the point of junction, have been studied in great detail.

Evaporation from a small liquid drop moving through a turbulent body of hot air under the influence of gravity and its own initial kinetic energy is a complicated function of the simultaneous conduction and convection of heat from the air to the drop surface and diffusion and convection of water vapor back into the body of air. Each droplet experiences a retarding force due to skin friction and form drag. The former is caused by viscous resistance of the air at the drop surface and the latter is caused by the bodily motion of the droplet, which produces eddies in the air on the trailing side of the drop, because of the separation of a boundary layer. The force acting on a droplet is defined by a drag coefficient which varies according to the shape assumed by the drop, and this shape is not only changing very rapidly, in wave-like pulsations, but is also changing materially and permanently as the solute in the drop becomes concentrated and finally solid. The time required for complete evaporation of a droplet of pure water was computed by Duffie and Marshall (1953) for various temperature gradients; for example, if the drop temperature is 55°C. and the temperature gradient is 250°C., a drop 0.06 mm. in diameter should evaporate completely in 0.12 sec.; at 0.15 mm. diameter, 0.7 sec.; at 0.4 mm. diameter, 5 sec.; and at 0.55 mm. diameter, 10 sec. The extreme importance of uniformly small drops is obvious. Of course when a solution of hygroscopic material is being evaporated the drying time may be very greatly lengthened. Equations derived by Ranz and Marshall (1952) for total drying time of drops containing a dissolved non-hygroscopic solid might perhaps be modified to take account of the great reduction of water vapor pressure seen in nearly dry hygroscopic materials.

The residence time of a given particle in the drying chamber and the history of air temperature and humidity in its immediate environment during that entire period are products of an interplay of chamber design and various operating factors that is too complex for analysis. In the absence of quantitative and detailed knowledge, design of spray driers remains in large part an art, based upon successes and failures in past experience. The design of the dust separation and collection system which forms the final essential piece in the spray drier picture depends almost as completely upon cautious extrapolations from past experience with successful driers.

Numerous modifications of the spray drying technique are being studied by various groups, generally with the aim of fitting the properties of the dry product to specific end uses. In one of the early procedures applied especially to milk (Heath and Washburn 1922) a somewhat soluble inert gas, such as carbon dioxide or nitrogen, was dissolved in the feed liquid under pressure. Its liberation at the point of spraying was said to reduce the bacterial content of the dry product and improve its flavor. Modifications of the procedure have recently been described by Chase and Laursen (1956), Reich and Johnston (1957), Hanrahan and Webb (1961), and Sugihara et al. (1962).

A dramatically different spray drying method developed by P. Hussmann and the Birs A. G., Basel, Switzerland, has been put into operation by I. D. I. T., Siena, Italy, and was very recently described by Ziemba (1962). Tomato juice or concentrate, or other liquid food product, is sprayed into the top of a gigantic empty tower (50 ft. in diameter, 220 ft. high, larger diameters planned) in very uniform small droplets. Dehumidified and filtered air at essentially room temperature (not over 86°F.) rises through the tower at a velocity carefully controlled to give the droplets a free-fall time of about 90 to 200 sec.—sufficient to reduce the material to dryness in a single pass, even at this moderate temperature. The 50-ft. tower evaporates 2,200 lbs. of water per hour from 3,000 lbs. of tomato concentrate. Air leaves the top of the tower at a relative humidity above 80 per cent.

The dry product settling to the bottom of the tower is recovered in a cyclone separator, and the finer fractions are returned to the tower for recycling in order to control the particle size. Particles are said to be spherical and extremely porous, but not hollow like most spray-dried material. Dry product reconstitutes readily in cold water.

VACUUM DRYING

Vacuum drying, applied for many years on a relatively small scale to certain fruit products (Falk *et al.* 1919; Havighorst 1944) has recently received wider attention through development of puff-drying and freeze-drying processes. These make use of the fact that the boiling point of water is lowered below 212°F. if the atmospheric pressure is reduced. They differ in that in freeze drying the system pressure is maintained so low that the boiling point is kept below 32°F. so that the water in the material remains frozen and must sublime away from the dry solids, while in ordinary vacuum drying, including the special technique of puff drying, system pressure is somewhat higher so that the water is always evaporated from the liquid state.

Published descriptions of the vacuum drying process used to produce such foods as "apple nuggets" (Havighorst 1944) contain little information that would throw light on heat transfer relations or the mechanism of moisture removal under these conditions. Ordinarily the moisture content of the fruit is brought down to the "dried fruit range," 20 to 25 per cent, in a conventional dehydrator. Then the pieces are chopped to small slices or dice. These are loaded on trays and dried to a moisture content of only 1 to 3 per cent in a vacuum shelf drier. Pressure and shelf temperature are both controlled according to an empirically determined time schedule meant to secure rapid drying without perceptible heat damage. At one stage of this schedule the system pressure may be reduced suddenly so as to produce an instant boiling effect in each piece, thus expanding it materially. The somewhat porous condition of the product is maintained all the way to dryness, being highly advantageous in promoting rapid rehydration when the product is used.

Two related processes, under investigation by the Eastern Utilization Research and Development Division, U. S. Department of Agriculture (Anon. 1962; Eisenhardt *et al.* 1962) are "pressure-puff" drying and the "vacuum-foam" method. In the former, which has produced good results on certain vegetables, partially dried pieces of the material are heated in a closed vessel until a pressure of 40 to 60 lbs. per sq. in. of pressure builds up; when the pressure is then released suddenly, as in the well known process for puffing cereal grains, the pieces expand materially and maintain a porous structure during final drying. The "vacuum-foam" process has been successfully applied to concentrated whole milk (Sinnamon *et al.* 1957). The concentrate is chilled, foamed by dispersing nitrogen gas into it, and the foam is fed through special nozzles onto a belt drier operating at a pressure of about 16 mm. absolute.

Still another vacuum process, also introduced by the Eastern Division, produces dry powders from fruit juices which will stand concentration at a relatively high temperature without damage, such as apple, Concord grape, and Montmorency cherry juices (Turkot *et al.* 1956) or honey (Turkot *et al.* 1960). The process for fruit juice comprises first stripping out the volatile flavoring compounds and recovering them as a concentrated "essence"; depectinizing, filtering, and evaporating under vacuum to about 75 per cent solids; dissolving additional sucrose to the extent of from 50 per cent (grape or cherry) to 100 per cent (apple) of the weight of juice solids, and adjusting the acidity; concentrating the warm solution continuously in a single pass through a mechanically agitated thin-film evaporator, operating at about 3 to 4 in. of mercury absolute pressure, and discharging the molten and nearly anhydrous product at a temperature of 225° to 235°F. The molten product is mixed with a metered quantity of the recovered volatile essence and is immediately solidified in the form of flakes on a chilled roll. The flakes are coarsely crushed and then sealed in a can with an in-package desiccant.

Less and less of the heat required for evaporation can be supplied by convection of air as the system pressure is reduced, so greater and greater reliance must be placed on heat transfer by conduction from a heated support or by radiation from a high-temperature source. Both of these expedients have characteristic limitations. The difficulty of transferring heat by conduction was graphically shown by Ernst *et al.* (1938) for the vacuum shelf drying of a gelatinous pigment which had been spread uniformly on the tray while wet and which shrank materially upon drying. As it shrank it pulled away from the tray and curled up, losing its heat transfer contact. The drying rate fell almost to zero. Radiative heat transfer, which always proceeds in a straight line from the hot source to a cooler surface it can "see," faces the inherent difficulty that if the source is raised to a really high temperature in order to increase its heat output, any momentary failure of automatic control exposes the product to risk of surface scorching. On the other hand, the thermal inertia of heavy shelves heated by steam or circulating oil is so high that close control of product temperature is difficult; the low inertia of a radiative heat source, and the consequent rapid response to control, is advantageous in that way.

Types of equipment used for vacuum drying, including freeze drying, are described by Marshall and Friedman, pp. 853–856 (1950), and Kröll, pp. 496–529 (1959). The application of radio-frequency heating is described briefly by Marshall and Friedman, pp. 870–871, 874.

Puff Drying

A special technique of vacuum drying known as "puff drying" (see especially Strashun and Talburt 1953; Kaufman et al. 1955; Copley et al. 1956; Notter et al. 1959; Fixari et al. 1959) is being used for the dehydration of fruit juices whose delicate flavors are especially subject to heat damage. Much earlier work by many investigators had developed many of the necessary techniques, but had not resulted in products that were fully satisfactory in flavor and stability. Experimental work has generally been done in a vacuum shelf drier. Eventually the design and techniques of operation of a continuous drier were mastered, mainly by empirical methods. Little has been published that can be related to the physical mechanisms of heat and mass transfer.

The puffing phenomenon itself, observed by several of the earliest experimenters, has been recognized to be important to successful operation of the technique, not only because of the ease with which the flaky, porous dry product can be reconstituted to beverage juice consistency in cold water, but also because the rate of drying of a layer of concentrated juice is much greater if the puffing is allowed to take place than if it is prevented.

Freeze Drying

The degree of public interest in the freeze drying of various foods and the extent of scientific and popular publication about its development are indeed extraordinary in view of the fact that regular commercial production of freeze-dried food products has become a fact only during the past ten years. In some respects the process is still feeling its way as a means of food preservation, and many workers are trying to discover its true potentialities for large-scale use. For many years it was regarded as applicable only to biological materials like blood plasma and penicillin, and inherently too expensive to have any practical significance for foods; this is no longer a realistic appraisal.

We shall attempt to summarize some of the significant contributions to understanding of the principles involved, but not to abstract the numerous descriptive articles that have appeared in popular and scientific publications.   Especially pertinent are the books by Flosdorf (1949), Harris (1954), Neumann (1955), Rey (1960), and the British Ministry of Agriculture, Fisheries, and Food (1961), and technical articles by Campbell *et al.* (1945), Ede (1949), Zamzow and Marshall (1952), Gane (1954), Gersh and Stephenson (1954), Greaves (1954), Cooke and Sherwood (1955), Harper and Tappel (1957), Kramers (1958), Ginnette *et al.* (1959), Harper and Chichester (1960 A, B), Seltzer (1960), Brockmann (1960), Gröschner *et al.* (1960), Tchigeov (1960), and Ward (1961).

The drying of a substance from the frozen state (variously called "freeze drying," "sublimation drying," or "lyophilization") depends basically upon creation and maintenance of a difference in water vapor pressure between the very dry immediate surroundings of a piece of substance and the ice in the frozen interior of the piece, so that water vapor is continuously transported away from the piece but the ice in the piece never melts.   The result is that surface forces are unable to produce shrinkage as drying proceeds.   When the product is frozen water is withdrawn from the highly hydrated colloids of the food substance, first by crystallization of pure ice and then, if temperature is low enough, crystallization of the remaining more concentrated solution, in the form of one or more eutectics; evaporation removes water from the surface of a piece, most rapidly from the exposed crystals of pure ice, somewhat less rapidly from exposed eutectic because the vapor pressure of the latter is somewhat lower than that of ice.   Sublimation of the water, the solid constituents being completely immobilized, leaves behind a light, microporous structure of substantially the same dimensions as the original piece.   Reabsorption of water into this spongy material is not only very rapid, but is usually quite complete as well because little denaturation of proteins and other sensitive colloidal constituents takes place.

Ordinarily the necessary vapor pressure gradient is produced by operating the equipment at a moderately high vacuum (generally in the range of 0.1 to 2 mm. of mercury, absolute pressure), providing a low-temperature condenser in the vapor space, with wide and unobstructed passage for vapor coming from the evaporating surfaces of the frozen body, and supplying a steady flow of heat to the frozen body so as to keep its temperature higher than that of the ice at the condenser, but not high enough to cause melting anywhere within the body.   However, the vacuum is not theoretically necessary; Meryman (1959) and Lewin and Mateles (1962) showed that the necessary vapor pressure gradient can be obtained by circulating desiccated cold air over the frozen material at atmospheric pressure. Not enough work has been done with this procedure to indicate whether it is practically feasible.

Heat equal to the latent heat of sublimation of ice at its temperature in the zone of evaporation within the body being dried (see Table 11) must be continuously supplied to that zone in order to keep the temperature there from falling and thus diminishing the vapor pressure gradient and the rate of further drying. In all commercial freeze drying the transfer of this necessary heat is the major rate-limiting factor.

TABLE 11

VAPOR PRESSURE AND HEAT OF SUBLIMATION OF ICE

Temperature		Vapor Pressure (mm. Hg.)	Heat of Sublimation (B.t.u./lb.)
°C.	°F.		
0	32	4.58	1,220
−10	14	1.95	1,210
−20	−4	0.776	1,200
−30	−22	0.286	1,192
−40	−40	0.097	1,186
−50	−58	0.030	1,181

Note: European terminology often expresses a pressure of 1 mm. Hg. as "1 Torr." 1 atmosphere = 760 mm. Hg.

Some divergence of opinion exists regarding the importance of rapid freezing of the material and storage at a very low temperature, so as to create and maintain very small ice crystals, but there is no doubt that the rate of freezing does have an effect on the subsequent rate of drying. According to Gane (1954) slow freezing has an adverse effect on the quality of freeze-dried meat and fish, because, as pointed out also by Greaves (1954), the sensitive proteins are partly denatured by long contact with the increasingly concentrated liquid phase as ice is frozen out. All the water in meat is frozen at −37.5°C. Residual liquid phase, of eutectic composition, finally freezes out of fruit juices at about −25°C., while the solutes from coffee extract freeze out at about −10°C. Of course it is advantageous to accelerate the drying by maintaining the temperature within the frozen body at the *maximum* safe level. Ordinarily, the upper temperature limit will be that at which melting just does not occur; melting would cause collapse or coalescence of the partly dry product, destroying the finely porous structure needed to promote rapid and complete reconstitution when the product is used.

The lower limit of temperature of the ice phase within the body will be that temperature for which the saturation vapor pressure of ice equals the system pressure; for example, if the latter is 0.3 mm. of mercury, the ice in the pieces of material will be in equilibrium at $-22\,°F$. (Table 11), and the temperature must be higher than that. The pressure of water vapor in the porous surface layer must be greater than the system pressure in order to produce flow of vapor from the interior to the surface of a piece, and from thence to the condenser or vacuum pump. In the foregoing example, suppose that pressure at the evaporating zone within a piece were 1.95 mm. of mercury. This is the vapor pressure of ice at $14\,°F$., and if the melting point of a eutectic in the frozen material were, say, $0\,°F$., some thawing would be occurring within the body of material. In order to operate properly, heat input from all sources would have to be reduced so as to lower both the temperature and the vapor pressure within the frozen pieces; rate of drying could not be forced that much without damaging the quality of the product.

Even when all the ice phase is gone, the spongy solid will still contain a small amount of water adsorbed in the internal structure of carbohydrates, proteins, and other high-molecular weight constituents, but its structure will not now collapse if the temperature is raised. The moisture content at this point, corresponding to equilibrium with almost-saturated water vapor at the temperature of the solid, will ordinarily be too high for satisfactory stability in food distribution. Whether the process should be continued all the way to a satisfactorily low-moisture level (for example, one to four per cent moisture) in the same equipment, possibly accelerated by a deliberate increase in temperature, or had better be broken off as soon as the last of the ice phase is gone, leaving a final drying stage to be done in a bin-drying operation or by in-package desiccation, would depend on a balance of economic factors.

The quantitative study of freeze drying has been approached either by analysis of the water vapor transport mechanism, with experimental study of particular rate-determining factors (Ede; Cooke and Sherwood; Harper and Tappel; Kramers; and Harper and Chichester A, B) or by empirical correlation of results obtained under conditions simulating practice (Ginnette et al.). An advantage of the latter is that results are immediately applicable to design or operation for the particular raw materials that have been studied; its drawback is that its predictive value for conditions that are a little different is quite limited. We shall give a summarizing sketch of the approach through analysis of transport mechanisms, and describe the correlations reported by Ginnette et al.

Analysis of Mechanism.—The physical mechanisms involved

most critically in freeze drying include: (1) the transport of water vapor from the ice core to the surface of a frozen product through the finely porous outer layer from which ice has already been vaporized; (2) the transport of water vapor from the surface of the body to the vacuum pump or low-temperature condenser; and (3) the supply of the necessary amount of heat to the zone of ice evaporation.

Evaporation takes place directly from an ice surface only at the very beginning of drying; almost immediately this ice disappears from the surface, leaving there a finely porous ice-free solid. The rate of sublimation thereafter is determined to a large extent by the resistance to flow of the water vapor from the boundary of the ice phase inside the piece through this porous solid layer. This resistance in turn is a function of the number, arrangement, and size distribution of the open pores or voids left in place of the ice.

Harper and Tappel and Harper and Chichester report studies of the resistance of freeze-dried beef, peach, and apple to flow of water vapor and several gases. Porosity, or proportion of voids, for the three materials averaged 0.64, 0.91, and 0.88, respectively, and the mean diameter of the voids was generally in the range of 50 to 300 microns. Increasing the rate of freezing decreased the mean pore diameter, corresponding to a decreased growth of the ice crystals. Isothermal flow of water vapor through such a material is described by the following equation:

$$G = \frac{\mathbf{P}M(\Delta p)}{\mu l T}\left[p_m + \frac{0.269}{\mathbf{P}^{1/2}}\right] \tag{61}$$

where, if we adopt Harper and Chichester's units

G = mass velocity of vapor (gm.)/(hr.)(cm.)^2
M = molecular weight, 18
(Δp) = pressure drop producing flow (mm. Hg.)
μ = dynamic viscosity of the water vapor (centipoise)
l = length of path (cm.)
T = absolute temperature (°K.)
p_m = mean pressure of water vapor in the porous body (mm. Hg.)
$\mathbf{P}$ = permeability of the porous material (gm.)(cp.)(°K.)/(hr.)(cm.)-(mm. Hg.)^2

Numerical value of the permeability for the freeze-dried beef, peach, and apple was found to range between 0.0004 and 0.003 in the above units.

This vapor flow through the porous solid can best be described as taking place by two separate flow mechanisms, as is suggested by the form of the above equation. The first of these is governed by the same factors that govern the flow of fluids through capillaries in laminar (*i.e.*, streamline) flow, following Poiseuille's law, or in the flow through porous solids, following Darcy's law. Fluid in contact with solid walls is pictured as remaining stationary, so that a diagram of the velocity of motion versus distance from the centerline of a capillary would contain a maximum at the centerline, and would show the velocity falling to zero at the solid boundaries (see Fig. 8, p. 39). At atmospheric pressure and down to a pressure of, say, 10 mm., this is the only significant mechanism for laminar flow of air or water vapor. At lower pressures the motions of individual molecules begin to be significant, and "slip-flow" at the solid boundaries begins to play a part. When the mean free path of a molecule becomes longer than, say, twice the diameter of a capillary or pore opening, as it does when the system pressure is very low, free molecular motion, or "Knudsen flow," becomes the principal flow mechanism. In this region the rate of flow of water vapor through a porous solid layer, per unit of pressure difference, is almost unaffected by a change in the mean pressure; thus, little advantage in rate is gained by reducing the system pressure to a very low value, such as only a few microns of mercury. Ultra-high vacuum is unnecessary.

The thermal conductivity of the freeze-dried material, a vital factor in determining how rapidly external heat can safely be supplied to the zone of ice sublimation, was determined experimentally by Harper and Chichester. At pressures near atmospheric, heat is transferred in part by conductance through the water vapor in the pores and in part by conductance through the porous solid structure itself. At low pressures only the latter pathway remains and the conductivity is lower. Harper and Chichester found the conductivity of the freeze-dried apple, peach, and pear flesh to be approximately 0.01 (B.t.u.)/(hr.)(sq. ft.)(°F.) at low system pressures, about 0.025 at atmospheric pressure. The conductivity of the freeze-dried beef was about 0.02 at low pressure, 0.04 at atmospheric pressure. Conductivities at a pressure of 1 mm. were just about midway between these two levels.

Much experimentation has been devoted to the key problem of transferring heat rapidly and controllably to the evaporating zone. The methods now in commercial use rely upon contributions from both conducted heat and radiated heat. Some experimentation with radio-frequency, or dielectric, heating has been reported, but difficulties of temperature control and injury to the surfaces of the food product due to ionization of the low-pressure vapor (apparently leading to accelerated oxidation of the product) have combined to keep this promising way of putting the heat energy exactly where it is needed from becoming a practical success.

Correlation of Drying Rates.—Ginnette *et al.* (1959) considered the freeze drying of solid tissues represented by $1/2$ x $1/2$ x $3/16$-in. pieces of carrot, apple, and lean beef, and $1/2$-in. cubes of carrot. Single layers of the frozen pieces were supported on a horizontal heating platen with their smallest dimension vertical. Weight changes were recorded continuously. Drying runs were made at system pressures of 0.5, 1, and 3 mm. of mercury, and with constant platen temperatures of 0°, 45°, 90°, 135°, and 180°F. The condenser, parallel to the layer of frozen material and only a few inches away, was kept at a temperature as low as −40°F. Temperature of a piece of the drying material was measured throughout each run. Drying was carried only to removal of 90 to 95 per cent of the initial moisture content— that is, it included only what has been called "rough freeze drying," on the assumption that the remainder of the necessary drying is more economically carried out by bin-drying or in-package desiccation Hendel *et al.* (1958). The initial moisture content, W_0, of the three materials averaged 2.7 (lbs.)/(lb. dry) for the beef, 5.3 for the carrots, and 6.7 for the apples.

Drying rate as a function of time and moisture content was correlated with system pressure, with the difference between temperature of the platen and temperature of the drying piece, and with the difference between the vapor pressures of ice at the temperatures of the drying piece and the low-temperature condenser.

Drying rate in all cases started out very low, but increased to a maximum as the material warmed up to an equilibrium temperature, and this warm-up period occupied an appreciable part of the total time at the higher platen temperatures. Immediately after reaching the maximum, the rate began to decrease steadily; no constant-rate period was seen. Fig. 50 presents unsmoothed results from carrot drying experiments at five different platen temperatures.

Material temperature, beginning in all cases at temperatures in the range of −20° to +5°F., rose almost linearly with change in moisture content until only about 10 to 20 per cent of the original moisture remained, and then rose very rapidly. In the experiments on carrots, the melting point of ice was reached when about 80 per cent of the initial moisture had been removed in the runs at platen temperatures of 180° and 135°F., but not until the moisture was almost completely removed when the platen temperature was only 45°F.

The authors consider the geometry and physics of the situation and base correlations upon the simplifying assumptions that the pieces are spherical and that the remaining moisture content at any time is entirely contained in the frozen spherical core of each piece. Resist-

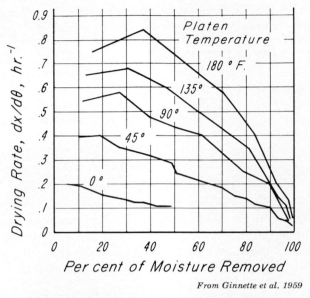

Per cent of Moisture Removed

From Ginnette et al. 1959

FIG. 50. RATE OF FREEZE-DRYING OF CARROT
HALF-DICE AS A FUNCTION OF PLATEN TEMPERATURE

ance to flow of the water vapor from this constantly shrinking surface
through the finely porous "dry" shell constitutes the only significant
resistance to vapor flow.   Under these conditions the ratio of the
vapor pressure difference (between the ice core and the ice on the
condenser) to the drying rate should be a linear function of the following expression:

$$\frac{1 - (1 - x)^{1/3}}{(1 - x)^{2/3}}$$

where x is the fraction of the moisture content removed.   This correlation can be written as follows:

$$\frac{p_{ip} - p_{ic}}{dx/d\theta} = \frac{k_2 r_0}{3} + \frac{k_1 r_0^2 [1 - (1 - x)^{1/3}]}{3 \quad (1 - x)^{2/3}} \tag{62}$$

where

p_{ip} = vapor pressure of ice at the temperature of the core of the piece (mm.
          Hg.)
p_{ic} = vapor pressure office at the temperature of the condenser (mm.
          Hg.)
r_0 = initial radius of the piece (cm.)
k_1 = constant (mm. Hg.)(hr.)/(cm.)^2
k_2 = constant (mm. Hg.)(hr.)/(cm.)

For the conditions of their experiments on carrot pieces, the authors found constant $k_2 r_0/3$ to be approximately 1.0. Experimental data clustered closely around a straight 45° line on a plot of

$$\log\left[\frac{p_{ip} - p_{ic}}{dx/d\theta} - 1.0\right] \text{ against } \log \frac{[1 - (1 - x)^{1/3}]}{(1 - x)^{2/3}}$$

thus lending support to this analysis. For this lot of $^1/_2 \text{ x } ^1/_2 \text{ x } ^3/_{16}$-in. carrot dice the empirical drying rate expression thus found, as a function of vapor pressure difference and moisture content, was as follows:

$$\frac{dx}{d\theta} = \frac{p_{ip} - p_{ic}}{1.0 + 7.58\{[1 - (1 - x)^{1/3}]/[(1 - x)^{2/3}]\}}$$

The vapor pressure difference is completely determined when the temperatures of the condenser and the ice core in the piece are known, and the latter can be deduced from the experimental data relating difference between platen temperature and piece temperature to the drying rate and moisture content. When data from all the runs on carrot, apple, and beef pieces were correlated by plotting

$$\frac{t_p - t_{ip}}{dx/d\theta} \text{ against } \frac{1 - (1 - x)^{1/3}}{(1 - x)^{1/3}}$$

where

t_p = temperature of the platen (°F.)
t_{ip} = temperature of the ice core in the pieces (°F.)

the straight regression line led to the following empirical expression for the temperature of the ice core in terms of drying rate and moisture content:

$$t_{ip} = t_p - \frac{dx}{d\theta}\left\{216\left[\frac{1 - (1 - x)^{1/3}}{(1 - x)^{1/3}}\right] + 120\right\} \tag{64}$$

The total pressure maintained in the drying chamber had a decided effect on the piece temperature at any given moisture level; for example, in carrot pieces, raising the system pressure from 0.5 to 3 mm. Hg raised the temperature of the pieces from 8° to 23°F. at the point where 0.4 of the moisture had been removed. The drying rate was also increased at that point from 0.48 to 0.72 hr.$^{-1}$. The reason for the increase in drying rate appears to be that an increase in heat transfer from the platen to the sample occurs which outweighs the decrease in temperature difference.

The authors conclude that the rate of drying is primarily determined by the temperature of the platen and the size of the piece. Heat transfer from the platen to the piece is virtually independent of the nature of the material.

FOAM-MAT DRYING

The very new procedure given the name "foam-mat drying" by the group of workers at the Western Regional Research Laboratory who developed it, has been applied to the production of high-quality powders from a very wide variety of liquid food concentrates prepared from fruits, vegetables, milk, meats, coffee, and also from certain starch- or pectin-based puddings (Morgan *et al*. 1959; Ramage 1960; Morgan *et al*, 1961; Lawler, 1962). Essentially the process is convection drying in warm air, the concentrated material being first converted to a stable foam which is spread in a thin layer on the supporting surface. Under these conditions complete drying is accomplished in from 2 or 3 min. to $^1/_2$ hr. Data from which the effects of pertinent system variables can be evaluated have not yet been published.

BIBLIOGRAPHY

ANON. 1962. Foam dehydration techniques. Food Eng. *34*, No. 2, 42.

BABBITT, J. D. 1940. Observations on the permeability of hygroscopic materials to water vapor. Can. J. Research *18(A)*, 105–121. NRC No. 907.

BECKER, H. A., and SALLANS, H. R. 1955. A study of internal moisture movement in the drying of the wheat kernel. Cereal Chem. *32*, No. 3, 212–226.

BRITISH MINISTRY OF AGRICULTURE, FISHERIES, AND FOOD. 1961. The Accelerated Freeze-drying (AFD) Method of Food Preservation. H. M. Stationery Office, London. *See also* Hanson, S.W.F., Editor.

BROCKMANN, M. C. 1960. Time requirements for processing freeze-dehydrated foods. Proc. 10th. Int. Congress of Refrigeration *3*, Rept. 4–55, 35–39.

BROWN, A. H., LAZAR, M. E., WASSERMAN, T., SMITH, G. S., and COLE, M. W. 1951. Rapid heat processing of fluid foods by steam injection. Ind. Eng. Chem. *43*, 2949–2954.

BROWN, A. H., and VAN ARSDEL, W. B. 1944, 1951. Drying rate nomographs. III. White potato strips—vertical air flow. U. S. Dept. Agr. Bur. Circ. AIC-31-III.

BURTON, W. G. 1944. Mashed potato powder. II. Spray drying method. J. Soc. Chem. Ind. *63*, 213–215.

CAMPBELL, W. L., PROCTOR, B. E., and SLUDER, J. C. 1945. Development of dehydrated citrus powders. Ann. Rpt. QM Contracts 1944–1945. OQMG, Mil. Planning Div., Res. and Devel. Branch, Mass. Inst. Technology, Cambridge, Mass. 2–181.

CHARLESWORTH, D. H., and MARSHALL, W. R., JR. 1960. Evaporation from drops containing dissolved solids. A.I.Ch.E. Jour. *6*, 9–23.

CHASE, F. A. and LAURSEN, G. E. 1956. Carbonation of coffee extract. U. S. Pat. 2,771,364. Nov. 20.

CONRAD, R. M., VAIL, G. E., OLSON, A. L., TINKLIN, R. T., GREENE, J. W., and WAGONER, C. E. 1948. Improved dried whole egg products. Kansas State Agr. Coll. Expt. Sta. Bull. *64*.

COOKE, N. E., and SHERWOOD, T. K. 1955. The effect of pressure on the rate of sublimation. Proc. 9th Int. Congress of Refrigeration *1*, Rept. 2–79, No. 2, 133–141.

COOLEY, A. M., SEVERSON, D. E., PEIGHTAL, D. E., and WAGNER, J. R. 1954. Studies on dehydrated potato granules. Food Technol. *8*, 263–269.

COPLEY, M. J., KAUFMAN, V. F., and RASMUSSEN, C. L. 1956. Recent developments in fruit and vegetable powder technology. Food Technol. *10*, 589–595.

CORDING, J., JR., WILLARD, M. J., JR., ESKEW, R. K., and EDWARDS, P. W. 1954. Potato flakes, a new form of dehydrated mashed potatoes. I. Pilot-plant process using double-drum drier. U. S. Dept. Agr., Agricultural Research Service, Circ. ARS-73-2.

CORDING, J., JR., WILLARD, M. J., JR., ESKEW, R. K., and EDWARDS, P. W. 1955. Potato flakes, a new form of dehydrated mashed potatoes. II. Some factors influencing texture. U. S. Dept. Agr., Agricultural Research Service, Circ. ARS-73-9.

CORDING, J., JR., WILLARD, M. J., JR., ESKEW, R. K., and SULLIVAN, J. F. 1957. Advances in the dehydration of mashed potatoes. Food Technol. *11*, 236–240.

DEOBALD, H. A., MCLEMORE, T. A., MCFARLANE, V. H., ROBY, M. T., PERYAM, D. R., and HEILIGMAN, F. 1962. Precooked dehydrated sweet potato flakes. U. S. Dept. Agr. Circ. ARS-72-23, and QM Food and Container Inst. Coop. Paper No. 2115.

DIEMAIR, W. 1941. The Preservation of Foodstuffs. (In German.) F. Enke Verlag, Stuttgart.

DLOUHY, J., and GAUVIN, W. H. 1960. Heat and mass transfer in spray drying. A.I.Ch.E. Jour. *6*, 29–34.

DUFFIE, J. A., and MARSHALL, W. R., JR. 1953. Factors influencing the properties of spray dried materials. Chem. Eng. Progr. *49*, 417–423, 480–486.

EDE, A. J. 1949. Physics of the low-temperature vacuum drying process. J. Soc. Chem. Ind. *68*, 330–332, 336–340.

EISENHARDT, N. H., CORDING, J., JR., ESKEW, R. K., and SULLIVAN, J. F. 1962. Quick-cooking dehydrated vegetable pieces. I. Properties of potato and carrot products. Food Technol. *16*, No. 5, 143–146.

ERNST, R. C., ARDERN, D. B., SCHMIED, O. K., and TILLER, F. M. 1938. Drying commercial solids. Ind. Eng. Chem. *30*, 1119–1125.

ESKEW, R. K., REDFIELD, C. S., CORDING, J., JR., WILLARD, M. J., JR., CLAFFEY, J. R., EDWARDS, P. W., and SULLIVAN, J. F. 1956. Potato flakes, a new form of dehydrated mashed potatoes. III. Estimated commercial cost. U. S. Dept. Agr. Circ. ARS-73-12.

FALK, K. G., FRANKEL, E. M., and MCKEE, R. H. 1919. Low temperature-vacuum food dehydration. Ind. Eng. Chem. *11*, 1036–1040.

FIXARI, F., CONLEY, W., and BARD, G. 1959. Continuous high vacuum drying techniques. Food Technol. *13*, 217–220.

FLOSDORF, E. W. 1949. Freeze Drying—Drying by Sublimation. Reinhold Publishing Co., New York.

FOGLER, B. B., and KLEINSCHMIDT, R. V. 1938. Spray drying. Ind. Eng. Chem. *30*, 1372–1384.

GANE, R. 1954. The freeze-drying of foodstuffs. *From* Biological Applications of Freezing and Drying. Academic Press, Inc., New York.

GERSH, I., and STEPHENSON, J. L. 1954. Freezing and drying of tissues for morphological and histochemical studies. *From* Biological Applications of Freezing and Drying. Academic Press, Inc., New York.

GINNETTE, L. F., GRAHAM, R. P., and MORGAN, A. I., JR. 1959. Freeze drying rates. National Symposium on Vacuum Technology, American Vacuum Society, Inc., Trans. V., 268–273. Pergamon Press, New York.

GREAVES, R. I. N. 1954. Theoretical aspects of drying by vacuum sublimation. *From* Biological Applications of Freezing and Drying pp. 87–127. Academic Press, Inc. New York.

GRÖSCHNER, E., HAMANN, O., and SCHARNBECK, M. 1960. Freeze-drying, a modern preservation method for highly perishable foods. Proc. 10th Int. Congress of Refrigeration *3*, Rept. 4–29, 39–44.

HANRAHAN, F. P., and WEBB, B. H. 1961. USDA develops foam-spray drying. Food Eng. *33*, No. 8, 37–38.

HANSON, S. W. F., EDITOR. 1961. The Accelerated Freeze-Drying (AFD) Method of Food Preservation. Great Britain, Ministry of Agriculture, Fisheries, and Food. H. M. Stationery Office, London.

HARPER, J. C., and CHICHESTER, C. O. 1960 A. Micro-wave spectra and physical characteristics of fruit and animal products relative to freeze-dehydration. Contract Research Project Report, QM Food and Container Inst. for the Armed Forces, Contract No. DA-19-129-QM-1349, O. J. 9088, Rept. 6, final, July 14.

HARPER, J. C., and CHICHESTER, C. O. 1960 B. Freeze-drying—application of dielectric heating. *In* Symposium on Freeze-Dehydration of Foods—Military-Industry Meeting, Chicago, Ill., Sept. 20–21, 1960, 11–14.

HARPER, J. C., and TAPPEL, A. L. 1957. Freeze-drying of food products. *In* Advances in Food Research 7, 171–234.

HARRIS, R. J. C., EDITOR. 1954. Biological Applications of Freezing and Drying. Academic Press, Inc., New York.

HAVIGHORST, C. R. 1944. One per cent moisture attained by vacuum dehydration. Food Inds. *16*, 258–262.

HEATH, W. P., and WASHBURN, R. M. 1922. Process of manufacturing powdered milk and other food products. U.S. Pat. 1,406,381. Feb. 14.

HENDEL, C. E., LEGAULT, R. R., TALBURT, W. F., BURR, H. K., and WILKE, C. R. 1958. Water vapor transfer in the in-package desiccation of dehydrated foods. *In* Fundamental Aspects of the Dehydration of Foodstuffs. Soc. Chem. Ind. 89–102.

HUKILL, W. V. 1947. Basic principles in drying corn and grain sorghum. Agr. Eng. *28*, 335–338.

HUKILL, W. V., and SHEDD, C. K. 1955. Non-linear air flow in grain drying. Agr. Eng. *36*, 462–467.

JOHNSTONE, H. F., PIGFORD, R. L., and CHAPIN, J. H. 1941. Heat transfer to clouds of falling particles. Univ. Illinois Eng. Expt. Sta. Bull. *330*, Vol. 38, No. 43.

KAUFMAN, V. F., WONG, F. F., TAYLOR, D. H., and TALBURT, W. F. 1955. Problems in production of tomato juice powder by vacuum. Food Technol. *9*, 120–123.

KRAMERS, H. 1958. Rate-controlling factors in freeze-drying. *In* Fundamental Aspects of the Dehydration of Foodstuffs. Soc. Chem. Ind. 57–66.

KRÖLL, K. 1959. Driers and Drying Processes. (Trockner und Trocknungsverfahren.) (In German.) Vol. 2 of Trocknungstechnik, O. Krischer and K. Kröll. Springer-Verlag, Berlin-Göttingen-Heidelberg.

LAPPLE, C. E., and SHEPHERD, C. B. 1940. Calculation of particle trajectories. Ind. Eng. Chem. *32*, 605–617.

LAWLER, F. K. 1962. Foam-mat drying goes to work. Food Eng. *34*, No. 2, 68–69.

LAZAR, M. E., BROWN, A. H., SMITH, G. S., WONG, F. F., and LINDQUIST, F. E. 1956. Production of tomato powder by spray drying. Food Technol. *10*, 129–134.

LEWIN, L. M., and MATELES, R. I. 1962. Freeze-drying without vacuum; A preliminary investigation. Food Technol. *16*, No. 1, 94–96.

LOWE, E., RAMAGE, W. D., DURKEE, E. L., and HAMILTON, W. R. 1955. Belt-trough, a new continuous dehydrator. Food Eng. *27*, No. 7, 43–44.

MARSHALL, W. R., JR. 1954. Atomization and Spray Drying. Am. Inst. Chem. Eng., Chemical Engineering Progress Monograph Series, No. 2. New York.

MARSHALL, W. R., JR., and FRIEDMAN, S. J. 1950. Drying. *In* Chemical Engineers Handbook. Third Ed. Edited by J. H. Perry. McGraw-Hill Book Co., New York.

MARSHALL, W. R., JR., and SELTZER, E. 1950. Principles of spray drying. I. Fundamentals of spray drier operation. Chem. Eng. Progr. *46*, 501–508. II. Elements of spray drier design. *Ibid. 46*, 575–584.

MERYMAN, H. T. 1959. Sublimation freeze-drying without vacuum. Science *130*, 628–629.

MORGAN, A. I., JR., and CARLSON, R. A. 1960. Steam injection heating. Ind. Eng. Chem. *52*, 219–220.

MORGAN, A. I., JR., GINNETTE, L. F., RANDALL, J. M., and GRAHAM, R. P. 1959. Technique for improving instants. Food Eng. *31*, No. 9, 86–87.

MORGAN, A. I., JR., GRAHAM, R. P., GINNETTE, L. F., and WILLIAMS, G. S. 1961. Recent developments in foam-mat drying. Food Technol. *15*, No. 1, Notes and Letters, 37–39.

NEEL, G. H., SMITH, G. S., COLE, M. W., OLSON, R. L., HARRINGTON, W. O., and MULLINS, W. R. 1954. Drying problems in the add-back process for production of potato granules. Food Technol. *8*, 230–234.

NEUMANN, K. 1955. Fundamentals of Freeze Drying. (In German; Grundriss der Gefriertrocknung.) Second Ed. Musterschmidt Wissenschaftlicher Verlag, Göttingen-Frankfurt-Berlin.

NOTTER, G. K., BREKKE, J. E., and TAYLOR, D. H. 1959. Factors affecting behavior of fruit and vegetable juices during vacuum puff-drying. Food Technol. *13*, 341–345.

O'CALLAGHAN, J. R. 1956. Contra-flow drying of beds of wheat. J. Science Food Agr. *1*, 721–728.

OLSON, R. L., and HARRINGTON, W. O. 1955. Potato granules; development and technology of manufacture. *In* Advances in Food Research 6, 231–256.

PHILIP, T. B. 1935. The development of spray drying. Trans. Inst. Chem. Eng. (London) *13*, 107–120.

RAMAGE, W. D. 1960. Foam-mat drying—recent development. *In* Symposium on Freeze-Drying of Foods—Military-Industry Meeting, Chicago, Ill., Sept. 20–21, 15–18.

RANZ, W. E., and MARSHALL, W. R., JR. 1952. Evaporation from drops. Chem. Progr. *48*, 141–146, 173–180.

REICH, I. M., and JOHNSTON, W. R. 1957. Spray drying foamed material. U.S. Pat. 2,788,276. Apr. 9.

REY, LOUIS, EDITOR. 1960. Treatise on Freeze Drying. (In French; Traité de lyophilisation.) Hermann, Paris.

SELTZER, E. 1960. Accelerating freeze dehydration. *In* Symposium on Freeze Dehydration of Foods—Military-Industry Meeting, Chicago, Ill., Sept. 20–21.

SELTZER, E., and SETTELMEYER, J. T. 1949. Spray drying of foods. Advances in Food Research 2, 399–520.

SIMMONDS, W. H. C., WARD, G. T., and McEWEN, E. 1953. The drying of wheat grain. I. The mechanism of drying. Trans. Inst. Chem. Eng. (London) *31*, 265–278.

SINNAMON, H. I., ACETO, N. C., ESKEW, R. K., and SCHOPPET, E. F. 1957. Dry whole milk. I. A new physical form. J. Dairy Sci. *40*, 1036–1045.

SMITH, D. A. 1949. Spray drying equipment. Factors in design and operation. Chem. Eng. Progr. *45*, 703–707.

SPADARO, J. J., and PATTON, E. L. 1961. Continuous pilot plant process produces precooked dehydrated sweetpotato flakes. Food Eng. *33*, No. 7, 46–48.

STRASHUN, S. I., and TALBURT, W. F. 1953. WRRL develops technique for making puffed powder from juice. Food Eng. *25*, No. 3, 59–60.

SUGIHARA, T. F., MEEHAN, J. J., and KLINE, L. 1962. Application of instantizing methods to egg solids. Presented at 22nd. Annual Meeting, Inst. of Food Technologists, Miami Beach, Fla. June 11.

TCHIGEOV, G. B. 1960. Investigation and application of freeze-drying of foods. Proc. 10th. Int. Congress of Refrigeration *3*, Rept. 4–14, 31–35.

TURKOT, V. A., ESKEW, R. K., and ACETO, N. C. 1956. A continuous process for dehydrating fruit juices. Food Technol. *10*, 604–606.

TURKOT, V. A., ESKEW, R. K., and CLAFFEY, J. B. 1960. A continuous process for dehydrating honey. Food Technol. *14*, 387–390.

UNITED STATES DEPARTMENT OF AGRICULTURE. 1959. Management Handbook to Aid Emergency Expansion of Dehydration Facilities for Vegetables and Fruits. Western Utilization Research and Development Division, Agricultural Research Service, Albany, Calif.

VAN ARSDEL, W. B. 1955. Simultaneous heat- and mass-transfer in a non-isothermal system; Through-flow drying in the low-moisture range. Am. Inst. Chem. Eng., Chem. Eng. Progress Symposium Series No. 16, Mass-Transfer, Transport Properties, 47–58.

WARD, K. 1961. Accelerated freeze drying. II. Fundamental design problems. Food Manuf. *36*, No. 2, 60–63, 66.

ZAMZOW, W. H., and MARSHALL, W. R., Jr. 1952. Freeze drying with radiant energy. Chem. Eng. Progr. *48*, 21–32.

ZIEMBA, J. V. 1962. Now—drying without heat. Food Eng. *34*, No. 7, 84–85.

Symbols and Units

Most of the symbols used in this book are defined in terms of one consistent set of English engineering units. The symbol for a quantity remains the same, however, even if a different set of units is used; for example, heat transfer coefficient retains the symbol h whether its numerical value is given in (B.t.u.)/(hr.)(sq. ft.)(°F.) or in (kcal)/(hr.)(sq. m.)(°C.).

The notation is, unfortunately, not completely consistent with any one standard system, because some symbols have become so firmly entrenched during the past 50 years of engineering studies of drying that complete adoption of even such excellent systems as those of the American Standards Association for Letter Symbols for Chemical Engineering, ASA Y 10.12—1955, and Letter Symbols for Heat and Thermodynamics, Including Heat Flow, ASA Z 10.3—1943, would impose unnecessary burdens on many readers. The divergence from the standard usage is not extensive.

TABLE 12

EXPLANATION OF SYMBOLS USED IN THIS VOLUME

Name	Symbol	Unit
General		
Area	A	(sq. ft.)
Density		
General	ρ	(lb.)/cu. ft.)
Bulk density	ρ_s	(lb./gross cu. ft.)
Density of dry substance	ρ_d	(lb. dry)/cu. ft.)
Diameter	D	(ft.)
Differential operator	d	. . .
Diffusion resistance factor (Krischer)	ϕ	. . .
Distance, thickness, or other linear dimension	l	(ft.)
Drying time constant (Jason)	τ	(hr.)
Efficiency, thermal	η	. . .
Loading per unit area	L	(lb.)/(sq. ft.)
Mass	m	(lb.)
Molecular weight	M	. . .
Porosity	ψ	. . .
Radius	r	(ft.)
Reynolds Number	**Re**	. . .
Spreading potential in adsorbed film	Π	(lb._f)/(ft.) or (lb.)/(hr.)^2
Surface tension	σ	(lb._f)/(ft.) or (lb.)/(hr.)^2
Time	θ	(hr.)
Tunnel constant	b	(°F.)

Name	Symbol	Unit
Velocity	u	(ft.)/(hr.)
Viscosity		
Dynamic	μ	$(lb._f)(hr.)/(ft.)^2$ or
		(lb.)/(hr.)(ft.)
Kinematic	ν	(sq. ft./(hr.)
Heat		
Chemical potential (Gibbs free energy		
change)	Δg	(B.t.u.)/(lb. mole)
Coefficient in recirculation Equation (21)	f	$(°F.)^{-1}$
Cooling line slope ($\Delta t/1{,}000 \ \Delta H$)	z	(°F.)
Emissivity for radiation	ϵ	....
Energy of activation (Arrhenius)	$\mathbf{E}$	(B.t.u.)/(lb. mole)
Enthalpy		
Moist air	E	(B.t.u.)/(lb. dry air)
Air saturated at the thermodynamic		
wet-bulb temp.	E^*	(B.t.u.)/(lb. dry air)
Condensed water	E_w^*	(B.t.u.)/(lb. water)
Entropy	S	(B.t.u.)/(lb.)(°R.)
Gas constant	R	(cu. ft.)(atm.)/(°R.)
		(lb. mole)
Gibbs free energy	g	(B.t.u.)/(lb. mole)
Heat quantity	Q_h	(B.t.u.)
Heat transfer coefficient	h	(B.t.u.)/(hr.)(sq. ft.)
		(°F.)
Heat transfer rate	q	(B.t.u.)/(hr.)
Heat usage of a dehydrator	F	(B.t.u.)/(lb. water
		evap'd.)
Humid heat	c_s	(B.t.u.)/(lb. dry air)
		(°F.)
Latent heat of evap'n. at t °F.	λ_t	(B.t.u.)/(lb.)
Mean specific heat of gas or vapor at con-		
stant pressure	c_p	(B.t.u.)/(lb.)(°F.)
Mean temperature difference	$(\Delta t)_m$	(°F.)
Specific heat (liquid or solid)	c	(B.t.u.)/(lb.)(°F.)
Temperature		
Absolute (Rankine)	T	(°R.)
Air	t_a	(°F.)
Air entering drying section	t'	(°F.)
Air leaving drying section	t''	(°F.)
Adiabatic saturation	t^*	(°F.)
Difference	(Δt)	(°F.)
Outside air supply	t_0	(°F.)
Surface	t_s	(°F.)
Thermodynamic wet-bulb	t^*	(°F.)
Wet-bulb (physical)	t_w	(°F.)
Thermal conductivity	k	(B.t.u.)/(hr.)(sq. ft.)
		(°F./ft.)
Thermal diffusivity	α	(sq. ft.)/(hr.)
Total heat transferred	Q_h	(B.t.u.)
Transfer coefficient, heat	h	(B.t.u.)/(hr.)(sq. ft.)
		(°F.)
Wet-bulb depression	$t_a - t_w$	(°F.)
Moisture		
Coefficient in constant-rate equation	a	....
Concentration of moisture in material	C	(lb.)/(cu. ft.)
Diffusivity of water vapor in air	$\mathbf{d}$	(sq. ft.)/(hr.)
Diffusivity of moisture in material	$\mathbf{D}$	(sq. ft.)/(hr.)
Equilibrium moisture content	W_e	(lb.)/(lb. dry)
Fraction of total moisture removed	x	....

Name	Symbol	Unit
Humidity		
Absolute, or humidity ratio	H	(lb./) (lb. dry air)
Absolute, of saturated air	H_s	(lb.)/(lb. dry air)
Absolute, of air sat'd at temp. $t*$	$H*$	(lb.)/(lb. dry air)
Relative	r_h	. . .
Humid volume of air	V_h	(cu. ft.)/(lb. dry air)
Moisture content—		
Material, "dry basis" or "moisture ratio"	W	(lb.)/(lb. dry)
Material, initial	W_0	(lb.)/(lb. dry)
Material, final	W_f	(lb.)/(lb. dry)
"Wet basis," percentage	ξ	(lb.)/(100 lbs.) ("as is")
Mole fraction of water vapor in moist air	w	. . .
Permeability of water in moist solid	$\mathbf{P}$	(lb.)/(ft.)(hr.)(atm.)
Permeability of porous material to gas flow	$\mathbf{P}_a$	(lb.)/(ft.)(hr.)(atm.)
Recirculation, proportion of, in a dehydrator	r_d	. . .
Saturated volume of air	V_s	(cu. ft. sat'd. air)/ (lb. dry air)
Transfer coefficient mass		
Through gas film	k_g	(lb.)/(hr.)(sq. ft.) (atm.)
Through liquid film	k_l	(lb.)/(hr.)(sq. ft.) (atm.)
Pressure		
Partial pressure of water vapor in moist air	p_w	(atm.)
Partial pressure of dry air in mixture	p_a	(atm.)
Partial pressure difference	(Δp)	(atm.)
Saturation vapor pressure of water	p_s	(atm.)
Saturation vapor pressure of water at the wet-bulb temperature	p_{sw}	(atm.)
Total or barometric pressure	P	(atm.)
Vapor pressure of ice in freeze-drying piece	p_{ip}	(mm. Hg.)
Vapor pressure of ice on surface of condenser	p_{ic}	(mm. Hg.)
Volume or Flow		
Air flow rate	Q_a	(cu. ft.)/(hr.)
Mass velocity	G	(lb.)/(hr.)(sq. ft.)
Saturated volume of air	V_s	(cu. ft.)/(lb. dry air)
Specific volume of air	V	(cu. ft.)/(lb.)

Moisture Determination in Dehydrated Foods

The magnitude of the "moisture content" of a dehydrated foodstuff or its raw materials depends in part upon the method used to determine it—*i.e.*, all definitions of this term are operational. Many different methods of determination have been proposed, and several have some kind of status as "official" methods for one purpose or another. Choice of a method is based on the importance attached to accuracy, precision, or reproducibility, time required for a determination, availability of necessary equipment, degree of skill or training required, and several other factors, as discussed by Stitt (1958). Purchase specifications frequently include definition of the moisture determination method that is to be accepted as conclusive, even though the method is a deliberate compromise between the accuracy demanded and the time required.

Methods used for various purposes are classed as (1) vacuum oven drying, (2) entrainment distillation, (3) Fischer volumetric, (4) nuclear magnetic resonance, and (5) dichromate oxidation. We give the detailed procedures only for the first three of these, which have been rather widely used either for procurement specifications (military, federal, or industrial) or in precise scientific investigations. Several kinds of "rapid" method are also rather widely used for control purposes. Some of these employ the rapid heating of a small weighed sample for a specified arbitrary length of time. Others indicate the electrical resistance of a sample or its dielectric constant as that affects the tuning of a radio-frequency circuit. All such instruments are calibrated against samples of a similar product whose moisture contents have been determined independently. The catalogs of many laboratory equipment manufacturers describe commercial instruments of these kinds.

VACUUM-OVEN DRYING

Seven distinguishably different vacuum-oven procedures are currently specified or recommended for determining moisture content of various dry food commodities. The results they give differ from one another for reasons that are not entirely clear. We summarize the seven methods here in order to bring out the major distinctions between them.

(1)   Drying to constant weight (about 5 hr.) at the temperature of boiling water, oven pressure not over 100 mm. mercury.   (Used for dry milk, A.O.A.C. (1960) methods 15.101 and 15.102.)

(2)   Drying to constant weight (about 5 hr.) at 98°–100°C., oven pressure not over 25 mm. mercury.   (Used for egg solids, A.O.A.C. (1960) methods 16.002 and 16.003, and Quartermaster Corps specification MIL-E-25062, June 30, 1961.)

(3)   Sample ground in blender 1 min., sifted through 20-mesh screen, caught on 40-mesh screen.   Drying 6 hr. at 70°C., oven pressure not over 100 mm. mercury.   (Used for potato and for green beans, Quartermaster Corps specifications MIL-P-1073A, December 12, 1950, and MIL-B-35011, December 19, 1955, respectively.)

(4)   Sample ground in blender 1 min.   Drying 16 hr. at 60°C., oven pressure not over 100 mm. mercury.   (Used for cabbage, Quartermaster Corps specification MIL-C-826A, April 8, 1960.)

(5)   Sample ground in a food chopper, Hobart mixer, or blender. Drying 6 hr. at 70°C., oven pressure not over 100 mm. mercury. (Used for dried and dehydrated fruits, A.O.A.C. (1960) methods 20.002c and 20.008;   and for dehydrated onions, same A.O.A.C. methods.)

(6)   Grind sample in Wiley mill through 40-mesh screen.   Drying 30 hr. at 60°C., oven pressure not over 5 mm. mercury.   (Research and reference methods for onions, cabbage, and leafy vegetables; Makower *et al.* 1946.)

(7)   Grind sample in Wiley mill through 40-mesh screen.   Drying 40 hr. at 70°C., oven pressure not over 5 mm. mercury.   (Research and reference method for potatoes, carrots, beets, and sweet potatoes; Makower *et al.* 1946.)

We refrain from quoting all seven of these methods in full;   the following directions for the dried milk method (A.O.A.C. 1960) and for the "40-hr., 70°C." reference method (Makower *et al.* 1946) provide a framework on which the specific variations prescribed for the other methods can be readily placed.

MOISTURE IN DRIED MILK PRODUCTS

Official A.O.A.C. Methods Nos. 15.101 and 15.102.

Preparation of Sample

Sift sample through No. 20 sieve onto large sheet of paper, rubbing material through sieve and tapping vigorously if necessary.   Grind residue in mortar, pass through sieve, and mix into sifted material.

Discard particles that cannot be ground (wood, etc.). Sift sample two more times, mixing thoroughly each time. To avoid absorption of moisture, operate as rapidly as possible, and preserve sample in air-tight container.

Moisture

Weigh 1–1.5 gm. sample into round flat-bottom metal dish (not less than 5 cm. diameter and provided with tight fitting slip-in cover). Loosen cover and place dish on metal shelf (dish resting directly on shelf) in vacuum oven kept at temperature of boiling water. Dry to constant weight (about 5 hr.) under pressure not over 100 mm. Hg. During drying admit slow current of air into oven (about two bubbles per second), dried by passing through sulfuric acid. Stop vacuum pump and carefully admit dried air into oven. Press cover tightly into dish, remove from oven, cool, and weigh. Calculate per cent loss in weight as moisture.

MOISTURE IN DRIED POTATOES AND OTHER ROOT VEGETABLES

Preparation of Sample

Carefully sample the material, grind coarsely in a Wiley mill equipped with a U. S. 10-mesh sieve (Makower *et al.* 1946). Pass the ground material through a quartering funnel, regrind a 25-gm. portion through the same mill with a 40-mesh sieve. Place sub-samples of the reground material in weighing bottles with tightly fitting ground glass covers. If the material was so moist that it clogged the mill, predry prior to grinding, determining loss in weight quantitatively.

Moisture

Dry in a vacuum oven maintained at a pressure of 5 mm. mercury or less. The temperature setting refers to the temperature of the oven shelf, which should be copper. Covers of the weighing bottles should be cocked. Dry potatoes, carrots, beets, or sweet potatoes for 40 hr. at 70°C. Stop vacuum pump and carefully admit dried air. Close the weighing bottles tightly, cool in a desiccator, and weigh. Report loss in weight as moisture.

TOLUENE DISTILLATION METHOD

Official method for dry milk products. American Dry Milk Institute, Chicago, Ill. Bulletin 916 (undated).

Procedure

Transfer a 50-gm. sample to a clean, dry 300 ml. Erlenmeyer flask as quickly as possible and immediately pour approximately 75–100 ml. toluene (technical, moisture-free) into the flask to cover the sample. Rinse down any milk particles on the inside of the flask when introducing the toluene.

Insert a dry distillation trap into the flask and fill the trap with the toluene.

Note: Toluene is readily inflammable and the utmost care must be exercised to keep supplies of it away from flames and heating elements.

Shake the flask with the sample thoroughly before connecting the trap and flask to the condenser. Heat the contents to boiling, making sure that the sample does not scorch on the bottom of the flask. The amount of heat should be so regulated that the toluene will condense into the trap at a rate of about 4 drops per second.

Forty-five minutes after distillation has begun, and without interrupting distillation, dislodge water droplets in the condenser tube by means of a condenser brush. While the brush is in the upper part of the condenser, flush the tube with 10 ml. of toluene.

Read the moisture level in the trap to the nearest half of a scale division (0.05 ml.). Be sure that the meniscus between the toluene and water is sharp. Droplets of water in the toluene or droplets of toluene in the water may be dislodged by a long, stiff wire inserted down through the condenser into the trap.

Continue the distillation for an additional 15 min. period (making a total time of 60 min.) and again dislodge water droplets from the condenser tube as before and note the water level in the trap. If this reading agrees with the previous reading within 0.05 ml. water in the trap, discontinue the distillation and report the determined moisture content. The milliliters of water in the trap multiplied by two equals the percentage of moisture in the sample.

If readings fail to agree as required, continue the distillation for additional 15-min. periods until successive results agree within a half scale division.

MOISTURE DETERMINATION BY FISCHER REAGENT

Rapid method, suitable for use in a well equipped laboratory with skilled operator, McComb and McCready (1952), McComb and Wright (1954). Gave good agreement with standard vacuum oven method in tests on beans, cake mix, egg powder, egg noodles, rolled oats, potato starch, rice, wheat, and garlic, onion, orange, and tomato powders.

Fischer Reagent

For each liter of reagent, dissolve 133 gm. resublimed iodine in 425 ml. of reagent-grade pyridine (<0.1 per cent water) in a dry glass-stoppered bottle, add 425 ml. of anhydrous methyl Cellosolve (Peters and Jungnickel 1955), and cool in an ice water bath. Add, in small increments, and with constant swirling, 70 ml. of anhydrous sulfur dioxide from a graduated cylinder, and mix thoroughly, or add 100 gm. of gaseous sulfur dioxide at a rate of about 40 gm. per hr. Stopper the solution tightly and store for two to three days before use. The water equivalence of this reagent is approximately 6 mg. of water per milliliter of reagent.

Water Equivalent of Reagent

Determine the water equivalent of the Fischer reagent and the blank titer of the formamide daily or each time a series of determinations is made. To determine the blank, titrate 10 ml. of formamide in a 250 ml. Erlenmeyer flask. To the same flask add, by means of a weight burette, 70–100 mg. of water, and titrate. Calculate the water-equivalent of the reagent, milligrams of water per milliliter of reagent. The electrometric end point is used, employing a titrimeter whose indication should remain steady for approximately 30 sec.

Determination

Weigh a quantity of the sample, calculated to give a suitable titer, into a dry glass-stoppered 250 ml. Erlenmeyer flask which contains a magnetic stirrer. Add 20 ml. of formamide with slight agitation to disperse the sample and prevent clumping. Stir for 10 min., then titrate directly with the Fischer reagent.[1] The per cent water is calculated as follows:

$$\text{per cent} = \frac{100\ (\text{sample titer} - \text{blank titer})\,(\text{water equivalent})}{(\text{sample weight in milligram})}$$

BIBLIOGRAPHY

AMERICAN DRY MILK INSTITUTE (undated). 221 No. LaSalle St., Chicago 1, Ill. Bulletin 916. Standards for Grades and Methods of Analysis for the Dry Milk Industry.

ASSOCIATION OF OFFICIAL AGRICULTURAL CHEMISTS. 1960. Official Methods of Analysis. W. Horwitz, Editor. 9th Edition. The Association, Washington, D. C.

---

[1] Beans, oatmeal, rice, and wheat must be heated with the formamide in the flask to 70°–80°C. for from 5 to 30 min. to complete the extraction of water, then cooled and titrated.

178   FOOD DEHYDRATION

McComb, E. A., and McCready, R. M. 1952. Rapid determination of moisture in dehydrated vegetables with Karl Fischer reagent by use of formamide as an extraction solvent. J. Assoc. Offic. Agr. Chemists *35*, 437–441.

McComb, E. A., and Wright, H. M. 1954. Application of formamide as an extraction solvent with Karl her Fiscreagent for the determination of moisture in some food products. Food Technol. *8*, 73–75.

Makower, B., Chastain, S. M., and Nielsen, E. 1946. Moisture determination in dehydrated vegetables. Vacuum oven method. Ind. Eng. Chem. *38*, 725–731.

Peters, E. D. and Jungnickel, J. L. 1955. Improvements in Karl Fischer method for determination of water. Analyt. Chem. *27*, 450–453.

Stitt, F. E. 1958. Moisture equilibrium and the determination of water content of dehydrated foods. *In* Fundamental Aspects of the Dehydration of Foodstuffs. Soc. Chem. Ind. 67–88.

Name Index

A

Aceto, N. C., 155
Ackerman, G., 61
Aikawa, Y., 67
Allen, R. J. L., 2, 85
American Society of Heating, Refrigerating, and Air Conditioning Engineers, 15, 22
Ardern, D. B., 155
Arnold, J. H., 20, 59
Australia Dept. of Commerce and Agriculture, 5

B

Babbitt, J. D., 54, 55, 146
Badger, W. L., 37, 128
Banchero, J. T., 37
Bard, G., 156
Barker, J., 2, 85
Bateman, E., 43, 67
Bate-Smith, E. C., 67, 68
Beavens, E. A., 85
Becker, H. A., 146
Benson, S. W., 67, 70
Bergelin, O. P., 64
Beuschel, H., 76
Bosworth, R. C. L., 40
Bourne, J. A., 85
Brekke, J. E., 156
Brewer, R. C., 16
British Dept. of Scientific and Industrial Research, 5
British Ministry of Agriculture, Fisheries, and Food, 157
British Ministry of Food, 5, 102, 119
Brockmann, M. C., 157
Brombacher, W. G., 20
Brooks, D. B., 20
Brooks, J., 81
Broughton, D. B., 122, Food, 127
Brown, A. H., 102, 104, 119, 128, 129, 146, 152
Brunauer, S., 55, 68
Bryan, L., 84
Buckingham, E., 45
Burr, H. K., 162
Burton, W. G., 84

C

Campbell, W. L., 157
Carlson, R. A., 168
Carman, P. C., 61
Carrier, W. H., 16, 22, 110
Carslaw, H. S., 38, 52
Ceaglske, N. H., 43, 76
Chace, E. M., 3
Chapin, J. H., 151
Charlesworth, D. H., 152
Charm, S. E., 33, 45, 57, 98
Chase, F. A., 153
Chastain, S. M., 71, 174, 175
Chichester, C. O., 157, 159, 160, 161
Chilton, T. H., 59
Christie, A. W., 3, 133
Claffey, J. R., 155
Colburn, A. P., 59, 64
Cole, M. W., 148, 149
Comings, W. E., 16, 44, 53
Conley, W., 156
Conrad, R. M., 147
Cooke, N, E., 61, 157, 159
Cooley, A. M., 148, 149
Copley, M. J., 156
Cording, J., Jr., 151, 154
Coulson, J. M., 37
Crank, J., 52, 75
Cruess, W. V., 3, 133
Culpepper, C. W., 102

D

Davis, H. N., 18
Davis, M. E., 81
Dehority, G. L., 67
Deobald, H. A., 151
Diemair, W., 2, 76, 151
Dlouhy, J., 152
Downes, N. J., 67, 68
Drake, R. M., Jr., 22, 40
Duckworth, R. B., 73
Duffie, J. A., 151, 152
Durkee, E. L., 150
Dusinberre, G. M., 38

E

Earle, P. L., 76
Eckert, E. R. G., 22, 40

Ede, A. J., 27, 53, 61, 91, 98, 102, 104, 105, 108, 109, 110, 111, 112, 115, 157, 159
Edwards, P. W., 151
Eidt, C. C., 106, 134
Eisenhardt, N. H., 154
Ellis, G. P., 84
Emmett, P. H., 55, 68
Ernst, R. C., 155
Eskew, R. K., 151, 154, 155

F

Falk, K. G., 3, 154
Ferrel, W., 20
Fish, B. P., 44, 56, 57, 58, 67, 68, 97
Fisher, C. D., 102, 128
Fisher, E. A., 43
Fixari, F., 156
Flanigan, F. M., 21
Flosdorf, E. W., 157
Fogler, B. B., 151
Frankel, E. M., 3, 154
Friedman, S. J., 37, 41, 43, 51, 53, 146, 147, 151, 156

G

Gane, R., 67, 68, 81, 157, 158
Garber, H. J., 22
Gardner, W., 45
Gauvin, W. H., 152
Gersh, I., 157
Gilliland, E. R., 44, 127, 128
Ginnette, L. F., 157, 159, 162, 163, 165
Girdhari, L., 67
Gnam, E., 61
Goff, J. A., 11, 15, 18, 19
Gooding, E. G. B., 137
Goodman, W., 15, 22
Gore, H. C., 84
Görling, P., 43, 48, 49, 50, 67, 69, 76, 94, 95, 100
Graham, R. P., 157, 159, 162, 163, 165
Gratch, S., 11, 15, 18, 19
Greaves, R. I. N., 157, 158

Subject Index

A

Absolute humidity, 14, 18, 21, 22
Activated diffusion, 52
Activation energy for water diffusion in starch gel, 97
Adiabatic cooling line, slope, 120
Adiabatic drier, 118
  air temperature decrease proportional to change in moisture content, 119
  constancy of wet-bulb temperature, 119
Adiabatic process, 24
Adsorption, multimolecular, 55
Air-suspension drying, 147–149
  egg solids, 147
  potato granules, 147–148
Amagat's law, 13
Analogue determination of drying time, 122–127
Apple nuggets, 154
Ascorbic acid, oxidation of, 76
Avogadro's hypothesis, 13

B

Barometric pressure, 19
  effect of altitude, 32
Belt-trough drying, 150
"B-E-T" adsorption theory, 68
Bin drying, 146–147
Boer War, 2
"Bound water," 34
Boundary layer, 39
Boyle's law, 13
Break-point in drying rate, 94–95
Browning, 73, 83–86
  conditions to minimize, 144–145
  rate of, 84–85
Bulk density, effect of drying conditions, 80

C

Capillary flow, 43, 45, 47, 53
Capillary rise, 32
Case hardening, 73–75
Charles' law, 13
"Chuño," 2
Coefficient of restoration of weight, 82
Concentration, distinction from drying, 11
Concurrent tunnel, 133
Constant-rate drying, 92
Conveyor drying, 146
Cooling effect of evaporation, 27
Critical moisture content, 98

D

Dalton's law, 13
Definitions, dehydration, drying, 1, 11
Dehydrated foods, production in World War II, 4–5
  value of production, 6–7
Dew-point temperature, 18, 19, 20
Dielectric heating, 161
Diffusion resistance factor, 49–51
Diffusion of water vapor, 49
Diffusional transfer, 43, 51–52
  analogy with heat transfer, 44
Diffusivity, dependence on moisture content, 52
Diffusivity of moisture, 52, 56
  in potato, 57
Direct heating, effect on recirculation, 30–31
Distortion accompanying shrinkage, 78–79
Drier, experimental, 90–92
  pilot-scale cabinet, 122
Drum drying, 150–151
  of potato flakes, 151
  of sweet potato flakes, 151
Dry-bulb temperature, 22
Drying conditions to minimize browning, 144–145
Drying costs, 137–140
Drying potential, 26, 110
Drying rate, effect on, 102–116
  by air velocity, 112–113
  by barometric pressure, 113–115
  by composition, 104
  by initial moisture content, 104
  by material, 102–104
  by material arrangement, 106
  by piece shape, 105
  by supplementary heat supply, 115–116
  by temperature, 110–111
  by thickness, 104
  by tray design, 115
  by tray-loading, 107–109
  by wet-bulb depression, 109–110
  in freeze drying, 162–164
Drying time, in experimental drier, 125
  by nomographs, 128–131

E

Enthalpy, 14, 22
Equilibrium moisture content, 56, 67
  see also Sorption isotherm
Erbswurst, 2